WHAT A LIFE!

WHAT A LIFE

A Conversation

Jeffrey M. Walton

'This do and thou shalt live'

Book Guild Publishing
Sussex, England

First published in Great Britain in 2009 by
The Book Guild Ltd
Pavilion View
19 New Road
Brighton
BN1 1UF

Typesetting in Times by
Nat-Type, Cheshire

Printed in Great Britain by
CPI Antony Rowe

A catalogue record for this book is available from
The British Library.

ISBN 978 1 84624 317 2

(age 7?)

One with the vintage port on 2007!

To start with although I was there at the time, I was not aware of it – at least I was to some extent, in fact I had been there for some 9 months or thereabouts, I was later to learn from a very reliable source, also waiting, with me waiting, apparently not patiently, for me to be born. My dear mother! I arrived, as they say, on Sunday, 28th December 1919, at approximately ten minutes to six in the evening (for the astrologers amongst you) at 66 St Catherine's Street in the Parish of Sandal Magna, Wakefield, a town which at that time was the proud capital of Yorkshire's West Riding. My dear mother, Mrs Gertrude Walton, was a SRM/DN (state registered midwife/district nurse).

My earliest memories are of visiting my maternal grandma and grandpa, who lived in one of two adjacent cottages on the east side of the Aire and Calder Navigation Canal on Heath Common, Wakefield. Another early mental snapshot is of Nora, a girl who was a little older than myself and lived next door. We had our den in the ample shrubbery boundary of the lock-keeper's cottage across the green, and here I remember we used to play house. At the time Irish navvies were clearing the mud from the drained section of the Aire and Calder, and they would give us thrupenny bits or even sixpenny bits they had dredged out of the mud. It probably felt like a fortune in those days! It was here that one morning I was playing with a boot or shoebox, on which I had drawn and then cut out doors and windows, to make a house, my first efforts I suppose at building construction. I had also erected a pole on my house for a radio aerial and thinking back, that was very unusual because at that time, before the 'wireless' was widespread, only a very select few residences had a wireless aerial stretching over their land. But it turned out lucky for me, a visiting insurance collector who saw it gave me a big silver coin, perhaps a two shilling piece or half-a-crown. This was an even larger fortune than the thrupennies and sixpennies. As we shall see, this was an omen for ten years later! On race days at local racecourses as a small child I remember waiting with older children at the main Doncaster and Pontefract Road, below the lock-keeper's cottage, to wave to passengers in charabancs, buses and the occasional car, who threw Doncaster butterscotch or Pontefract cakes, whichever was the race day to the excited children.

Recollections of my childhood at St Catherine's Street are entirely of my mother. I have no memories of my father, I suppose because I was too young. Of course, I now know why this was so. I clearly remember my first day at school, which was at the local Council School, and it is still there. It seemed big and wonderful, and I was given crayons to draw with and a bag of matching seashells, which were new to me. I ended the day with a prize for the best design made with the seashells, and was sent home, and told to 'come back when I was five'. I was apparently three years old at the time!

During this period I particularly recall the couple or so visits by the rag and bone man, with his donkey and flat cart, calling 'any old iron, bones' etc. and giving children a gift when they took useful items to him. Gifts from the rag and bone man that I treasured were a coloured tin Alpen mountain railway, and a stuffed doll called Mr Force, which I think was a breakfast cereal sales promotion toy.

About this time my family moved to a house at East Avenue, Horbury, due to mum having been appointed to the position of District Nurse, and I later went to a nearby school for a very short time, just some few weeks. The headmaster's name was Holliday, which was also another good omen as, it turned out. I also became aware that I had a brother, Ronald Douglas Walton. My strongest early memory of him was that he accidentally gashed my upper lip while he was cutting tree branches for the garden bonfire with my father's World War I bayonet and I came up behind him, while he was down on one knee, hacking away. This would be the very first near miss of meeting my maker. Thank the Lord! There was also a further incident that was probably much closer to a near miss than the last one. I had been taken to my uncle's farm, where he bred shire horses for agriculture, industry and transport, and for towing barges on the then much-used canal system in the north of England, and waterways such as those from the Humber to inland ports like Wakefield, which is now a Europort. The farm was situated alongside the River Calder, close to the present Double Two Factory on Thorns Lane Wharf. So close, in fact that you could go straight out for a dip in the water. The very fine main stable for the shires had stalls for perhaps ten horses on each side of a granite cambered roadway – although I wouldn't have used the word 'cambered' at that age, let alone know what it meant – and high, wide gates opening onto the yard and a very large galvanised drinking trough, I was to lead the huge horse from its stall at the far end of the stable, and take it to the water. This started off well, but the horse could probably smell the water, and started galloping. I remember huge hooves crashing down past, and it

2

seemed only just past, my head. Don't forget, I was a small boy! Fortunately, my much older cousin just happened to be behind the stable door, and managed to grab me out of harm's way. The angel on my shoulder came to my rescue!

Other visits to the farm were most enjoyable, particularly trips on the barges. On some of these barges the man and wife, and sometimes children, lived with an open brazier-type fire on board. Health and safety 'experts' wouldn't allow that sort of thing today. I remember their small barrels of monkey nuts and other goodies, acquired from who knows where. I thought it wonderful, towed by my uncle's shire horses one way along the canal and then returning back to my uncle's farm on another barge with the same shire horse. Wonderful: I felt like a water gypsy!

My mother, brother and I were soon on the move again, to a better house in the centre of Horbury. It was a semi-detached house with a bay window and out-buildings at Co-operative Street, off Highfield Road. My father, who was born in Rotherham, Yorkshire, had enlisted in the Prince of Wales West Yorkshire Infantry at the beginning of World War I in 1914, and served until the end of the war in 1918. He was in nearly all the major battles of that conflict. He fought as a sniper, and also took part in the first tank battle of the war, and was mustard gassed eight times! I treasure his miniature Bible (New Testament), which was one of those handed to soldiers leaving for the front, by the British and Foreign Bible Society 1804. In pen and ink he has written in it:

Sydney Walton, 66 St. Catherine's Street, Sandal, Wakefield, of the 17th Service Prince of Wales Own West Yorkshire Regiment No. 967 'A' Company.

Unfortunately, I cannot 'see' my father in my mind's eye the way I can these other snapshots from my earliest years. All I can remember is sitting on his knee when he was talking to another man in our kitchen at Co-operative Street, and him saying that he would rather have the Germans than the French fighting alongside him in war! He was probably speaking to a fellow, ex-service comrade, whose face and name are long forgotten by me. What I do know is that my father was ill at the time and it was to be some few years later that I was to fully understand how much he had suffered during the war (1914–1918) after four years of hell!

One fateful day I was standing on the stone step up under the sweetshop window, on the right side corner entering St Catherine's Street, when two children my own age started saying that my father had died! With the benefit of hindsight this is one the most unforgettable incidents in my life. I now realise they must have heard their parents talking. My feet must not have touched the ground, as I flew to my Gran's cottage a third of a mile away, where I was staying, happily, and all unknown to me, until after the funeral. I was utterly distraught and apparently inconsolable. Maybe this is why I cannot see him in my mind's eye. My father contracted pneumonia apparently, and he had virtually no lungs left, due to the mustard gas in World War I. I do remember him standing in the back yard as he was showing me two rabbits in a hutch and I also later overfed them, or as I was told 'pogged' them, a word I always remember. I think he had worked at the quarry on Quarry Hill, after the war, for a very short time, as it must have been, and he may have worked in the coal mines, there were dozens of them before the war.

Quarry Hill, Horbury, by the way, is the hill up which the Rev. Sabine Baring-Gould was leading his procession of Sunday School children to St Peters Parish Church for the 'Whit Walk', singing his hymn 'Onward Christian Soldiers', to a tune by Haydn, on Whit Monday 1865. He wrote it in 15 minutes.

By the time I was seven, my family moved again. My mother was a very hard worker, dedicated to her profession, and we moved to a large detached house on Benton Hill, Horbury, which she equipped as a nursing home called Danum Mount. She was, of course, now a widow and she would remain so until the early 1940s. My mother once informed me that there were probably more babies called Jeffrey in her practice area, due to mothers asking for the names of her sons, after the delivery of their own babies, than any similar size area in the country!

There was my brother, aged 13 and eight-year-old me. Working full time and raising two young boys must have been a huge strain for my mother, and something obviously had to give. Elder brother Ronald, more able to look after himself, was doing well at school and less in need of attention. So my mother arranged for me to be a pupil at the Crossley & Porter Schools, Saville Park, Halifax, a school endowed by the famous Crossley carpet manufacturers, and the Porter family, for children of both sexes who had been orphaned. The school had boarders as well as day boys, but only the orphaned boys and girls were boarders. The school is a noble Georgian stone building in a superb location, symmetrically planned and centred on the line of the dominant clock tower, the main entrance hall and the dining hall. It has three storeys with roof turret rooms, and an extensive brick-vaulted basement of rooms and tunnels. I was taken from Danum Mount by my mother and a friend by car to Halifax in the early

My dear Mum, SRM, DN

afternoon of May 2nd 1928 (I think), suitably equipped with a large suitcase full of schoolboy requirements. I remember it was a pleasant day, but I wasn't at all happy to be leaving mum and home.

The policy of the school was to select a guardian for each new pupil – or newk as we were now called, preferably from our local area. Mine turned out to be an older pupil (they were seniors), whose name was E. Vincent Broadhead from Wakefield. He was a nice chap, I'm pleased to say, and his duty was to generally advise me on the school system, traditions and facilities, and to keep me from being bullied, I suppose. Fortunately, I was not. Within a short time he decided that I was apparently able to manage, and got on with his normal activities whilst remaining a good friend to me.

Having just now been browsing through the September 1933 edition of *The Crossleyan*, the magazine of the Old Scholars Association, under 'The Headmaster's Letter Box', E. V. Broadhead (1764, school entry number) is with Dobson & Gigalls, Architects, Horbury, and all these years living in both Horbury and with a Wakefield Office. I had no idea that he was an architectural draughtsman or technician, although we met very occasionally on the street – but only to reminisce.

During my first few days at Crossley's I was desperately homesick and unhappy. The school's matron was in charge of the new entry children, she was very kind and took me to her sitting room for tea and cakes. I remember her as a tall, elegant lady, kind and efficient in her numerous duties. I never knew her real name. Matron's assistant was Sister. She was a much sterner and officious person, a kind of sergeant major to the matron's colonel, but always fair and helpful. Myself and the other 10 or so Newks were required to assemble daily in the large playroom, which was also the school gymnasium. It had beechwood floor, a high open-truss roof with steel braces and was equipped with wall-bars and, climbing ropes. Significantly, along one side and end, there were blocks of numbered lockers, one for each pupil, and they were sacrosanct – our locked, private space until we became seniors. There were also doors to the adjacent swimming pool, with shower rooms etc., on one side and changing rooms and storage for PT equipment such as vaulting horse, and then main corridor access on the other side. As will be referred to again later, there was also access diagonally across the playroom to the library, above which there were music rooms, and a billiard room (used by seniors and staff). The preceding paragraphs make me realise that more information is required if some words I have used are to be understood more fully by you, dear reader, namely 'Ahr Shant' language.

6

English is, in Rochdale for example, not the same tongue as is spoken in Arundel or Stephney. There is more than a little difference between the sounds from the mouth of a Halifax boy and those of a fellow East Anglian or an English-Welsh Bangorian (such as the head prefect of my house). Even in Yorkshire, it is possible to tell the boy who was brought up in Grassington from the boy who lived in Pocklington. The cultured southern speech is worse, or better, amongst suburbanites of Balham or Slough than the people of Bognor or Bournemouth, but it's not so much the sound that makes the difference as the actual phrases. Naturally, many of the pupils at the school were Yorkshire in type and origin, but it's interesting to notice how Yorkshire words of the time become transmuted. Thus, for example, 'Are yo leikin outside?' became 'Are ya lahkin inside?' It probably means 'stop larking on', but sometimes this Yorkshire phrase took the form of repetition of one word. There are, for example, no 'girls' in the school, only 'lasses'.

'Ahr Shant' lasses lived on the 'lasses side'. If some boy was successfully smiled upon, he was said to have 'got a lass'. A girl by another name is just as sweet, and it's a good old English poetical word, by no means derogatory, as witnessed by a certain charming repeated rendering of 'The Lass With the Delicate Air'.

I was smiled upon and got a lass some few years later. In fact, two 'lasses.' Molly Kay was a dainty brunette, Barbara Thomkins a blonde, unfortunately they sat next to each other at dining table so it was not easy to say who was successfully smiled upon and by whom! The matter was resolved some time later when, one very dark night in winter, three or four dressing-gowned girls arrived in my dorm, (yes I was still a junior). One of them woke me, and half awake, the first thing I felt in my hand was – an unwrapped pat of butter! Followed by various comestibles (apparently acquired from the remains of their mistresses' dinner)! Sufficient for a 'chew' and yes, it was my favourite – Molly Kay – and no, nothing else happened!

'Broad Yorkshire' seems to be fighting a losing battle, and these days many phrases of bygone days are heard no more. Yet since Ahr Shant in some ways is a small isolated community, there were phrases which were scarcely understandable to the outside world, mostly concerning places within the walls of Crossley's or some everyday event. You did not, for example, go on the fort to defend yourself, nor in the glass house to ripen. Neither did you boil in the pan or write under the clock, nor find much wool in the playroom rug – that was playing rugby, union, not league. Incidentally, a large proportion of Ahr Shant phrases are prepositional.

The Whitsuntide Reunion 1933

8

You strived to keep off the 'blacklist', but to be first on top pitch. You may be on the wall, on the reading room, on little pitch, down town, down Broomfield, down I.S. or be found in little prep – you did 'prep' in the evening, before you went to bed. Others were in Cobby's shy and in Pa Oyle's shy.

For variety you might be up King Crow, that was up Kings Cross, the area of Halifax where the school was sited, or up the billiard shy. If you do not care for any of these prepositions you may go to inspection or to music, or to sister. If you prefer a preposition to end the phrase off with, then you may dry up or proceed all down or all up or even try your hand at 'snivelling over' or 'scheming in', or out.

A new kid, as I have said, becomes a newk. An outside boy a little Bill, a good meal a chew, a driver of hard bargains a Jew, an Isaac or an Ike. Small boys who cannot be held responsible for their personal cleanliness were known as scrubbites and they (in common with others) attended bug scratch, all supervised by matron or sister, perhaps the most revolting phrase of all is to hear that someone has 'gone in the sick'.

Tiles and sawdust are hardly what they sound to be, or to hear of a feller cogging a shy or even making a bed for a curney supper. Another one, 'It grits', can trace its origins back to Milton – 'shepherds grating' upon their 'scrannel pipes'. 'What an Arab' is directly descended from medieval French farce of *Maître Pathelin*, which some ascribe to Villon – who knows? In our slang carelessness of speech we be entertaining other angels unawares.

Sister's domain was dispensary, from which she dispensed, compulsorily, cod liver oil and white mixture, etc. to newks, as well as general first aid and medication. We would try and sneak past the door to avoid, at all costs, having to suffer these things. A dentist visited the School each term for a check-up and gave dental treatment should it be required. There was the occasion when Sammy Wright, like Berty, from the Tyneside/Northumberland area, and whose teeth were perfect whenever the dentist visited, was asked what he cleaned them with. Sammy replied, 'Salt and soot' – and he really did! The dispensary was situated on the 'half-landing' at the foot of the very fine york stone paved square hall, with staircase, a cast-iron balustrade with oak hand-rail and cast iron reclining lions at intervals. Some of these are missing because some old boys, on leaving, pinched them as souvenirs. They were there to prevent pupils sliding down from the second- and third-floor dormitory landings.

Ablutions was a room with two back-to-back rows of wash basins, with an adjacent separate room with WCs on each dormitory floor. The large ground floor area comprised the rear entrance hall, dining hall used jointly by boys and girls, an internal courtyard with access to the main entrance corridor which connected the headmaster's residence at one end and at the other end the staffroom and private staff dining room. Off the corridor were prefect studies and corridors to all classrooms, toilets, playrooms, swimming pool, as well as the library and workshops buildings.

Outside were the playgrounds and well-maintained garden areas, including 'little pitch' in the Tarmaced corner area of roadway to the woodwork and metalwork workshops, followed by a full-width 'rough dirt' area, with Tarmac 'top pitch' above, and the rear high stone walls, with caretaker's house and the rear access roadway to playgrounds for both schools etc. On top pitch we played football with a tennis ball! We were a rugby union school, and proper soccer was not allowed. Little pitch was where we played 'little cricket', a game devised by 'Bertie' Ernest Berner Bertleson, 'Dougie' Douglas Egglestone, and myself; they were my best friends throughout my schooldays. (We were known as the Three Musketeers, not very original I am afraid.)

Little pitch was on a Tarmac area only 12 feet by 10, open on one 12-ft side and enclosed on the other three sides by stone walls of the library and

Dougie – JMW - Bertie

10

the pool's end wall. There was also a very short passage entry, four feet wide, on the pool or 'bowler's end'. That's clear I hope? The game and its rules were a moveable feast, played only by juniors of similar ages and subject to change with the passing years, allowing later-arriving newks to think they devised it – including we Three Musketeers. The scoring and boundaries were also laid down. Balls played over the chalk-line of the 'open' side were 'half out' – two 'halves' and you were out, probably because someone had to fetch the ball! Balls played through the passage-way earned four runs; those played onto the swimming bath, bowler's end wall, got two runs, three runs were for hitting the library wall, and six runs for hitting the 4ft by 2ft window in the only corner of the pitch immediately behind the right-handed batsman. Fortunately wire mesh protected it from balls hit from the playground. Clearer now, getting the hang of it?

On top of all this, and I mean top, at the rear of the school and across the Kings Cross Road stands the Wainhouse Tower, with internal staircase, a magnificent stone-built spectacle constructed in Victorian times. One legend claims it was built to ensure that the mill owner who erected it would always be able to look down over the high walls built by his neighbour, also a mill owner, to protect his privacy, they must have been very high walls.

The pupils were organised into four 'houses': Paladins, Vikings, Trojans and Spartans – with dining tables for each house, allowing prefects and seniors to educate newks in table manners, etc. The house captains sat at the head of each table on one side of the dining hall, and the lasses, with their house tables etc., were similarly accommodated on the other side of the dining hall. All our food was very good varied and plentiful, including tiles and sawdust served by matron, sister and kitchen staff from the two serving tables, (one for boys and one for girls) at the kitchen end of the hall. There was a masters' dining table at the main entrance end of the hall on the paladin side (I was a Paladin). The hall was also used for special occasions, such as entertaining various visiting school sports teams, old boys reunion dinners, and dances, sports day games guests, etc., and also by the lasses side, teachers and pupils, for whatever purposes they may decide. We rarely knew, our side doors were kept locked most of the time!

The sports grounds were at Broomfield, off Broomfield Avenue, three-quarters of a mile away across Savile Park, where rugby, cricket and other field games were played by all pupils, practically daily. The lasses also played lacrosse, and whatever else lasses played. Our personal Sunday

11

walks were taken 'on the rocks'. Dougie, Berty, and me, after rugby on Saturday and with some 'illicit' legal tender in our pockets. The school currency consisted of the 'shekal', a brass coin, size of the original penny, and stamped with the letters C.P.S and issued by the headmaster, Mr G.B. Newport – assuming we had credit covered by the money provided as pocket money by our sole parent, and only for use at the school tuck shop!

'The rocks', one of the best areas in Halifax, is accessed by Albert Promenade over, at a lower level, Delph Hill, and is a rock-faced escarpment with a not easily accessible cave and the rock shop. It was here where Bertie bought his Woodbines, paper packet of five, and I bought a small tin of Heinz baked beans in tomato sauce with, at that time, a nice little piece of bacon on top, both not on the menu at Ahr Shant. Well below the rock face was woodland and grass, bordered by Scarr Bottom and Bird Cage Road, and all a long hard way if you fell off! The Promenade was a wide road with seats at regular intervals, and magnificent views over the canals, River Calder, the railway, and the wide area of countryside to the Pennines. I recall one summer term walk on the rocks, Bertie having had his fags and I my baked beans. Returning, we had arrived at the school wall, with the entrance gates 100 yards further on, and the swimming sports day a week away, and Bertie announced, 'If it had been much further I couldn't have made it, must give up smoking.' His party piece at the sports day, was three lengths of the swimming bath, under water, and he would not have come up sooner, if he had drowned. When he did come up he was purple! He was a first class all round sportsman, rugby, cricket, swimming, fives, shooting, etc. In the fives team, playing against Leeds University – a much older team – he came off the court with his right gloved hand swollen to twice its normal size. He was very fast and seemed to be able to bend his right arm somewhere behind his left ear! Our team beat Leeds University, home and away!

Bertie's mother ran the Sun Hotel, Walkworth, Northumberland, just north of Newcastle and after each summer hols we needed an interpreter to translate from his Geordie brogue, with its 'Hack-away man' and his tales of 'the wee-Scots lad, best centre forward Newcastle United ever had'. When he left Crossleys he became a midshipman on, I believe, a ship of the Bertelson family merchant shipping line. We later met in Halifax in 1941, both now in uniform, Bertie merchant navy, me in the RAF. By that time he had already been torpedoed eight times and it was to be the last time we would meet. I visited the school in 2003 but his name was not on the War Memorial Boards of the First and Second World Wars along with those who also died in WWII – D. Egglestone, and D. Nicoll

12

1933 Cricket Team

1933 Fives Team

(on HMS *Hood*), my friends, but no Bertie. The possible reason is that the merchant navy, I think, was not included in WWII, along with the army, navy and air forces and regrettably, the merchant navy did not get a suitable memorial until some few years back, and 3500 merchant ships sunk!

Time has a very bad habit of passing, perhaps by now you too have noticed, so as I gradually fitted in or whatever, my involvement increased. For example, juniors did prep after tea and were in dorm by 8.30 pm, summer and winter, with the duty master and duty prefect on patrol only sporadically. So the simple pastimes of pillow fights etc., could be short run, terminated, and in their place came 'Tell us a story Wally'– no guessing who Wally was, also summer and winter – me!

I suppose I was interested in learning about some things, most things probably, but was also very interested in doing things, things that I read about happening. Now, making things myself I felt I could do, and imagining and doing things I read about, things such as at that time published by *National Geographic* magazine (in my view, the worlds finest monthly periodical publication, both in quality of production, content, photography and text). In this case, Professor Pickard's descent into, I think, the Mariarnas trench in the Far East in the 'bathysphere' and the pictures of marine life in colour. Terrific! (I have been subscriber all the years since then – 80!) Similarly, I was also intrigued by astronomy and space, but at that time you could only imagine it, no one had been there except perhaps Professor Pickard.

I started a story about space, due probably after holding forth in a discussion before we got off to sleep, and say, perhaps, '186,000 miles a second speed of light' (still find hard to imagine). So I started there and then and imagined, and told them a story, on the hoof, without any pre-written draft, day after day, asking first, 'Where had I got to?' Immediately came the answer, in detail, so I had to get on with it! With hindsight, my regret is that tape recorders for general use were only invented some years later. Had I had a recorder then, to record the story as I spoke, who knows, I might even have become a writer!

I was also interested in radio, science and physics, and had made various items of laboratory equipment at the request of 'Puffer' Smith, (science master, tuck shop controller and an all round interesting fellow), such as a magnetometer, and a portable radio in an oak dovetailed box, with leather handle, and clasps, purloined from my mother's Pye portable battery-powered radio at home (I still have the box in my workshop). It was used to monitor, among other things, an induction coil transmitter, with telegraph type key and, according to the usage instructions, 'for use only across the laboratory'. It turned out to be practically all over the radio dial as the key was pressed in the lab on my testing walks circuit a mile away, and that was illegal, then as now!

I also had a 'small business' producing crystal radio sets using toilet roll cardboard tubes or match boxes, whichever I had most of, with a crocodile clip connection to the metal flat wire-mesh bed with side springs under the mattress as the aerial, with a permanent crystal detector and a coil of DCC (double cotton covered) copper wire wound round the cardboard tube, tapped at intervals, and with another metal clip to tap the coil to get the different station frequencies. I made these every Friday night, for Harry Roy and his Orchestra, from the Dorchester Hotel in London, late night dance music: 'Tiger Rag', Al Bowley, etc., all while someone else did my prep. This was repeated Friday after Friday, as some sets had been confiscated by Saturday! Happy days!

Improvements occurred. I later was able to build a Class B portable radio and connect up a few individual sets of ear phones, in series or parallel in the dorm, bed to bed. When my business caught on, the external wall of the school became hung with a web of insulated wire aerials lines, as only one license was needed for the whole building then. I also started to build a John Logie Baird TV set, instructions as published in the 'Peto–Scott Radio' magazine at the time, and being tested by Baird in London. I didn't finish. Baird used mirrors on a drum at that time but I got to know something about cathode ray tubes, which came in useful in later years. Hopefully, if I get there, you will learn how useful they were. The last two lines of the previous paragraph remind me of another happenstance. Boys of different denominations went to different places of worship, I was Church of England. Each Sunday morning we processed to St Jude's Parish Church, a quarter of a mile away, at the corner of Saville Park where we had reserved pews facing the altar; on the front rows on the right hand side of the nave with the pulpit on the left. The resident vicar's sermons were the same style each week and boring, some of us even took books to read, risking severe comment from the vicar! One Sunday, the vicar being on holiday, it was a scientist (vicar) and possibly, because Professor Rutherford had already split the atom at Cambridge, he said in his interesting sermon that the time would come in the future, when the energy contained in a pin head would drive the Atlantic liner, *Mauritania* across the Atlantic ocean! Years later, in the UK and overseas, and in the various RAF messes, I would occasionally mention this sermon, and after the atomic bomb, ('top–top' secret until then) was dropped on Hiroshima, Japan, and I was still in the RAF, I received a number of letters from officers wanting to know how I knew about 'the bomb', was I a spy, or what?

Around this time, I had my first experience of going 'in the sick', a junior, not newk. I do not know what was wrong with me, but I was definitely not well. I was the sole patient on the ward, in the smaller, five bed ward, the other ward was three times bigger but empty. I was in the corner bed, under the long narrow windows, like swords over my bed, and also facing more swords in the opposite external wall. It was also winter and a dark night!

When one went in the sick, the first thing that you had to do was have a bath. This was supervised by the 'sick room maid' on duty, and in my case a very cheerful Irish girl. Later, when I presented to her with my autograph album (the iPod of those days amongst boys and girls), she wrote: 'Thy friend has a friend, and thy friend's friend has a friend, so be discreet.' Typically Irish, short and sweet, it has stayed with me ever since, and has been much used!

I apparently went on my first and only bout ever of sleep walking, out of the ward, down a short corridor, down about three steps, along the corridor to the first door. I came to sister's room, I checked all that later, in the morning sister took me back to my bed, probably feeling better. My only other occasion of going on the sick at Crossley's was probably about two years later. It was much more serious, I passed out, (the only time in my life that I have done so, so far,) in a WC cubicle, in the middle of the night, on a hard terrazzo solid floor; I was found by someone and taken back to bed, then to the sick room, and eventually, by ambulance, to Clayton Hospital, Wakefield, where I was operated on for acute appendicitis, and after about 10 days' duly released from hospital.

I returned to Danum Mount to my mum and Ron to recuperate. At this time she had as companion and assistant nurse a lady, Miss Dorothy May Capp. She had a rose named after her, by her father who was head gardener with some twenty bothy boys under training at Nostel Priory, one of England's finest stately homes, and experts, then as now, in rose growing and marketing, situated about five miles from where I am sitting writing this at Sandal Magna. Unfortunately, she helpfully erected a folding deck chair on the rear lawn for me to enjoy the sunshine, I sat on it, and it collapsed, trapping the fingers of my right hand. I yelled, she came dashing out to assist me, and started pulling the timber frame in the wrong direction and made matters very much worse. It was convenient that I was there to recuperate and not at school. Eventually back at

Crossleys, I was still not allowed to take part in sports or PT – had to sit and watch!

The Scientific Society was one of my interests. We paid visits to various locations, by coach or on foot, depending on the distance, but usually by coach. The place I will remember always was the Halifax Royal Infirmary, just less than a mile down the road from Crossleys. We visited the Bacteriological Department and were shown, through their very powerful microscope, various types of bacteria. The one that I found to be the most amazing, and I like to be amazed, was the deadly typhoid bacteria, like strings of sausages altogether, but each one splitting in halves, and the halves splitting in halves, apparently ad infinitum, before your very eyes, and your nose and mouth only about twelve inches away from the living organisms, multiplying in the slide!

Littleborough, Lancashire, was another interesting visit to the very first sliced bread manufacturer in the UK, and virtually all automatic (so you now know how to calculate, reasonably accurately, how some new invention, is the best thing since sliced bread!). Here we were shown round the large production machines with sliced loaves endlessly flowing, fully wrapped, along conveyor belts for daily distribution by a fleet of vans over a wide area, and shown other departments, until we came to the cakes, pastries and other good things dear to children's hearts. Here there was a huge table covered with a similarly huge slab of sponge cake, being spread with jam by ladies in white coats and cooks caps, by hand, and then cut into Swiss rolls! In the same department were other cake and pastry products or sweets being produced, and alongside were large metal drums, approximately three feet high by eighteen inches diameter, one with the lid cut off like a household tin of baked beans, and full to the brim with eggs – but only the unbroken yoke, and the clear white, NO shells. There must have been hundreds in each drum, from China. Ready for us was a first class tea consisting of sliced bread with various sandwich fillings, ice cream and various cakes and sweets etc., and a good time was had by all! A later and very different visit was on the same main road as the previous visit to Littleborough but a few miles nearer to Halifax. This time it was a factory producing toilet rolls, and how's that for variety for young minds? My main memory of this visit was of the huge bath of water at least ten feet wide with a similar width of toilet roll paper on a roller bar, but at this stage uncut into roll size, propelled from the water and being taken up by a similar roller, and at the same time being cut into roll size by continuous overhead jets of water, under pressure, some twenty of them (approx), a very different system from the sliced bread!

17

We also had unfortunately, two outbreaks of diptheria, during my time at school. Trying to be brave but casual I suppose, we would accuse anyone sitting on the steam heated, cast iron radiators in classrooms under the windows, (a favourite place to chat or 'grit' in winter) and looking a bit peekish, of having 'dip'. I particularly remember us accusing Cuthbert Chapman, and he went in the sick, next day. A few days later we were dispersed to our homes to avoid further contamination, and I don't know, even now, whether he got it, but I still feel guilty! Cuthbert, by the way, was the newk who came two years later than me, and who was queuing up at Puffer Smith's tuck shop and asked us what the jar full of barley sugar sticks were called. 'Charley Bugger Sticks' came the rapid reply, so he then asked Puffer for two Charley Bugger Sticks please, and got a very stern look from Puffer!

A gentleman, F.E. Bowman Esq., Founder Director of the Halifax Building Society, no less, of Priory Cottage Friars Cliff, East Christchurch, Dorset, had, I presume, asked the headmaster to select two pupils from the school for a summer holiday at his home in Dorset. Alan Goodfellow and I were duly selected. Mr Bowman was retired, a keen golfer and a very interesting person as his later letters to me at school (and I suppose also to Allan) show. He also had a BSA (Birmingham Small Arms) car, a well made saloon of the day, in which we progressed in a very stately manner. He was adamant that the red line on the speedometer at 30 mph was the maximum speed of the car – this was the time of Mr Hore-Belisha, MP, Transport Minister, of Belisha Beacon fame and also the 30 mph speed limit! On one local journey, I sat in the front seat with Mr Bowman driving, when smoke started issuing from under my seat. I said something like 'It must be the battery.' He had no idea there was a battery!

My above mention of the transport minister, reminds me that I sent him drawings of my earliest invention while I was at school, an illuminated number plate for motor transport, He wrote thanking me, saying it was good idea, but Rolls Royce had recently patented it. Ah well, at least I was in very good company!

The time came for me to leave Crossley's and the excellent headmaster, teachers, staff, facilities etc., who had been part of my life for years. Previously, in my younger years, we made day hour, minute and in some cases even seconds end of term lists to cross off, but not this time! I regret that I am unable to remember any detail of this event and I wonder why? I was about to start the third section of my life and raring to get on with it, I had been there, done that, with older school friends, leaving! I was later to

18

learn that parting was not always such sweet sorrow, – *many* times in WWII!

However, I must remember, my teachers, all of whom were all there, from the time I was there, to the time I left, and to whom I have always felt greatly indebted: MR. G.B. NEWPORT MA, Headmaster – Latin and most other things. A solid, imposing gowned figure, firm, fair etc., only the odd one or two canings. When on one occasion we passed each other mid-way, in the inner courtyard area, I with my hands in my trouser pockets, he gowned and mortar boarded, from under his gown like lightning appeared his cricket pad cane, covered in lambskin, to stab me firmly, but fairly, in the body. Defenceless boy – defenceless!

MR 'EGG' BOLTON MA, Maths, (Cambridge). Deputy head, mathematics. With his way of teaching, not the most popular of teachers. Before my time, he had been head prefect, rugby team captain, etc., at the school and came back to Crossleys, after Cambridge, as senior mathematics master. Mr Bolton was possibly, after more experience in later years, one of the earliest reasons for my later coined, lesser known phrases or sayings, including: 'You can have an educated fool, you cannot have an intelligent fool.' (Mr Bolton was *not a fool*!) He was educated and intelligent. The other saying, 'The world is over populated with schoolmasters, but there are not many teachers about!'

MR HANSON – French – languages 'thasser', 'Tubby Odd Boots' (I don't know why either)! Pleasant gentleman, good teacher, always sat on a desk, short and rotund, dry wit, one occasion when I expressed achievement in my eight out of ten marks for French prep, announced, 'Charity, Walton, Charity!'

('Captain') MR HARRISON – Geography – Ex World War I, captain (army). All round good chap, had the habit of saying to his class, and only when *not* gowned, 'I am going to take my coat off to you boys' and proceeded to do so, but only when he had on a new sports coat, pullover, watch or belt, Expert in the freezing cold nights on the North African desert etc., A lovely man!

MR MARGERISON – History, and other subjects. Again another good chap, he was a member of Lord Baden-Powell's own Scout Troop! and organised the schools Cub and Scout troops who met in the school basement. Dressed in full regalia, say for attending 'Jamboree' he was immaculate, full uniform of rank, ribboned hat, sporran, skean dhu, knife, etc. In the classroom he was prone to lose his patience occasionally with a pupil, cuff him on the head, and spend the rest of the period full of remorse!

MR NEWBOULD – Music, Singing etc. A distinguished organist, music teacher etc., I am afraid I blotted my copy book in singing lesson by maintaining I was tone deaf. I probably did not know what it meant as a newk, and was only using this as an excuse to avoid more singing classes and choir, but it worked! Later, in the first year of WWII he was a passenger on the *Athenia* the first passenger liner to be torpedoed, off Southern Ireland, en route to Canada, Mr Newbould was going to be the Organist at Toronto Cathedral, I believe, and he was one of the few rescued, I think!

MR CHARLES ('CHARLEY') PLAICE – PT (Physical Training.) A first class person and PT instructor, demonstrator advisor, and liked by everyone, would parade each class in three columns, at ease, give a five minute good advice lecture, demonstrate rapid climbing of the ropes, first with one hand only, then with two, 'Muscle control laddie, muscle control!' Arriving unfortunately with a bad cold, he would move the class back from himself, place the large plywood tea chest (used as a waste bin in the gym) at his side, complete with box of tissues. Every time he beat the sneeze with a tissue, then into the bin it went, Good example, good fellow!

MR RUCKLEDGE – MSc. Chemistry, Art. (RUCKS) etc., Mr Ruckledge lived locally, near the school, a charming gentle man with many interests. Unfortunately he suffered from very bad halitosis (both his subjects required, at times, some close contact), fortunately for me, I managed, somehow, to come out top in Art; all my time at Crossley's, in my last year in the art exam I sat looking at my blank 'Whatman' paper for half the exam time. He came up behind me, 'Get on with it Walton', and I did, and it has stuck with me ever since. 'Rucks' also had a great interest in and knowledge of, Hadrians Wall. He lectured on the subject over a wide area of the county, and asked me if I would make a model of the wall, coast to coast, in relief, and also a larger scale model of a fort on the wall. I agreed. The job of course took some time, and only in my spare time, after studies, in the evenings, in a room adjacent to the masters' private dining room from which I was regaled by items Rucks produced from the masters' evening dinner, my late supper! The 'coast to coast' model was built on a ¾-inch thick square of blockboard on which I drew a map of the area in pencil, and also inserted pin-wire of various lengths, to indicate elevation of terrain. OK, mixed a small bucket of plaster of Paris, near disaster, what would happen to the map? Revised thinking, got on with it!

MR SMITH – Science ('PUFFER'). Always the same in all respects, calm, solid, dignified, science, one of my favourite subjects. At the other end of the scale, he also officiated at the tuck shop, as previously mentioned – an excellent teacher.

MR TOLSON – English Literature/Language, History. A charming man, had a slight impediment in his speech. As he felt in various pockets with one hand, he would point the forefinger of the other hand, 'I will put you on the "bwak" list Walton!' But he was often unable to find his list! Mr Tolson lived in at the school and just before the start of the summer term he became engaged to be married. Apparently he had decided to spend his honeymoon canoeing down the River Elbe in Germany. I became involved in this matter early, in the usual exclamation of 'Walton, I would like a word with you.' No, it was not the bwak list, but the 'folbot', a collapsible, fabric and wood, canoe boat, which had arrived at his rooms. He had tried to assemble it and he had broken some of the plywood cross braces etc., could I help him? I made him replacements for the few damaged components, assisted him in assembly of the folbot and how it should be unpacked and repacked in the two large 'golf' type bags, one for each of the two canoeists to carry. From then on, at least once a week, at the end of the lesson, it was, 'First Mate, join me on the river.'

The boat house was situated at the foot of Salterhebble Hill, on the Huddersfield road, on the left side, and adjacent to the Calder and Hebble Navigation, and from there we both gradually improved our canoeing skills. On one occasion we were about one mile away from the boat house when the sky became very black and we were deluged by a thunder storm. We did our best paddling hell for leather to get back to the boat house, lifted out the canoe, and then stood under cover, watching the storm and a thunderbolt burst in front of our eyes, or so it seemed. I have not seen another, before, or since!

The Tolsons went on their honeymoon on the Elbe, but, before they left, he gave me a memento, a fourth verse to John Masefield's *Cargoes*:

> Collapsible canoe boat with stream-lined body,
> Paddling down the river with alternating stroke,
> With a cargo of tent pegs, sleeping bags, cooking pots,
> Water proofs, Heinz beans, and spare pairs of socks –

And that is as near as I can remember!

MR UMPLEBY – Workshops, Joinery, Engineering. A very active man who drove an Aerial square four motorbike, state of the art at that time, when we had the best in the world in all types of road transport – we were also close behind in air transport as well

Mr Umpleby and I made the solid oak dining furniture for his home. I have no idea now if he was getting married or not, but I enjoyed it and it was good practice. The main item was the triangular dining table, with three triangular let-down leaves, forming a larger triangle. I had not seen one before, or since! He was a part-time teacher, three days per week, so I was promoted and given a key to workshops, allowing access for me and others to build various items for PT and sports, such as the curved and slatted, wood and metal 'practice catching frame' for cricket team practice. Later there was a fire in the covered cycle park, and the Aerial square four was a write off!

'ARETHUSA.' An acknowledgement should also include non-teaching staff in contact with pupils, Arethusa, I never knew his real name. He had served on the HMS *Arethusa*, in World War I, hence his name, and was general factotum for teachers and pupils, and full of stories of his navy experiences! 'Arry's cure for a pupil complaining of having a stiff neck in the morning was to leap onto a desk, stand the patient in front of him, and lift him up by his head, it seemed to work, at least no one ever asked for more! 'Arry also turned a blind eye to our boiling eggs in handkerchiefs under the taps of the steam heated (very hot!) taps in the classroom ablutions.

'COBBY' – 'COBBY'S SHY' – (resident Cobbler). Cobby was the most useful of all. He repaired, fitted and generally looked after our various boots, rugby boots and shoes, etc. His shy was called 'I'S' and entered from the ground floor by steps under the main staircase, and in the basement, to an area also having access to the rifle range (·22 calibre rifles) adjacent. Again, I am afraid, I never knew his real name, but Cobby was a very helpful little man, out of a Disney cartoon, the leader of the seven dwarves!

'PA OYLE' – 'PA OYLE'S SHY'. Again I never knew his name. Mr Oyle I suppose, but I am only guessing. He was in charge of the steam boiler system that heated the entire school. Lasses and boys, headmaster's home, swimming bath, showers, ablutions, egg boiling taps and all – (I nearly wrote oil)!

So, back to me leaving Crossley's, again! I have in front of me the Holy Bible – Old and New Testaments, bound in black leather, gilt-edged paper, on the back of the front cover a label with the Crossley's badge coat of arms, and motto, *Omne Bonum Ab Alto* (All Good From Above). This Bible was presented to Jeffrey Walton – This do and thou shalt live. – Signed G.B. Newport, Headmaster, December 1935.

Inside the Bible I found a postcard, posted to J Walton, Danum Mount, Benton Hill, Horbury, with two halfpenny stamps, King George V, the day and month on the franking stamp are indistinct, possibly 29, 1936 (I left in December 1935) – the message on the other side is, to me, both intriguing and a reminder!

The situation regarding permits is that we have a case of scarlet fever in the school. If there are no more cases by Saturday, permits will be given on Sunday, Monday and Tuesday. But the boy must be fetched. Why not come on Monday, to the reunion and see him then?

Yours,
G.B. Newport.'

I regret that I have no recollection of this incident. There had been no outbreak, to my knowledge, of scarlet fever in my years at Crossley's, and who the pupil was who 'must be fetched' I have no idea I am sorry to say – the reminder is the word 'permits'.

The next book to the Bible on my study shelves is *The Kings Grace* 1910–1935 by John Buchan (no less, ex. Ambassador to Canada, among other talents!). The label on the inside cover reads, Presented by the Mayor and Corporation of Halifax to commemorate the Royal Jubilee 1910–1935. Presented to J. Walton 6 May 1935, Miriam Lightowler, Mayor. This has reminded me that I was still living at Danum Mount, and well remember hearing on the wireless that King George V had died. In this book John Buchan has quoted twice, once at the beginning, and again at the end, the following: 'The Englishman is taught to love the King as his friend, but to acknowledge no other master than the laws which himself has contributed to enact' – Goldsmith: Citizen of the World. And since then, over 73 years ago, I have only opened them both six times to show someone, and I would not even have got them, if my Mum had not given them back to me when I left home!

Today, it is not a king but a queen, Elizabeth II (we were together in World War II, together along with a lot of others)! But we must all remember, 'The price of liberty is eternal vigilance.' I wish I had said that! But then, I know what happened, with Stalin, Hitler and Mussolini, along with many others. I was there when they were there and they 'got-rid' of many millions of people, including many more millions of their own people – so be very vigilant!

Some few years earlier, perhaps two years, the Mayor of Halifax, I am fairly sure it was not Mayor Lightowler, came again into my life when I was invited to be present at the official opening of the BBC Moorside Edge transmitter building, near Slaithwaite, or 'Slawit' as the locals have it. I was the only boy there, how I was picked, why I was picked, I have no idea. Moorside Edge is more in the Huddersfield area than the Halifax area, and both are of similar importance, and I would guess, with hindsight, that both towns were involved. Perhaps it was that I was the only school boy messing about with wireless and radio at that time, but I don't think so, there were millions of people in the country who at least had wireless sets and even splendid automatic radiograms.

I had a smashing day! In the morning, the various dignitaries, and yours truly, were shown round the station and then driven to a good pub in Slaithwaite, where we had a very good lunch. I have since been many times through the area and failed to find the pub, maybe it has been demolished or converted, I don't know. The pub was on a higher level from the road and alongside at the same level was a good bowling green, where I competed with my elders, but not very well!

At school permits were a personal thing, applicable only to boarders – with only one parent, mother or father, who if able to, according to circumstances and geography, could visit their children, by arrangement with the headmaster, then the pupil was given a permit. Obviously a very sensible arrangement, allowing parents, siblings and friends to enjoy a change of scene and probably, as in my case in my early days, tears all round at the end of the day! In my case there were difficulties. In my early years my brother Ron was either too young to visit alone, or later as a pupil at Wakefield's Queen Elizabeth I Grammar School, was involved in studying for his matriculation for university entry, and in my later years he was at Leeds University, studying English Language, English Lit., English History, and also at the Carnegie College of Physical Training, Leeds. His various degrees in those days meant serious work on serious subjects at high levels. Not as now, when, after ten years of 'Education, Education. Education!' and 'Universities' offering subjects such as Media Studies, (T.V. watching)! Sociology (How to get a job in 'Local Government, read the Guardian') 'Elf 'n safety', (don't play conkers and don't 'hang' hanging baskets of flowers), and there is probably somewhere offering Handloom weaving and Flower arranging – with Hons!

My mother was virtually always 'On call' in her professional medical field, nursing home, outside patients, and general medical emergencies in the area. This meant she was coming if she possibly could, which she did when she could! My brother Ronald, now at university, and perhaps understandably, had other irons in the fire and also came when he could, and as permits tended to be given on Saturday and Sundays, again for obvious reasons, this depended on whether he was winning, in which case he was *not* allowed to leave, that is from the poker game in progress, or he was at a very critical stage, in or out, with his present girlfriend, take your pick! At Crossleys, the side gate entrance on the 'town side' has substantial cast iron and oak fixed seats. On my last visit they were still there, where I sat waiting and looking, all the way down the main road to St Jude's Church and Halifax for Mum or Ron to appear, sometimes yes sometimes no, there were no mobiles then. Mum was on the phone of course, Horbury 164, but it was pointless for her to ring as the headmaster's phone would not be monitored at weekends, and of course I was out on 'permit', and no answering machines!

This phase passed, with passing terms and holiday periods, from junior to senior, and my *own* irons in the fire but at that time it was up with what I had to put. Today I would have to be taken into care, headmaster suspended on full pay for a couple of years, while lessons had been learned, and Mum taken to court as not being fit to have children! It is a funny old world, sorry, planet, to be politically correct! I am sorry, as with everything else in this Conversation, Discussion, Dissertation, call it what you will, and it is all the *truth*, and I *mean it*! All of it!

It is now Monday 19 February 2007 – I started, you will recall, on 9 January 2007 (no, not a New Year resolution)! and still I am desperately trying to complete this first section, and the more I write, the more I remember, items I should have included at an earlier stage. There is a list of notes, I have already done and included, three separate inserts so I have no place to insert any more.

Since penning or, in my case pencilling, that last diatribe, the phone has rung, it was Penny Holiday, she is a bank manager, Lloyds, daughter of my companion. 'Have I included the Marmite stink bomb story?' No I haven't, damn it – do it now!

In my junior years, mum sent me various tuck box items, Wilkin & Sons, Tiptree, Essex: cherry marmalade, they don't seem to have it now, raspberry jam, clotted Devonshire cream and home made scones etc., on occasion, also a jar of Marmite, one of my favourites still. In one special case I had kept a nearly empty jar, the usual last bits still clinging to the jar and over some time, I augmented the contents with various ripe items of food, cheese, bits of this and that, etc. With the lid off the smell was, as Damon Runyon would say, 'more than somewhat', and I would threaten to open the jar and let out the appalling smell, to quell some insurrection.

Another person who figured in this period of my life was Ikey Bradshaw, he was truly a one off, highly intelligent, secretive, a loner, but also in his way a good friend to a few. Fortunately, I was one of the very few. In appearance, he was fourteen to fifteen years old, dead ringer for Shylock in The Merchant of Venice, and I assure you I do not say this with any intension of belittlement, or disrespect, it just happens to be *true*, today he would be in high demand for J.K. Rowling's Hogwarts School or Shakespeare! The main classroom corridor is nine or ten feet wide, york stone paved, and with pitch pine, vertically V jointed boarding to dado height, if I remember correctly. Ikey always walked with the panelling on his right side up and right side down, very close, never in the middle, in complete silence and concentration, and rarely a word to anyone passing, not exactly gregarious! There were a few times, in my experience, while playing indoor cricket in the playroom/gym, and we had managed to get our cricket tennis ball wedged in the V joints of the open queen post timber roof truss, when, fortunately, Ikey would appear from the aforesaid corridor door, heading for the diagonal exit door to the library. I would ask: Ikey, will you please get our ball down? it's up there – and Ikey would then walk to the wall bars on the opposite long side of the room, climb to the top of the bars, grasp a half-inch diameter metal gas pipe running from floor to truss, tie-beam level, bracketed from the wall with metal pipe clips for the six or seven feet to a metal truss tie-rod, grab it with one hand, then two, swing slightly then pull himself up onto the tie-beam, walk along it, reach for wedged ball, throw it down, walk back along the beam to tie-rod, lower himself down onto the tie-rod again, swing for a second time, then drop to the hard beechwood floor, a sickening height, land on his feet, turn round and continue his interrupted walk to exit door to the library. From start to finish, he had not spoken a word! Those days, and for many years to come, not many people had heard the word anorexic. In PT strip, Ikey was almost skin and bones, mainly bones! No, I can't believe it either, but it happens to be true!

Then there was the business of the shoe laces and top floor of the main staircase, three stories above the york stone paving slab floor, – but you would not believe that either, so why bother, and anyway it was madly dangerous!

Then there was the business of the mercury, but I am not sure I 'saw it' even though I have always remembered it, and was there in the chemistry laboratory, during a class with Mr Rucklidge. Ikey drank some mercury and lived! – sleight of hand or what, I am not sure. Ikey was a very 'Krafty' chap!!

26

I am sure about this instance, I still have the scars to prove it. We were in the glass house, a large classroom with three walls panelled to desk top level, including the access door, off the entrance corridor, during the change period, waiting for the teacher. I cannot remember what the reason was, but I was being pursued by Ikey at some speed, but I was faster than Ikey, going for the exit door, and reaching out with my left hand, for the door jamb, to push off from, at speed, down the corridor, when Ikey, with outstretched arm, pushed me in the back and my left hand and arm went through the plate glass, and for a time there was blood everywhere, mine. Off to sister, in dispensary, with glass shards in my hand and arm. Some very small bits are still in there now! The last I heard of Ikey was some few years later, probably during my last meeting with Berty during the early years of WWII, this was that he was in a home or hospital, I am sorry to say.

However, on my last visit to the school in 2004, and my only visit since I left, to say the least, things have changed, basically in the educational area. In 1985 Heath Grammar School (founded 1597) and less than a mile away, was amalgamated with Crossley Porter Schools (my *Times Educational Supplement* says, 'the school is currently housed in Porter Schools Victorian Building'). About time Heath Grammar moved into the twentieth century! But it was a very good day school, and it is now called Crossley Heath School, so you can see which is still in front!

The school was partly refurbished in the 1990s, a new technology block opened in 2002 with a language college extension in 2004 and an extension to the technology block (2005). The head is Helen Gaunt, Mrs, Miss or Ms it does not say, and these days it pays not to ask. She was '(Appointed 2001)' – and therefore must be very capable. 'Staff: Twenty-four men, thirty-six women. Total number of pupils 1,025. Gender of sixth form mixed, number of sixth form pupils 250.'

Woke at six, normally wake at seven, and get up at seven-thirty, mind starts working, thank the Lord! It is Tuesday January 23rd 2007. Start thinking (as usual, not able to sleep any more). What CHANCE have I of finishing what I started on January 9th 2007? Not Much! Will try, see how it goes!

On Sunday January 7th I had a phone call from a life-long friend (His lifetime, not mine)! Dr J. B. Stoker, cardiologist, recently retired to Scotland (to be with his family), as government ministers and MPs say for dubious reasons. I floated my intentions for this project, and his advice, always being very good, was: 'Knowing you, you will be too comprehensive.' (It was his phone call, a long one, embarrassingly so, over an hour, although I offered to ring him back a number of times.) He continued: 'I try to keep my papers shorter and don't cover so much. But please, let me have a copy when it's published. E&OE.' ('Errors and Omissions Excepted' as building contractors usually add on to their Bills of Quantity Tenders.) In John's case, going to Scotland is understandable, with one son a (doctor), two daughters (one a doctor), and all with wives or husbands and some grandchildren. I have designed for various weddings, and John has made (first class) the clever bits, Charles Rennie Macintosh style chairs to support the tiered wedding cakes in one case, and for the more modern millennium years of space orbit, a cake stand, with a stainless steel orbital arc sweeping over the rosewood base and the three tiered cakes, both at an angle to the base, and with millennium dated coins of the Realm inlaid in the base, also first class (or it should have been). They are all living in Scotland, and as with Wales both have their very expensive parliament buildings paid for by England's taxpayers, including this poor Yorkshire boy.

Another good friend is Paul Pearce, who recently moved in across the road 100 yards away from my home in Sandal Magna – we also have mutually good friends, of long-standing, some of whom, like me, were Apple computer converts in the days of the Apple Lisa and long before Bill Gates came along to steal the Apple 'Macintosh' operating system, mouse and all!

Paul also gets around a bit, works very hard and sooner or later answers all my phone calls. I have an email from him on 29 April 2006, from Beijing, China – and he wasn't on holiday! His valued observations were very interesting. 'Beware of people who try to use or con you,' but his parting shot on leaving my study, referring to my memoirs, was: 'Reserve me a copy' – E&OE again!

In consequence I will do a quick recce, hopefully into my future. Immediately, it now also dawns on me that I have already started, and hopefully got well on into my youth period, and I have omitted the most important near-miss of my life, I contracted, somewhere between the ages of 5 and 6, meningitis!

Actually, I was not 'all there' at the time and can only repeat the information I was given when I was 'all there' a few years later, which was that I was either in a coma or unconscious (I still don't know the difference if there is one) for two weeks with my dear mother virtually in constant attendance. my pulse stopped! My mother had a bag of ice pieces, which she immediately 'plonked' on the back of my neck, I assume after lifting up by my head by my hair! From there on, thankfully, the angel and my mother continued to sit on my shoulders and I gradually recovered from this terrible and often fatal disease, which is still virulent in the twenty-first century!

I hear you say – But where did the ice cubes come from?

The refrigerator, at that time, was probably the latest thing from America and only available to the well-off few, and we were not well-off. It was only a few years later while on my hols from Crossley's, that I became aware of a new butchers, or in this case, meat shop in the High Street called the Argenta, which sold pre-butchered and packed beef from the Argentine, and only frozen beef in all its forms, sirloin, fillet steak, rib-eye, from refrigerators and only 200 yards from our home in Co-operative Street. Mum, and Me! – and it was to be in the year 2003, driving past the shop, no longer the Argenta, that it dawned on me that this was where the ice cubes came from! My doctor was Dr Simson, who had his home and surgery lower down the High Street – a sole practice long before Mr Ernest Bevin's NHS.

A convalescent period followed. My mother had arranged, among other things, for me to be taken down to the large LMS Railway Horbury Bridge goods station, from where goods of all types were delivered over a large area from the adjacent railway marshalling yards. I was to accompany the driver in his solid-tyred Leyland lorry to the various mills, factories, businesses, warehouses in the area. It was good fun, but as a small boy arriving with the goods at these very exciting large buildings, it seemed very adventurous, and amazing. I was made welcome, fed with tea and cakes, or whatever, and made a fuss of I suppose, and I did my bit on the paperwork and fetching and carrying. One place on the list was the famous Sykes cricket bat manufacturers factory on Westfield Road, Horbury – in later school years, Sir Don Bradman, who used Sykes' bats, was a guest in Mr Sykes' house during the Leeds test matches with Australia, and our Danum Mount garden had a common boundary with Mr Sykes' house garden. Incidentally, as I write, the Sykes bat factory and the adjacent one of Ready Cut Rugs Limited, are being demolished, a comment on the times!

As the American writer (and later TV programmes, based on his work) Ripley, says in 'Believe it or Not!' I now realize I have omitted a number of anecdotes, now I am not threatening, merely perhaps, considering my appendix no, not that one! I dealt with that earlier, the one some writers often put at the end of books, and are then able to put in the things they forgot to put in. What do you think, good idea? Look in the back, no! not now, later!

I am sitting thinking, how to start again after the memory trauma of what I now call the first phase, so you will have realised that this is the second phase. It also buys me some time, believe it or not, and by now you know you had better believe it! The door bell has just rung, a delivery, some excellent shoes from ComfortSko Modbury, Devon, (Swiss made), and included is a free gift packet of small bulbs. On the front it says *Viel gluck, Veel geluck, Bonne chance*, Good luck! and a picture of the plant. I know a bit about two of the languages, they are bulbs of the four leaf clover Lucky clover, I have had this plant, as now, in my garden for years, given loads away, but it is nice to have reinforcements at memory block time, from my you know who. I am glad they are thought of as female, at least I do.

Having left school in December 1935, it would appear from some fortunate documentary evidence that my girlfriend Maria, we were the same age, and she had collected, unknown to me for many years, various other similar items that now sharpen my memories. I have a couple of foolscap letters, looking rather dilapidated, headed Charles Roberts & Company Limited – Railway Wagon Builders & Hirers, Horbury Junction, near Wakefield, and above this is a dominant aerial perspective of the entire factory, of some 36 acres extent, established 1856, Capacity: one wagon every 25 minutes. This heading occupies one third of the depth of the page, and in case I do not get round to including a scan, I have included the salient points.

Thursday, 5th March 1936

Dear Sir,

With reference to your interview at these works on Friday last with Mr. Henshaw, when we arranged for you to commence duty in the Drawing Office on Monday last, at a commencing salary according to scale, of 12/6 (twelve shillings and sixpence) per week, we now confirm this arrangement, and set out below, the terms and conditions of employment at these works.

Hours of Work: Commence 8.55 am. Dinner 12.30 to 2.00 pm.
Finishing Time, 5.00 pm. or as near as possible thereafter.

Annual Leave: One week with full pay first year; thereafter fourteen days per annum.

Kindly note that this engagement is subject to termination by 7 days notice in writing on either side.
Yours faithfully,

Signed
Russell Bailey,
Director and Secretary

My salary *per week* was the equivalent of 60 pence today. In my first six months I never left the office before 6.00 pm, and thereafter I was only rarely home for 8.00 pm and on one occasion there *all night* and as for holidays, I did not have any, and did not get double pay in lieu either, but I really enjoyed every minute!

The drawing office, where all detailed design drawings were made and stored, of all Engineering products made at the factory for world wide sale, was headed by the Chief Draughtsman, Mr Edgar Downing, who had been with the firm since he was a boy and knew everything about everything pertaining to the design office, and was also a first class person, then in his 60s I would guess, knowledgeable, dedicated and respected, and I learned a lot from him. I was always 'Laddie' to him!

The Senior Draughtsman was Mr Irwin, ex Bentley Motors, and again completely competent and an exquisite draughtsman, he used to both draw, rule and letter, using the same ruling pen for all three skills now lost with the advent of computers, as with the whole gamut of drawing instruments, beam compasses, double elephant drawing boards, chinese ink on transparent linen, tracing paper, brass-head drawing pins, parallel rules, etc. Mr Irwin's skills included being able to throw a large brass-headed drawing pin up into the sloping side of the timber boarded area of the north light glazed roof truss of our drawing office, and impale it at a single throw. And he was also very capable in the engineering design field. Now we have computers, the world is over run by alleged designers, experts, consultants, professionals, so called artists etc., mostly cribbing from the multitude of computer programs (some excellent) on the 'Internet'.

The drawing office staff consisted of those already mentioned, and eight others, including me – after about six weeks I got an assistant, straight from Grammar School, Leslie Bains, (remember the name, it will come up again later). He was a pleasant chap so I initiated him into the finer points of electro-photo printing, which I had at first found interesting, but was repetitive, and I do not like doing the same things over and over again, except perhaps in the design field, where when I have finished I see improvements, and want to start again and often do.

Mr Edgar Downing along with Mr Irwin had decided I would be more useful devoting all my time on the drawing board rather than producing prints in the print room. I could not have agreed more, hence the appointment of Leslie. The print room was approximately 20 feet by 10 feet with two doors diagonally in each corner of the long walls, one from the drawing office and the other leading to the photographer's office and the various administration offices, directors, and chairman's office. On one long near side wall was installed a large developing tray to take the large sheets of ferro prusiate paper, for engineering blueprints, to be fed into a conveyor roller oven to dry the wet prints.

On the opposite side was the splendid print machine, cast iron frame, glass carbon arc lamp with two, half-inch thick carbon rods pointed and adjusted for contact and when switched on, produces a blinding, (don't look at it) light, and when simultaneously traversed across, backwards and forwards, by steel chain drive and across the simultaneously unrolling roll of print paper, with a drawing on tracing paper or a similar linen paper on top of the print paper, the drawing is photographically reproduced on the sheet of print paper. The print is then transferred to the developing tray, developed, passed through rubber rollers, to remove most of the water, deposited on a moving heated metal mesh belt, to be deposited on a waiting tray for collection so now, if you ever come across one at PC World you will be able to tell the assistant expert how it works!

I mentioned in the paragraph above carbon, nowadays carbon dioxide as in global warming of the planet, carbon that after over 40 million years since the dinosaurs were apparently instantly, wiped off the face earth, according to some experts, although we are still digging up their fossilized remains. We are fed propaganda by politicians and other financial experts that carbon dioxide in the atmosphere is causing it and we must pay for it. It is going to be quoted on the Stock Market, millions of tons of it, and that is tons of a gas in the air! And a few years ago it was the holes in the ozone layer, causing the trouble – or so we were led to believe by the 'experts', what happened to them?

This world, this earth, not this 'planet' there is only one world, one earth, and apparently billions of planets. We are trying to get to Mars, it is not far away, only a few million miles away, but if and when we get there, it is barren, and we are at present trying to hydrogen bomb earth into a similar state for training purposes, of course, but try coming back, if we ever arrive on Mars, it is as they say, another ball game. The moon is the only place in space we have been to, and it is on our doorstep, compared with Mars, and there is nothing we can do about it, if it was global 'cooling' as in the ice age then we would really need to worry, but there is nothing we could do about that either. As a postscript to the last paragraphs, and another remarkable coincidence, in today's, *Daily Mail*, March 23rd 2007, Masterquiz, Question 5. Which is the principal gas in the atmosphere of Mars? ... Answer, carbon dioxide, now you know why we are so keen to get there, has any one volunteered yet?

My drawing board, now antiquarian size, was now full time, and I was fully involved in the design of major contracts for new types of rolling stock for various large companies, both in the United Kingdom, and abroad. One interesting contract, from ICI (Imperial Chemical Industries), was for the largest rolling stock on British railways at that time, and even now probably still are, a number of forty-two and a half ton double bogie steel hopper wagons, for use in transporting limestone from their mines in the UK. Another contract was for the Pulverized Fuel, Company, pressurised twin tank vehicles, we used this type of fuel for some of our furnaces, in the main forge, pulverised fuel (very fine powdered coal) which arrived at our works from the main line rail system, and they were then traversed across the lines to park against a furnace and start to blow in the fuel onto an already very hot fire, and this went on continuously!

Possibly an even more interesting contract I was asked to deal with was the manufacture of 20-ton tank wagons for Guinness. No problem, but these tankers were different, they had to be glass lined, and the lining was to be done by a firm in Denmark, after C.R. & Co. had built them, and also in this case all measurements, were to be in metric (not imperial), and who had to do the drawings and learn metric? Me. The metric system was apparently invented in Great Britain, not many people know that now, even less then, but a lot of people have been taught metric since then, and they know nothing about the imperial system, used for centuries, British Empire wide. By the way, maybe you also do not know, so be my guest, the largest empire the world has ever seen, just thought I'd mention it in passing, as the passing sun never set on the British Empire. Imperial is much more basic to human beings, yards, feet, inches all are human, a stride measures a yard, a man's feet, a foot, etc., try marching striding a metre, not very good is it, much better by the yard. I had better not go on, I might get into serious trouble now, not then.

The drawing office housed a vast collection of drawings going back to the mid 1800s. In various plan presses in the office were kept the more recent drawings as they were made, but we also kept drawings going back to the 1800s, in a large but I regret to say dusty roof space adjacent to the print room area, in which we had to scramble and get somewhat grubby, in search of drawings of ancient railway products for Indian, Chinese, African, and many other countries railway systems, requiring parts etc. These old and even older negatives were kept in rolled bundles, fortunately they were not often required. Mr Downing would occasionally ask for a certain drawing, from a series for a named contract, its code number, and we would spend time searching, without success, he would return eventually, and call out the alphabetical and numerical code and then remind us to remember or use the 'drawing number and contract book, laddie'. He had a phenomenal memory, and at that time, unlike now, lessons really were learned, or else!

A great day for me came when I was asked to accompany the chairman and directors on a tour of the works for their guest, Sir Nigel Gresley, the London and North Eastern Railways, (LNER, created in 1923), Chief Mechanical Engineer. He and his design department designed the first Pacifics for the network, the renowned A1, in 1922 (when I was 2!), the famous, The Flying Scotsman No 4472, with carriages in teak, and two coal tenders with corridors and rest room for the crew changes, etc. It was very hard work, after the coal in the first tender had been used, transferring coal from the second tender, at an average speed of 69.9 mph, and pulling 24 carriages, completing the 392¾ miles to Edinburgh in 5 hours 45 minutes. Later, the streamlined A4 locomotive first seen in 1935, Mallard, with a speed of 126 mph in 1938, beat the world speed record. My main job was to arrange a demonstration for Sir Nigel, of the stressing or tensioning of a main locomotive coupling, in short loading it to destruction if possible, but hopefully not. Sigh of relief by all parties! Twelve years later, my interests necessitated that I commute from Yorkshire to London on the Yorkshire Pullman, on a more or less a weekly basis. On a few occasions at Doncaster, Mr Pegler, then the chairman of Pegler Brass Products Ltd, Doncaster, boarded the train and joined me at the table. He was a dedicated railway enthusiast, and all the way to London had his stopwatch on the table timing the train, and we were together on the return journey and he timed it back to Doncaster. He later bought the Flying Scotsman, took it to America on tour, lost a fortune – and was to then become be the first greeter or major domo, on the Orient Express from Paddington station, London, to the continent. A lovely man who, I hope, is still around and happy.

The above paragraphs have also reminded me of another of my near misses at C.R. & Co., where it happened. I was standing waiting at the side of the 20-ft wide door opening with my back nicely fitting into the 24″ × 9″ recess, of one side of the rolled steel stanchions or columns forming the upright of the main door frame, waiting for a 20-ton coal wagon, loaded, on a traverse, to pass into the forge, which was being pushed by a tractor, on the blind side, far rear corner to me, with the two 12″ (approx.) diameter buffers, at about my chest height. When the second buffer was immediately opposite me, the wagon rolled off the traverse and deposited the buffer into my stomach, making a very large bang in doing so and causing me to pull in said stomach, more than somewhat (as Runyon said, remember?). Then I pulled in my stomach even more than somewhat, and walked off as usual, with my roll of drawings on my way, and it was only after going about 20 yards, I noticed that the even louder bang of drop stamps had stopped and the operators were standing looking at me, and only then did it dawn on me how near I was – well, to not being here, to write this. Fortunately, the reason for my survival was that the main yard was paved with granite sets, which earlier had been removed in a strip a yard wide, across the aforesaid doorway, and had been replaced with tarmac, and the wheels had dead dropped into this, and, being softer, stopped dead. Some near miss!

The roll of drawings I was carrying were for the foreman of the pattern shop for some item for which I had done the drawings, and I passed by some contractors' men installing yet another drop stamp huge foundation block of reinforced concrete in the forge, and all the Irish labourers, about six of them, were running at speed with full steel barrows of concrete mix in a continuous chain! A different world now!

An even bigger dead drop I had experienced in my time in the drawing office, the power for the above mentioned drop stamps in the forge was in the form of a weight-loaded accumulator in a very large tower, one hundred yards from the drawing office. One day, as I recall, mid-morning, there was one colossal BANG, the ground literally shook, drawing boards bounced, instruments went on leave all over the place. I do not wish to bore you with the construction detail of this machine but is briefly, a very large pressure cylinder with a load casing of heavy ballast of many tons, fortunately there were no casualties.

My progress in the firm was apparently being well monitored, unknown to me. I received a letter from the Chairman and Managing Director, Mr Duncan Bailey, OBE, MIMECHE, again, no less, and this time, unlike the previous letter from the secretary, Director Russell Bailey, (D.B.s Son)! This really was coming down from the Mount as with the Ten Commandments and I am not now, I see, addressed as Dear Mr Walton, but as Dear Walton, so he has come down and he really was. The letter is dated 17th November 1937,

(First paragraph): Mr Henshaw, (Works Director) – Has recommended you as a suitable young man to go into the Frame Department, and there, you should get some very valuable experience, and help to fit yourself for a higher position in these works. For the time being, I want you to become Progress Man, chasing up various parts for the different contracts running through the shops.

(Last paragraph of 4) – Remember that your future is in your own hands. Nobody can make a man of you except yourself. As soon as I get a further favourable report from Mr Henshaw, the question of your salary will receive my sympathetic and immediate consideration.
Yours faithfully,
Duncan Bailey.

Progress man meant that I was now in a freelance position in the works and particularly in the main frame department, the one that turned out one wagon every 25 minutes. I also wore a white linen coat as did all heads of departments, but I was the only one still in my teens! The frame department was the largest unit in the works, No.1 Bay, and was 200 yards (approx.) long and consisted of three longitudinal bays – two outer bays at ground floor level and the centre bay had a raised, steel framed platform, 6 or 7 feet higher, with a steel 'railway line' on which the wagons progressed, in stages, to completion and removal to Charles Roberts and Co.'s own railway system and marshalling yard for onward delivery to the customer on the national rail network, LMS, LNER. The building was steel framed construction with pitched roofing and continuous glazing on both sides to provide top lighting, and with two overhead travelling cranes spanning the three bays to feed the production lines.

The process, simplified, was for steel framed wagons to be assembled on the raised centre section, this again was divided into sections by the wagon's size, and was served by a small team of men and boys. The rivet boys, teenagers, were in charge of a Red hot brazier, on which they heated steel rivets, manipulated, using bellows and tongs, to the same heat as the fire, and then, still using the tongs, threw the hot rivet up to the riveter's mate, holding a catching bucket, and then transferring it to the pre-drilled rivet hole, for the two riveters to hammer home, and this was a continuous process, one team to one wagon – and made a lot of noise! So far, so good! But the main walkway, down the production line, was *between* the brazier and the catcher's bucket and continually being crossed, at regular intervals, by flying red hot rivets, timed by the boys immediately before anyone in a white coat, and particularly a new boy on the block was due to walk past. However, I was now in charge, so I at least made sure I managed to dodge the rivets with a casual air, until things quietened down, and I was accepted, or perhaps tolerated.

My duties continued to expand, as did my position in the company and in consequence my salary was expanded by the chairman. I was promoted to assistant to the works manager, Mr Henry T. Stead and the works director, Mr Henshaw. This now meant that I had to deal only with heads of departments. Our offices were at the main entrance end of the works and consisted of two offices, interconnected with the works director in one, and the other larger, for the works manager, myself and a very good secretary Stanley Fell. Stanley was an international level table tennis player, about 6' 4" tall and thin, and very quick, also at shorthand and typing! Mr Stead was a very pleasant person and perhaps a father figure to me, we got on well together and I certainly learned a lot working with him, and he obviously appreciated my efforts as the transcript below of one of his not unusual pencilled letters while on holiday at St Anne's-on-Sea, indicates. By chance I was to continue to be connected with his progress, and perhaps he with mine, until the late fifties, but we never actually met again after I left Charles Roberts & Co., and he left after me. In my case, further things happened including World War II, and other varied commitments, and I very much wish I had met him again. However I happen to have, amongst the papers previously mentioned, one of his many pencil letters,

'Friars Mere',
36 All Saints Road
St-Anne's-On-Sea

Dear Jeffrey,

I have been wondering this last day or two how the extension to No 1 Bay is progressing. Don't forget to have the men working week-end altering the track. But the point I wish to stress really is that J. Hawke must have the concrete pads fixed on the wall to carry the roof trusses. I arranged this matter with W. Milner as you know, and it is essential that they are in position before Bidgood & Co. are ready for them. Will you make sure this is done?

Next, of course, comes the furnaces and wall alterations for the 35 cwt stamps, but Mr Henshaw is so keen on this that he will see to it to some extent personally.

37

Please drop me a line by return giving me the position.

The weather here is quite good and we are enjoying the holiday very much.

Kind Regards

Henry T Stead.

So you will gather that I had responsibilities.

I lived with my mother and brother Ronald at Danum approximately two miles away from the works, and of course she, and thus we, were on the phone, Horbury 164. It may surprise some of you to learn, that in those days people did not, as now, walk about with a mobile permanently to the ear, take it to bed every night, and keep it switched on and provide one for each of their children, with a digital camera, again, for 'elf'n safety reasons.

One dark, but unfortunately not stormy night (it probably would not have happened if it had been) the phone rang, not as usual for mum, but it was for me. The works timber yard, in the open air, and stacked ten feet high over a very large area, with various types of timber was on FIRE! Mounting my Sturmy Archer, cable operated, multi-speed, gear change, front and rear lights powered by built in hub electric generator etc., transport, I arrived. Fire brigades in attendance, thank the Lord, but some chaos, and no sign of the works director or Mr Stead, although they arrived later, at least Henry did, and after a lot of effort, mainly by the fire services, we eventually welcomed the dawn. Next day we held a meeting in the director's office, to try to determine the cause of the fire and we soon had a main suspect, the waste heat boiler. This was sited at the far end of the main workshop bays including the Sawmill, where all the timber used in the building of all wagons of timber construction, with headstocks, sole bars, and the timber load container of various types, was prepared, sawn, planned, etc., with the sawdust, planer shavings and waste timber vacuum extracted in overhead metal ducting from each machine, and conveyed to a large hoppered container over the boiler to fuel the boiler and provide heating for the works.

There is no prize for guessing who was deputed to look into this, and come up with a solution PDQ: ME. There had apparently been complaints earlier, from workers in the sawmill, of pieces of glass dropping from the glazed side of the north light roof trusses, which ran across and at right angles to the main bays, but this was late summer, and there was a very large amount of glass up there, and when hot, metal frames and glass both expand, the glass cracks and pieces may break away simple science or whatever happens every summer everyone knows that, so it had not been reported, and even the unions accepted that.

Up I went, unattended, not even with, er, what are they called? Ah yes, a safety helmet, apparently they could be useful now in Iraq, but I didn't have one then, but neither do they have the best possible equipment, NOW, so that's all right then. Between each north light roof span was a metal drainage trough or gutter, in this case approximately 18″ × 6″, running the length of the span to deal with heavy rains, but in summer they were more often dry and now, in my case, they were on fire! The gutters, particularly the ones nearer the waste boiler were literally filled with charcoal or I suppose, charwood, small carbonised pieces of shavings, yes the same deadly global carbon, of today. It was black and warm on the top layer, but red burning hot 4″ below, and kept very hot along its not inconsiderable length by draught, as in a boiler, and this heat was also cracking the glass, which came down to the top of the wood shavings level, as it should for water drainage. What was happening at the waste boiler was that the shavings, were being deposited on the very hot fire, instantly lighted, but due to chimney draught were also being blown out to the open air, still burning, at above the height of the adjacent roofs and ending up in the dry gutters. There was a spark arrester hood on the chimney but this was worse for wear and obviously not effective so it was back to the drawing board, by now you know by whom.

My duties as progressor meant that I was dealing daily with the various heads of departments in the works, and this was to have some rather personal commutations in the future, about which I had no idea at the time. The head of the electrical department for the entire works was Mr Harry Watson, a man of many talents, ex. WWI, army, involved in the Russian Campaign at the latter part of the war, but now known for all his various interests and connections generally, and again an interesting person. Mr Watson was responsible for organising a visit to the Northern Command Coronation Tattoo at Roundhay Park, Leeds on Wednesday July 7th 1937. The tickets were for covered stand 10/6; the Official Programme, sixpence (see transport details below):

CHARLES ROBERTS & CO LTD
NORTHERN COMMAND TATTOO – AT ROUNDHAY
PARK, LEEDS, WEDNESDAY, JULY 7TH, 1937
    The 'Yorkshire' buses will pick up passengers at the following places and times :–
    7.15. p.m Market Place, Ossett

7.30. p.m Barclays Bank, Horbury

7.45. p.m Lupset Hotel

8.00. p.m County Hall, Wakefield

Passengers are requested to be at the respective places on time, as the buses will leave promptly.

The buses will be numbered, <u>AND THE NUMBER OF YOUR BUS WILL BE</u> : 1. which will of course, also apply to the return journey.

This visit was a great success in more ways than one, the Tattoo was very impressive, but for me even more remarkable in that 'uncle' Harry had arranged, unknown to me or his niece, Miss Kathleen Mary Maria Baines, (no relation to Leslie Baines of C.R. & Co, mentioned earlier), the only daughter of Councillor F.J. Baines, mill owner, of Addingford Mills, Horbury, Chairman of Horbury Council, for the two of us to meet, for the first time, and in interesting circumstances, to say the least. We were eventually to marry.

The head of 'the wheel shop,' Mr George Cass, was a very solid citizen indeed. He was, a few years later, to marry my mother, and, due to my circumstances in the coming WWII, when I left C.R. & Co., I was never to see him again. Unfortunately he died while I was on overseas service, a very trustworthy Yorkshire man. I also have a pair of Northern Command Tattoo tickets, for covered Grand Stand, (not 'Coronation' Tattoo), for Block D, row D.7 & 8, Saturday 16th July 1938, so it would appear we made a special, second anniversary visit with WWII coming in September 1939.

When I left school, I think, my mind was made up. I wanted to be an architect – I liked the arts field generally, and the imagining or devising and inventing and making etc. I had also considered the possibility of the medical profession, and with some hindsight, I would probably have taken it as a personal insult if one of my patients had died, whereas now, I point out to my medical friends (jokingly I hope) that doctors bury their mistakes, whereas mine are there for a long time (I hope), so I try to keep them as few as possible.

Hence my initial and fortuitous entry into engineering, particularly with a company as large and diversified as C.R. & Co., with all the various facets of the different trades departments, forges, foundry, pattern shop, machine shops, coach and body builders etc., construction methods, management and design fields, and I was soon to appreciate how very fortunate I was to have been presented with this opportunity by my dear

THE NORTHERN COMMAND CORONATION
TATTOO

JULY 1st, 2nd, 3rd, 6th, 7th, 8th, 9th and 10th, 1937

OFFICIAL PROGRAMME   -   -   -   PRICE SIXPENCE

41

mum, probably thinking it would help me, and do me good anyway, and how right she was – as usual.

The time had come for me to move on, as they say today, so I handed in my notice to leave C.R. & Co., in accordance with my previous appointment conditions then as they again say, all hell was let loose and the tablets came down from the mountain again. The chairman, Mr Duncan Bailey required my presence in his office, NOW. What was I thinking about, didn't I realise that my future in the company was assured, I would be running the company in due course, or similar words to that effect, but I had in fact already signed 'articles' as pupil, with a firm of architects. However, had I stayed I would have been in a 'reserved occupation', and not spent six years in the RAF in WWII. I did not see Mr Bailey again until eight years later, in very unusual circumstances, but we will come to that in turn later.

By this time my mother had sold the Danum Mount house and we were now living at another Danum, also in Horbury, on Elmwood Grove, off Northfield Lane. I had in fact prepared working drawings in my spare time while at C.R. & Co. for this house. It was a semi-detached house on a mixed private housing development, the developer, Mr Charlie Taylor who owned what would be called a motor service station today, (it is still there on Westfield Road, Horbury). I also did the drawings for his own house, which was sited opposite our house. Charlie probably owned the large field site for this development, I don't really remember.

My brother Ronald was doing his years' teacher training, following his history and English etc. degree successes, at the mixed local school on Northfield Lane 300 yards (approx) away, and having a whale of a time with his number one girlfriend, Mary, who was also a teacher, and the lady he married. Some years later he told me that when they were both teaching at the same school, and by this time he was headmaster, Mary had to leave before they were able to marry! They had a fine family and grandchildren, but unfortunately, they are both now no longer with us, I very much regret to say.

However, it is now, today, March 30th, Saturday 2007, and I am doing one of my paragraph insertions, out of time context with the last paragraph, but it is apposite. I have, fortunately, just remembered that their daughter Elizabeth, my niece, and also a teacher, said on a phone call just before Christmas 2006, that she would call in to see me, when the weather improves in spring, when she was also due to visit her two brothers, one lives in Horbury, the other in Emley, a small village, and each just a few miles away from me, at Sandal Magna. Elizabeth lives near Salisbury, and has no idea I am writing this, neither have her two brothers, or their children! IF, I tell her, I only hope it is a pleasant surprise!

To continue, I was now commuting daily on my trusty Raleigh Sports, the five or six miles to the firm of architects I had joined, Messrs Fox & Hill, Chartered Architects and Surveyors. Their offices were in a three storey building at the crossroads corner of Union Street and Bond Street, with offices on the second and third floors – on the third floor, there was also the office of 'Scotland' one of the national bookmakers of the day. The ride to Dewsbury, through Horbury and Ossett, was reasonable, with only about three inclined areas, until I arrived at the boundary and then the Dewsbury cutting, cut through very solid rock, and in a very steep and long decline, into the town below which was fine going down, but a very different ball game going up to home! The view from the cutting over-looking the town was in the those days amazing. To me, it was hell's kitchen, with a large number of mill chimneys, each belching volumes of smoke, and with also the possibility of fog, or smog in the valley.

The partners in the practice were two gentlemen who were very different. Mr Charles Fox was the senior partner, and probably twice as old as his partner Mr Erskin Hill, ARIBA, Diocesan Surveyor to the Bishop of Wakefield, and his father or uncle, I am now not sure which, was Canon Hill, Vicar, at Horbury's St Peter's Church, Carr of York, architect, (but born in Horbury, son of a stone mason), and a highly respected and successful architect, he also became Mayor of York, but his grave is at St Peters Church, Horbury!

Mr Fox's father had been partner in the earlier practice of Holtom & Fox, apparently a very good practice, designing various town halls and public buildings in the Victorian and Edwardian periods. One of their excellent perspectives, in the competition for the design of Wakefield Town Hall, along with the other entries, was on display in the bar of Wakefield's first class Under the Tower restaurant, in the town hall. The dining room is/was superb, as was the food, the best for miles around, including Leeds and Bradford, but eventually closed by the council, about four years ago. When I was a boy my mother used to say, 'If they put a red rosette on a donkey, they would vote it onto the council, in Wakefield!'

My first day at the office I went, as was usual in those days, properly dressed, with clean shirt, old school tie, suit and well polished shoes. It is, as you will know, somewhat different now, but then, we have to move on haven't we? Unfortunately for me, when I arrived, Mr Fox asked me to accompany him on a pre-arranged survey of a proposed site in Leeds, and it had by now started raining, fast, and neither I nor Mr Fox had rubber boots or any other protection, but we went, as arranged. The site was a recently crop-cleared field of earth, and it was still raining! Our client came a little later in his car to meet us, and tender his apologies, but stayed in his car to watch, for a while, and we got on with it. Shoe and suit cleaning and drying at home that night, ready for the next day. Mr Fox was the quantity surveyor for the practice, and did not have any formal qualifications in architecture, but of course had worked for many years in these fields, so his appreciation, knowledge of construction etc. were very good. He was also Catholic, and in consequence we designed various churches, presbyteries, church homes, and other buildings for the hierarchy, and the practice had done so for many years previously; a consequence of this was soon apparent to me, in that various Catholic Fathers used our waiting room as a meeting room while they made their various transactions with Scotland, the bookmakers on the floor above, on a fairly daily basis! We also had another version of the splendid print room at C.R. & Co. Here we had a room on the third floor with a small, open air balcony, to which I repaired with drawing board size, glazed frame, into which I inserted the negative, backed by print paper, backed, by thin sheet of plywood, held them up to the light or, sunlight if there was any, and how is that for progress? But it worked just the same!

Mr Fox lived at Boston Spa, near Tadcaster and drove to the office daily. His partner Mr Hill, informed me that he had won and lost two fortunes on the Stock Market so he had not done so bad, so long as he was now in the win position! He was primarily a quantity surveyor. I had not done architectural quantities before, and I learned the methods during my time with Mr Fox, which was to be only just over one year. Quantity surveyors, as my old friend, the late Harold B. Morris, ARIBA, Chief Architect for Tetley's Breweries, would remind them that they were, Just Bloody Scorers! He was reasonably right, except for the expletive, hence you will recall my use of 'E&OE' always included by Q.S. persons, including me, earlier! Mr Fox, being Catholic, was indeed valuable in the Catholic confessional field. Mr Hill, earlier, had suggested to me that I ask Charles, 'how high was the penitent's elbow rest', which was in the confessional, and, without further ado Charles would kneel on the floor and insist I measure from floor to his elbow, there and then and, if I was prevailed upon by Erskin to ask him again the next day, he would give a repeat performance, without question, and even the next day!

Mr Erskin Hill was of course *the* architect, and a very good one, and being Diocesan surveyor we were responsible for designing all aspects of

44

Church of England buildings for the diocese, from general maintenance to church building. Projects I was involved with included Denby Dale Church, Yorkshire, which is well sited, high on the side of the valley, and was also equipped with a Hammond electric organ, probably one of the first churches in the country to have one, and also has a lectern, pulpit, pews, chairs, and other items to our design, which were made by Mr Thompson (The Mouse Man of Kilburn), and had his trademark mouse carved on them in various places. Mr Thompson's workshop was well known to architects as a very good maker of first class items of furniture. Since then, he has become world famous as his workshops are today a tourist attraction in North Yorkshire, all due to good workmanship and the mouse!

The small Catholic church at the cross roads at Akworth, West Yorkshire, was also designed by Erskin and myself, although I had earlier learned a lesson, I was to live with for many years. Mr Fox and I did the survey of the site, prior to the design stage, and it was in summer, a bright sunny day, we left the office at 9 am, drove to the site in his car, arriving at 9.30 am, and did the survey OK, but about 12.30 or 1.o'clock I mentioned I was sorry, but I had a bad headache. Mr Fox immediately said: 'I know what you need, lunch!' We went to one, of the two pub restaurants there, and had lunch, out of the bright sunlight which was the real problem, and to cause me problems with migraine for some years, until I got to know all the triggers. Sunlight is one of my main triggers, particularly when unprotected by sunglasses, or as is the case today, shades worn by all and sundry, all day, and even night time, indoors and even in the dark!

My most satisfying work was on the famous Chapel on the Bridge at Wakefield, on the Calder River. St Mary's Chapel, probably the finest bridge chapel in the world, certainly the finest in the not now so United Kingdom or Queendom, even the French considered it superior to the one on the bridge at Avignon, France, and the people in Wakefield know, it is superior to the one in Rotherham, Yorkshire! The Chantry Chapel, as it is now called, at one time there were four chantries in the Parish of Wakefield, on the main roads leading to Doncaster, York, Leeds and Dewsbury in the thirteenth century, and the bridge at Wakefield was fractured, by heavy floods, in the second quarter of the fourteenth century, and the town bailiffs applied to the Crown for help in rebuilding the bridge in 1342, and it was decided not only to build a bridge, but also a chapel on it, as was done in many places at that time. That was in 1342 and since then, until 1843, the building had a very remarkable history of other uses such as cowshed, corn merchants' office, pawnbrokers, etc. I did my research then, in 1939, you pay Wakefield a visit soon, you will find it very interesting, and do yours, now!

However, during those four centuries the chantry fell into serious disrepair, and, to cut a long story short, the chapel was conveyed to Ecclesiastical Commissioners. The Yorkshire Architectural Society of the time undertook to supervise the restoration, and they advertised for designs to be sent to York, and those were exhibited in March 1843, and the plans submitted by architect, Mr Giles Gilbert Scott were selected for the restoration. The Hon. George Chapple Norton, in 1847, bought the west front of the chapel, and re-erected it at one corner of the artificial lake at Kettlethorpe Hall, to serve as a front for the boat-house. It is less than a mile from where I live, and not much more than a mile in the opposite direction, along the A61, to where the now, much blackened, new stone front stands, and with which I was involved, and was erected, and carved etc., by masons working on the very famous Liverpool Cathedral, Church of Christ, and still being built, in the early WWII years.

Mr Scott had specified both Bath, and Caen stone for the heavily sculptured west front, which was similar in design to the original, but with some change to one panel of the parapet, and other less prominent alterations. Unfortunately, Mr Scott chose Caen stone and, before the turn of the century, it was apparent that the above mentioned, old original front was in a better condition than its replacement. It was a few years later that the now Sir Gilbert Scott saw the condition of his choice of stone, and wrote in *The Ecclesiologist*, 'It was an evil hour that I yielded, and allowed the new front in Caen stone in place of the weather beaten old one, I never repented but once, and that has been ever since, I think of it with the utmost shame and chagrin.' He even offered to contribute to the cost of replacing the original if local Yorkshiremen would help. It did not happen, but demonstrates a truly concerned artist architect, and I am proud to have had, while still a teenager, the opportunity of following in his footsteps in researching, and producing, the drawings for this famous chapel.

Fox and Hill, as architects for the Wakefield diocese, were appointed to undertake the design (nothing was left of the carving, the main feature, of Sir Gilbert's west front) and construction of a new west front for the chapel and general improvement of the rest. As the artist draughtsman in the office I was made responsible for the research and final presentation of drawings of the project, I was delighted! Sir Charles Nicholson, in London, was appointed our consultant, and all the time I was completing my research

46

and drawings at the practice, the only letters that Mr Hill got back from Sir Charles were on odd pieces of plain white paper, hand written, in Indian Ink, and not one of us in the office could decipher *any* of the words, at all. None the less, I completed my contribution, and my drawings were to be displayed in the West Riding County Hall, later in the year.

At this time, my brother Ronald was on his teacher training year at the Northfield Lane school, as I have previously mentioned, and he had prevailed on me to prepare him some drawings, rendered in colour, on the people and things, etc., of the Saxon period. I had agreed, I don't *think* any money changed hands, in fact, on consideration, I am sure! Ron and I shared our living room together, some evenings, and at weekends, he with his books, and me at my drawing board, and all was peace and quiet, with a nice open fire and music of his choice, on the radio or the wireless as then, which was fine. His books consisted of, on average, at least four volumes per week, on loan from the Horbury, Carnegie Public Library – with 'Knowledge is Power', in cast iron, over part of the main entrance, and he would read them ALL, and then return them, and then take out four more! He was very well read in history, and particularly the first World War, and could become very engrossed, to the extent that I would have to call Ron, Ron, Ron, at least three times, and getting louder, to get his attention, until I found that all I had to do was switch off the wireless, and he would say: 'Switch it on, I am listening to that' instantly! And then, one day, came the bombshell, and, as they say now, the earth moved, and I *now* realise, it is also today (Sunday, 1st April 2007) and almost exactly to the day, it is 66 years ago, since we studied together in the living room at Danum, in 1939 when my brother casually announced, 'Did you know there are two top class scholarships in architecture to be won, in competition, in Yorkshire?' (He was remember, a 'teacher' and not a school master, and he should know these things!) No, I suppose I answered, and then the earth became a black hole, Horbury's first. 'Oh yes, I've got the details for you, held every year, takes a year, folio of 12 imperial size architectural drawings to be submitted before 5th May 1939'! (About a month away, and I was daily, up at seven, cycled to Dewsbury, busy all day, cycled home, arrived 6 pm had a meal etc., every working day, which sometimes also meant weekends). Also by this time, Maria and I were serious, she was a single minded redhead, more than somewhat, and, later in the day, when we met and I gave her the good news, all she said was to the effect of, 'Oh, you can do it!' She would sit with me in my box room studio, most evenings and at weekends, while I got on with it!

Started thinking, I could send two sheets from my Chantry Chapel drawings at the office, that leaves ten, design church altar, crucifix and candelabra, for St Mary's Church, Horbury Junction. Borrow Maria's Uncle Tom's (Vicar of St Mary's Church) episcopal regalia, for details of symbolic emblems etc., now eight. Design a village hall/church with the latest 'Lamella' Swedish, timber laminated floor to roof trusses, with a stage at the chancel end, and proscenium, removable screens or curtains, plus some perspectives and some working drawings etc., all done! I still have them, rolled up somewhere!

Three weeks passed. I asked Mr Fox if I could have two copies of the Chantry Chapel drawings to submit to the adjudicators. No! He could not allow drawings by the office pupil to be displayed in the town, or County Hall, where they would also be displayed, later in the summer! So, it was again back to the drawing board with only a week to go before submission day – I had two more drawings to produce – and also had to make a suitable portfolio! Now I come to think of it, I would very much like to recoup the money involved, in later years, in my own office, by some members of staff, in stealing prints, photocopies etc., without asking my permission, which, if asked, under similar circumstances, was always given! Came the day, had completed the drawings and it was 3 am, morning, and was finishing making the portfolio to be deposited at the West Riding County Hall before submission time at 10 am. – quick breakfast – no sleep!

Among the many applicants, Henry Liley and I were the two winners, as was later published in the *Wakefield Express* and the *Yorkshire Post* amongst other papers. Subsequently, we both entered The Leeds School of Architecture, one of the best in the country, as first year students. Henry was a superb draughtsman, but had not an original design idea in his head, in all our one-day esquisse programmes – he would casually walk over to my board, and some others, to see how we were all getting on and, next day early, submit a similar, but well presented scheme of one or the other of our, or other people's schemes. It got to the stage where we were all involved in finding which architectural, or other publication, he had copied it from, and display it above his submission, for the person doing the crit. (criticism), of our schemes, usually a staff tutor. I am pleased to say that Henry must have mended his ways as he qualified and practised in Wyke, Bradford for many years, but I was never to see him again after the first, and a bit of the second year. He was also a very nice chap.

In my first year, the war having started, I was daily travelling to the school from Horbury to Leeds on the County bus, single deck, and then the long walk, particularly when carrying a 42″ × 27″ × ¾″ thick double elephant drawing board, from and to the bus terminal, and through Albion Street to the School of Architecture all uphill, and particularly on a wet, cold, and windy day. I was also in my spare time working for architects on the teaching staff at the school, Mr Charles Light ARIBA, and his similarly qualified partner, who unfortunately had a serious heart attack, and was ill for the rest of my time there. Mr Light also lectured on structural engineering, and we always got on very well together. Mr Light had been commissioned by the local authority, to survey a large area of solid, well built late Victorian, back to back terrace houses, with cellar and coal cellar, and with granite sett roads, in the Harehills district of Leeds, Lambton Road, Lambton Terrace and Lambton etc. it is a big area and still all there, I am pleased to say, including a fine large, church of the period. The job was to knock on the doors, say we were from the Council, and it was a *free* service, and if they so wished, we would survey (measure up) their cellar, and design suitable reinforcements to protect the family, in the event of an air raid by Nazis. Most people said, come in, straight away! We surveyed, and produced the relevant drawings etc., and of course, the dwellings were mostly of the same design, with various minor differences, in maintenance or lack of it! In one particular case the lady of the house invited us in, after a short chat she escorted us down the cellar steps, as we reached the cellar I noticed a very strong unusual smell, the cellar had only one 60 watt lamp, I asked my assistant (the office boy and measuring tape end holder) to look in the corners, and see if there was a dead cat, rat, or something, and then look in the coal cellar, with his electric torch, but there was nothing, not even coal. Unfortunately, I continued to express my disbelief, quite innocently, and then the lady beside me was called upstairs, and fortunately the smell disappeared at the same time, it turned out to be one of our quicker surveys! But just part of life's rich full pattern, and, as they say today, lessons will be learned, they were, then!

Typically, at that time, all the students, year one to year seven, were an interesting and unusual mix of people, mostly male, and with only very few foreign students, and we even managed to put on a Christmas pantomime, lampooning Hitler and his gang, Himmler, Goering, Goebbels, etc., at Christmas 1940, after the first year of the war. The Phoney War, as it was called, because people thought nothing much had happened, but it had, and it was about to get very much worse. Together with about six students, we decided to beat the compulsory call up time, and volunteer for service in the Royal Air Force; instead of being later conscripted, without much choice, into one of the three services, Army, Navy or RAF, in either service, or occupation, even the coal mining industry. We could then choose what we wanted to do, hopefully, in the war. We duly presented ourselves at the recruiting office in Leeds, and I am not sure now, but I think it was all of us, asked for fighter pilot training, thinking, in my case, I would at least learn how to fly! No such luck, or, as it turned out, thank goodness, at that time, they had more than sufficient fighter pilots in training for some time to come, and would we care to consider other occupations? I asked to see the list, it was fairly long, but also listed was the rate of pay on joining. I looked down the list, saw some entries for wireless operators, navigators etc., then, one that had the highest rate on the list, I think it just said radio, I am not now positive, but decided that I knew something about radio, so that may have been right, I volunteered, and was duly called up!

Padgate, nr. Warrington, Lancashire, small village, with railway station (then), and an RAF enlistment base, on November 6th, 1940, the place and date I enlisted and became an AC2, (Aircraftsman 2nd Class) in the Royal Air Force, to be kitted out, issued with a very stout, linen 'kit bag'– into which was deposited, by a corporal, various items of kit such as boots, socks, shirts, knife, fork and spoon, hanks, fore and aft RAF cap etc., and on the table, battle dress and parade uniform, steel helmet, etc. My draft and I were then escorted to our dormitory hut, with beds for about twenty recruits, and then further instructed on various matters to our benefit during our short stay at Padgate, I was indeed fortunate in, having been there, done that before, even got the tea mug and T shirt, some years earlier, at dear old Crossleys, and knew all about being homesick, and under orders, etc.

However, and not withstanding, I made my first mistake. I sat on my bed, having made it, and started putting my name and new RAF, number, 1127296, on my stout, and rough kit bag, in Indian ink, and with a steel nib pen, in Roman lettering (as *carved* on Trajan's Column in Rome). My second mistake, I surmounted them with the full Royal Air Force crest, complete with Royal Crown, Albatross, PER ARDVA AD ASTRA (Through Hardship to the Stars), the lot, about 3″ diameter and crown on a woven kit bag, I needed my head examined! And it was back to dear old Crossleys time again, tell us a story Wally – this time decorate us a kit bag Wally, like yours, twenty of them, but it was nice to see, very occasionally, over the next six years in the RAF, one of my kit bags. I never had chance to talk to the owners, they were in transit I am afraid, and/or on the platform on other side of the railway line! Our days at

Padgate were few, but I remember particularly the very large, $12'' \times 6''$ Cadbury's chocolate bars in the very good NAAFI, (Navy Army Air Force Institutes). Such items were unheard of on 'Civvy Street' in 1940, and the NAAFI also served very good evening meals, and also ran a good Housey Housey session every evening in the bar!

We were soon on the move, to our various RAF stations as postings, in all cases this posting was to Initial Training Centres, for square bashing, as it was called by all ranks, which, in my case, was to West Kirby on the Wirrall, near Hoylake, on the coast. The squadron that I was to join comprised a total of 26, from various parts of the UK, and I know that is the correct number, as I have just counted them on the group photograph, officially taken, before we passed out, as the best squad in the parade of four squads, at the end of our training, and in front of the hut we had occupied for the last month. On reflection, I realise that the squad had been at least 28, one entrant was a chap who was apparently unable to march in the normal left, right, left, right, left etc., sequence, but put forward his right leg and at the same time his right arm – and similarly the left arm and leg – how long he had had to practice to get it right, or get it wrong, is as they say, anybody's guess, but he was discharged, or posted, we were never informed. So in his case, and ours, there was no weeping and wailing and gnashing of teeth. There was also the case of a very big, fit, and pleasant person, a Scottish highlands, game keeper, who, when we had our various inoculations, had a serious reaction, in that his already massive upper arm became infected and very swollen. He was sent to hospital, in the last week of our training, and did not rejoin us although we heard that he was recovering, I am glad to say. The photograph also does not show the corporal in charge of our squad at the start of our training, our leader, our trainer, our guide and friend, who gloried in the name of Corporal 'Tiger' Welsh! A complete moron, sadist, and totally unfit for his position and NCO rank, all of which became apparent to us all within the first few days at West Kirby. Something, unfortunately, had to be done about it! We were fortunate, as a squad, in that all of our group were all from responsible jobs: a family member of one of the larger, well known, sports goods manufacturers of the day, well educated and university level students, independent tradesmen, and particularly, one member of our squad, Lex May, he had been accepted, and enlisted for fighter pilot training, after initial training at West Kirby. I was to meet Lex again, not very much later, and under very different circumstances. We arranged for a meeting with the Commanding Officer on the station, and our evidence, carefully assembled, eventually led to the removal of 'Tiger' Welsh, a

51

short time before our passing out parade. It was not of course as easy as I may have made it sound, but he was removed from New Entry Training and posted.

And as far as West Kirby is concerned, that's it! Oh, very sorry, I forgot (not really just joking!). Maria and I got engaged to be married, over dinner at the nearby Hoylake Hotel, Wirral, on our 21st birthday celebrations, or should I say, at least, Maria was 21 on the 14th December 1940. Sapphire and diamonds ring, very good dinner under rationing conditions, my 21st birthday, December 28th 1940 – remember, then back to camp and subsequent posting.

My first posting was to RAF Cranwell, near Sleaford, Lincolnshire, the home of The Royal Air Force College, and one time home of T.E. Lawrence, Lawrence of Arabia. World famous, he had enlisted incognito, after the First World War as T.E. Shaw, as an ordinary airman. The hut he occupied was still there, for lesser mortals. I did not yet know for what purpose I was there, but not for long! I was allocated a bed space, along with about 40 other new recruits in a large hut and all 39 others, except me, had been employed by such well known radio set manufacturers as Ferranti, Cossor, Decca, Marconi, HMV, etc., and seemed completely unable to talk about anything else! I was back to my school days again, we learned a lot from various teachers, and our own efforts. They were mainly interested in upstaging each other, and it was non stop, dawn to dusk, mainly salesmen, I suppose.

However, within a few days we were all to take an examination to test our potential for the job we had originally joined for, we still had no idea, the examination paper was quite straightforward, but it had questions on cathode ray tubes which I happened to know a bit about, and it was a bit! Nevertheless I also happened to come out top and was, for my pains, also remustered (no, not Colemans), to another job, in a large Drawing Office, with civilian staff, except for a warrant officer (RAF Senior NCO rank) in charge of the secret section of Cranwell, and me!

My work was on the drawing board, with the civilians, dealt in general with theoretical circuits and details, and was very interesting, but I was also in my spare time co-opted on one occasion to design stage sets in the Cranwell Theatre for, at that time, a famous American popular stage artist and his performers. I do not remember his name, and I did not in fact see the show! I designed the sets of skyscrapers on the New York skyline, in modern form, and from the sea view, and I drew them out, full size in various shades of black and greys, to plain white, and helped to paint them all. Pay day at Cranwell was held on the parade ground, in the open air, and was paid by name, alphabetically, so Walton was one of the last with Y and not any XZ, in my experience. So, to a virtually empty parade ground, I was informed by the paymaster that I had been overpaid ever since I joined, and now owed money to the RAF, in pay deduction, so I was re-mustered I suppose, to pauper PDQ!

During my time at Cranwell, visits to nearby Sleaford, 3 miles distance, and to Heckington, a further 5 miles, and to Newark-on-Trent, 12 miles away, when off duty at weekends and could be a mixed blessing – on the way back from Sleaford and Newark-on-Trent on the bus after the pubs closed, or 'report back time' the wise thing to do was, be early, and ride in the back seats – with no one behind you, having drunk too much – you know the rest and also the emergency escape door is at the back! I bought, if I had the money, the best 'Plum Label' HMV swing music records, etc., at the music shop there. I had eventually, after the war, a stack of them here at Tree Garden, but then they went walkies, don't know where, or when – fortunately, when Grundig manufactured one of the first tape recorders, I taped them all before they were 'borrowed'. It's not the same – they're collectors' items now, Mead Lux Lewis etc., for the boogy woogie addicts amongst you.

At Newark I also had a surprising experience. I was walking along the main road side, through Newark, on the pavement outside a good hotel, I forget its name, the Trent flows past, and I think there was the brewery on the opposite side of that – and there was a much older gentleman walking towards me. He stopped me, and simply asked would I care to join him for dinner at the hotel. He was in fact a local, and probably a World War I veteran – I can't remember now, but I will always remember his generous hospitality. We had champagne, Roget I think but I may be wrong. I did have a very interesting evening – but I had the 'sick bus' to catch, back to Cranwell, and believe it or not, there was a war on!

From passing the test, in first place, and being promoted to the restricted drawing office, I was now in the poor house for some months to come, but help was at hand. The warrant officer in charge in the DO, a couple of weeks later, informed me that there was a notice posted on the Warrant Officers' Mess board, asking for entries for positions in the soon to be formed, Royal Air Force Works Squadrons, (similar to the Army Royal Engineers). It was a first class opportunity for someone with my background abilities, and would also enable me to get some promotion – I took his advice, and applied.

Also about this time at Cranwell, I had a not pleasant experience, backdated to West Kirby, and again, purely by chance, I was returning to camp after a visit to nearby Sleaford with friends in a car and we were checked at the guard post gate, routine, but I happened to notice in the adjacent dugout machine gun post, my old friend from West Kirby, Lex May, remember him? Here he was manning a machine gun, and said that as yet he had no hope of fighter pilot training, he was very bitter. I regret to say that I never heard of, or saw him again, and I only hope he survived the war. Another bitter experience, but not comparable with the above, was that one weekend I was taken very ill in my hut, maybe some kind of food poisoning, I didn't really know but, it was Saturday so I stayed in bed. I asked a friend to get me some Fennings Fever Cure pills, all I could think of at the time, from Sleaford; he duly returned, but brought not the pills but the Fennings Fever Cure Mixture. I had never in my life tasted anything so bitter and repulsive, so after one dose I decided I could only lie quietly, and hope. I had a thing about going on sick parade, since Crossley's I suppose, and in fact, I never ever went on sick during my entire six years war service, I even used a two-day leave to go back to my then dentist in Dewsbury, to have treatment, instead of the RAF dentist, a very big mistake on my part! Dentists were not into conservation at that time.

Cranwell was, as I may have mentioned, the main centre for RAF ground to air, radio telecommunications, and had boy entrant recruits, on course there, from about 14–15 years old. There was also a large twin engine, transport aircraft, probably late First World War design, called by the boys the Pig, in which about twenty trainees practised radio communication circling the base daily. One day, one bright boy sent up a message: All aircraft land immediately! Chaos! Aircraft in the area all trying to land at once on, fortunately, a large, mainly grass, landing area. There was an immediate search, obviously, for the young culprit – amid continuing chaos on the airfield with the Pig trying to land somewhere anywhere! Suddenly, shortly after the foregoing, Cranwell was surrounded by additional security, by the presence of a cordon of army soldiers around the station, and the one and only Sir Winston Churchill, Prime Minister, arrived in our midst! The occasion of the first flight test of the Whittle Jet fighter aircraft, over and around the station. It was quite amazing, very fast and very quiet, comparatively, in my opinion. Unfortunately, jet aircraft were not to be seen in action until the war ended, but it was top secret, and truly a day to remember!

By now my application for the RAF Airfield Construction Squadrons examinations had been accepted, and I was to report, along with a number of others of various ranks, to sit the examination. We were eventually informed of the results, some not accepted, passes for various NCO ranks up to corporal, sergeant to warrant officer. I had passed, warrant officer rank, the only trouble was that you could not go from LAC, which I was in, as they say, in one fell swoop, to warrant officer and I still had not even paid back my overpayment debt! However, I was then seconded to an RAF Wing Commander Dow, to assist him in his formation of the RAF Works Squadrons, as they were at first called, and later, RAF Airfield Construction Squadrons, similar in the field to the Royal Engineers in the British Army, although they had been at it about a century, or more, longer than the RAF, and in my experience, as with the US, army engineers, were very cooperative, when we had joint interests.

Eventually, I was posted to Air Ministry, Works Directorate at Acomb, York, and again to another, even larger drawing office, with civilian staff. I was the only service man but I was now to have at my disposal, a Humber staff car, complete with civilian chauffeur, and I was still only LAC, RAF, and very much a poor Yorkshireman! I was attached for pay purposes to a very small, two room, brick built, RAF Works Squadron office, that was just being completed and I think was mainly for a recruitment office for RAF Works Squadron's various tradesmen volunteers, etc. It was about 100 yards away from the large Shelley House (still there), with coach house, staff quarters, and large grounds with, at the main road frontage, the large barrack type hut, drawing offices, that together comprised the Air Ministry Works Directorate Headquarters at York. I was billeted with a Mr and Mrs Tessyman, in Acomb, York, about a mile from the AMWD offices, and nearer to the city. I could not have had a better home! I would guess they were then both in their early thirties. Mr Tessyman was an engine driver at the main depot in York, a lovely man, and young for his exacting job. Mrs Tessyman was a housewife, top class Yorkshire cook, and treated me, I can only suppose, as an only son. They had no children. All my laundry done, daily, socks mended, buttons checked on uniform, etc., and superb breakfasts, evening meals, and my bedroom, as with the rest of the house, one of a recently built, terrace of houses on short cul-de-sac, always immaculate, a real home from home!

Mr Tessyman and I had evening discussions, when he was not on night duty, usually on the state of the country. The only problem on my part was that whatever he heard on the radio, or read in the newspaper, irrespective of which countries the paper or radio came from, it must be true, simply because he heard on radio or read it in the newspaper! There was the time when he was on night duty at York station, and the next day Lord Haw

Haw, the British-born Nazi propagandist, (later executed as a traitor in London) said that York station had been bombed (when it hadn't) – he was there all night but still believed Haw Haw! But still a hard working, kind gentle person!

My civilian colleagues at the AMWD made me very welcome and the director explained to me what my position and duties would be at HQ starting with a more or less immediate problem at the RAF, HQ, at Heslington Hall, a fine stately home on the outskirts of York, and occupied by all the various ranks needed at HQ it now appeared there were various sanitary problems, requiring advice on, and attention to, the septic tank capacity, and improvement thereof, among other things, as soon as possible, due of course, to the large increase in the number of occupants, compared with before the hall was taken over by the RAF.

I was also allocated airfields across Yorkshire, from the coast down to the Humber, for which I would be responsible. All very impressive perhaps, but it had its problems. Airfields like Leeming and Topcliffe, alongside the A1, were fighter bases, and others, at Dishforth and Church Fenton, and other Yorkshire, RAF Stations, were very different, as I was soon to learn. My main problem was that my duties far outstripped my rank. For example I would arrive at a station, be checked in at the guard post on entry, seated in the Humber staff car with civilian chauffeur, not standard practice for an LAC! A typical example of my predicament was my arrival at Hutton Cranswich near the coast, another air defence airfield. Here I had decided to test the efficiency of the station security, at the main entrance guard post, possibly for a bet with colleagues back at AMWD, can't remember. I had temporarily covered my photograph on my identity card with a picture of Hitler. I held it up, open, to the armed guard, said I was from AMWD, (it said that on the side of the Humber). The sergeant at the post called me to the phone, it was the station CO, inviting me to lunch in the officers' mess. I thanked him, but regretted that I could not accept his hospitality, due to my rank, perhaps another time in the future. You cannot do that kind of thing, quite rightly, in the RAF, I suppose a person now, in my position then, and with the present Human Rights Act, and 'Elf 'n Safety' Laws and Guidelines, and in similar circumstances, will demand to see the menu, and then sell his story to the Press, before agreeing to accept! – In my case, I didn't tell the CO, I was Hitler, but I still got in undetected!

York Minster is one of the finest cathedrals in the world, the Archbishop of York is second only to the Archbishop of Canterbury, and it was from him that I had to get approval for Maria and I to marry on

December 11th 1941 at St Paul's Church, York. To say it was a simple ceremony is something of an exaggeration, the people present were Maria and me, the vicar and verger, and Mrs Tessyman (her husband was on duty) so there was no overcrowding, and it was a quiet wedding, neither of us wanting the publicity of the weddings of today, paid for by *Hello* magazine, but I admit, we could have used the money! But, no honeymoon, and again, believe it or not, on checking my wife's, or my, retained personal documents I find that we actually had a short honeymoon exactly two months later, for four days, at the Pavilion Hotel Scarborough, owned by Charles Laughton and three other Laughton family members. Unfortunately, it has long since been pulled down, to make way for improvements I suppose, they also owned the nearby Royal Hotel in Scarborough, and I think they still do. They were, and one still is, the best hotel in the town. There is, by the way, a fine collection of master paintings in the Royal. So, from our wedding on December 11th 1941, we go to February 7, 8, 9, 10, 1942. Pavilion Hotel Bill No 75., 2 persons; Full Board; 4 days, £8-16s-9d! Now look what has happened since, you can't even have the breakfast, for that price, even at a bed and breakfast!

Maria and me at the Pavilion Hotel, Scarborough

At AMWD HQ my work continued on various airfields. I/we removed a large hill from either Leeming or Topcliffe to extend the runway, using Civilian contractors – a communications system at Boston Spa Centering on the RAF admin centre in a large house, The Grange I think, the Leeds Road entrance to the village, which was also being extended by a local contractor, and now the house and additional buildings are no longer there, and the whole site area has been redeveloped and is private housing. Even at AMWD HQ we had our own problems, there was a large administrative staff of male and female civilians – and complaints about, perhaps, very overstressed toilet facilities. Blockages, requiring urgent attention. The contract plumbers reported to me on the cause of the problem, but, I won't go into detail about that now. I was the only one in uniform. It was rectified!

From the start of my Cranwell days, my postings had been arranged by Air Ministry, and this was to continue throughout my service in the RAF, as were my promotions. For example, I suddenly went from LAC to Sergeant and was posted to RAF Tower Hill Camp, Reykjavik, Iceland, C/O, Squadron Leader Cook. This time I was Sergeant-in-Charge of the Drawing Office and supervision of construction, at the main RAF Reykjavik airfield, completely occupied by the RAF, and requiring a very great amount of work to make it the major airport for both the RAF and the (USAAF) United States of America, Air Force, (although they were there, preparing their own air base at Keplavik), and as a staging post for aircraft, navy, army, governments, etc., en route to the UK and Europe, Russia, and most places north, south, east, and west, and the protection of all allied shipping, submarines etc., over the vast area of the North Atlantic and Arctic waters. The work required ASAP included existing runways to be stabilised and lengthened, and new runways built over the sea, hangars for large RAF and USAAF military aircraft, Fortresses, Wellingtons, Catalina, amphibious flying boats, etc., and even a Walrus high wing amphibious flying boat, just one! Late World War I not exactly Concorde, but as with the Catalina high wing, and the Walrus high wing, beautiful machines, of their time in RAF, and USAAF, History!

Tower Hill Camp RAF, was on a prominent hill, overlooking Reykjavik, and the large bay and harbour on the south east of Iceland, and was surmounted by a lighthouse tower next to the camp, hence the name. It comprised about 10 Nissen huts, corrugated steel sheet roofing and semi-circular section 16 feet wide, supported by T section mild steel ribs, curved, and bolted at 6'-0½" (!) centres, and 36'-0" long, although they could be any length, and with other standard widths of 24′, 36′ and with flat mild steel tie bar internally, with horizontal ¾″, fibre board insulation panels. As we were the first RAF Works Squadron in Iceland, at Tower Hill we were a small unit with officers' mess, sergeants' mess and other ranks, Nissens, with guard post and barbed wire perimeter, our main administrative offices and drawing office, again Nissens were at the foot of the hill on the edge of the town proper, the Reykjavik airfield was two miles away. The weather in Iceland can be very severe, very high winds, very cold, heavy snow falls, light all night, or dark all day, and with very rapid changes, as Icelanders say, when in a howling gale, no aircraft landing, 'Oh just wait a few minutes, it will change,' and it often does, but not necessarily for the better! On one occasion, during a snow storm on the hill, my bed was covered with dry snow, and also half the room, blown through the keyhole during the night! At Reykjavik airport, before the hangars were built, it was common practice to have airmen in duffle coats etc., hanging on the wings of aircraft, to hold them down during very high winds, and you had to crawl, on all fours, to get to them!

Icelanders are a seafaring nation, as we British are/were, but we are counted in millions, they are counted in thousands. We had the world's finest navy, they have no navy, but they managed to defeat us in the cod war about 30–35 years ago, and kept their fishing grounds free, unlike our fishing grounds and fishermen's livings. When I first arrived at Reykjavik I was most impressed by the fact that virtually all of the houses, buildings, shops, etc., are centrally heated and even the pavements are kept free of snow and ice, and also one very modern swimming pool, and one open air pool, with changing rooms, in the older area, are all supplied with boiling hot water from a 3′ diameter surface pipe line running from natural hot springs, 10 miles away, and it only drops about 5 degrees C. on final discharge into the sea. All the babies in Iceland swim! All the Icelanders can swim it is not possible for a person, male, female, baby, or adult, to get into the modern swimming pool without first having passed through the disinfected foot baths, with overhead disinfected showers, naked, and under the gaze of a male, or female, attendant, and then be careful before run-diving into the pool. There were very young babies chugging about, here and there under the watchful gaze of the parent! The old pool, which I am sure will not now be there, was open-air, old and basic, but still very well attended, and more or less in constant use, – day or night, and HOT!

My outstanding memory of my first tour of duty in Iceland was the telegram from my dear wife, Maria, with the wonderful news of the birth of my dear son, Timothy Baines Walton and all was fine for both of them. Actually the telegram was sent by her mother, my mother-in-law, and my son had been delivered by my dear mother, so how about that for keeping it in the families!

Iceland had been occupied by the British Army on 10th May, 1940, and they were not well received by the Icelanders, having been neutral, with open arms. They were themselves endeavoring to be independent of Denmark at this time, and almost exactly a year later on 16th May, 1941, the 'Althing' the oldest parliament in the world, decided to terminate the union with Denmark, the country having been occupied by the Germans. But Iceland is a most interesting country and people, about 120,000, total population, some of whom I am proud to call my friends.

The C/O, Squadron Leader Cook's admin sergeant, informed me that I was to be Mentioned in Dispatches, presumably this was for my work in Iceland under his command. However, it was not to be, a signal was received that I was to return to the UK, on an aircraft landing at Reykjavik in a couple of hours, so I was no longer under Squadron Leader Cook's command – ah well, so be it! Back in the UK, I was given some short leave, I could now see my dear son, and his dear mum, and in fact I started, and maybe finished, making him a wooden horse on wheels, a push horse also designed to have a set of rockers to turn it into a rocking horse. Of course he was not old enough to rock or roll anyway, but you could not buy toys, and as he grew older he must have pushed, or rocked it, for miles! My short leave came to an abrupt end, recalled to report at a small RAF station in the south of England, I can't remember exactly where, for a course on demolition explosives in various forms, from Bangalore torpedoes to PHE dynamite, Arctic dynamite etc, detonators, safety fuse, etc. I am afraid I am by now a bit rusty on these, not having used much, if any, since the war! Some like dynamite are wrapped in special protective papers, and even handling them, with unprotected hands can give you very bad headaches. Bangalore torpedoes, a string of cartridges, like strings of sausages, used dynamite to demolish coiled barbed wire trench defences. PHE, or plastic high explosives is a cutting charge, as is Arctic dynamite, they can cut and demolish steel stanchions, steel plates even cut steel ships in half! Safety fuse consists of a fabric tube, with a core of gunpowder, which burns slowly, and leads to a detonator, a small hard case explosive capsule, which is pressed into the end of the large sausage stick of wrapped TNT, or dynamite – the fuse burns at a rate of 2 ft per minute, to enable all concerned to get to a safe distance away – fast!

Various things continued to happen, from day to day, some good, some not so good, as is the case with most people in the armed forces, particularly in wartime, in fact, I often thought of my father's First World War, under vastly more terrible and inhumane conditions, and for four years, in those days! When I had served four years, I hoped I was getting the hang of things, and doing my bit, but compared with my father I probably hadn't even begun! Then out of the blue, I was selected for officer training, and posted to RAF Cosford, Shropshire as an officer cadet, White flash on my fore and aft cap, and virtually continuous supervision, day and night! There was never a dull moment, no time to relax, parades, lectures, demonstrations, field battle training, with explosives and live ammunition, aircraft recognition tests, ours and theirs, leadership tests, personal assessments, etc. Eventually, those who were accepted stayed, those who were not returned to their or other stations, the rest of the group were then allowed to submit to the ministrations of Savile Row uniform tailors, Gieves, in my case, for dress uniform cap, Crombie, greatcoat, etc. Bank representatives were also on hand to invite our custom for officer's pay purposes, Coutts Bank was my choice. Bomb disposal was my next appointment, I was to attend for training in more explosive applications, but this time attacks on airfields and RAF bases and how to deal with unexploded bombs. I duly passed out on this pretty quickly, as in this field models change very quickly indeed, or they did at that time. This meant that I was now an explosives officer and would have an X beside my name on the air force list of officers. The commanding officer of any station I was at, even as a visitor, could call on me to defuse any object or whatever, even if the bomb was a very new type, unseen before. Fortunately, for me and many others, I was never ever called upon to demonstrate my skills – good job we had not got round to atom bombs yet! I also attended a special course in soil stabilisation for airfield construction, in the field, and it did mean field, and also any other types of terrain beaches, sand and gravel areas, etc., in short, establishing a landing ground for aircraft, using the materials already there, along with such good ideas as Sommerfield Track – interlocking, hinged, and perforated, long by narrow, easily handled, steel plates on top of the stabilised soil, compacted using plant such as a sheep's foot roller studded with steel projections, like sheep's feet only larger, and other methods! Hey oh!

I was then posted back to Iceland, to continue with the development work there. There had been changes, the RAF Works Squadron had by now grown in numbers, and had been relocated at Camp Cook, (named after my original Commanding Officer, Squadron Leader Cook, at Tower Hill camp) and adjacent to Reykjavik air base, and now under the command of Wing Commander Earnshaw, RAF. His family had, and still have, a tree felling and sawmill business at Midgley, a small village near Wakefield, only two or three miles from where I lived, but of course he was much older than me and probably had joined the air force as a career and was now in an administrative position, due to the war. Neither he nor I was ever aware all the time I was there that we were neighbours and he was never involved in any technical matters. Unfortunately, he is no longer with us so, I am unable to check, he was however a pleasant man and I designed, some years later, a house near the sawmill, for a younger generation of his family.

By this time, the army and air force of the USA were now much more in evidence than on my previous tour and in fact we cooperated with them and we had the benefit of their heavy plant equipment, main manufacturer, Caterpillar Co. US of A, bulldozers backakters, blade graders, all not seen in the UK at that time. Later, one American manufacturer, and a firm similar, but smaller, makers of tractors etc., a very religious man, his business not doing very well and I regret to say whose name I can no longer recall, only it was a short name, promised to give a large proportion of his profits to God. He then designed a simple, but very good lifting crane to enable clearance of large aircraft, Fortress, Lancaster etc., that crash landed, blocking the runway, obstructing the landings of other members of the attack force. It consisted of two very large steel wheels, tyred, and a large steel, cranked, lifting lever crane, operated from a heavy bulldozer or tractor, using the rear windlass. Aircraft crash lands, blocking runway, tractor moves crane into position over lifting point on aircraft, windlass operated, lifts aircraft to hard standing on side, clear of runway. OK? He never looked back, and prospered!

The Icelanders, due to the size, amazing geology and geography, climate, and history of the country, have used light aircraft to get to various parts of this large island, most of the few roads are only passable in summer, and to rescue skiers and climbers, and other emergency needs. With the airfield at Reykjavik, at that time, the only one able to accommodate larger aircraft, the runways were laid on peat and would rise and fall with the weather! I have watched smaller, fighter aircraft, from one end of the runway, appear and disappear in the undulations of the runway, due to the peat expanding and contracting! A few miles out of Reykjavik, much of the terrain is lava fields, laid down over millennia, and over a vast area and in depth and height, there are still a very large number of dormant volcanoes. One, only about thirty years ago, erupted in the sea on the southern side of the country and there is now a very significant permanent island, at least until it erupts again, and makes it very much larger! We had arranged for as many owners of transport vehicles in the area as we could employ to transport, continuously, day and night, quarried lava from the fields to replace the peat on the whole area. The airport was of course always operational and very active, a staging post for allied aircraft. The Americans were starting to build their airport at Keplavik about 30 miles away.

The weather was always the problem, particularly in winter. On one occasion I had to go to Hofn, a small village with an RAF unit, both at the foot of the Vatnajocull the largest glacier in Europe and the aircraft landing area was the beach, a narrow strip of shingle and sand, acceptable for small aircraft at the right time, but not for a twin engine American light bomber at the wrong time. We had minor damage but at least we had arrived. However, we had still to cross the ice-laden shallow water area, in the dark and in an outboard-engined small boat, with five people on board and no idea which way to go, or for that matter how to get off the sandbank on which we were fully grounded, and probably no one knew we were there. I did not think of it then but the angel, previously mentioned, was certainly in attendance. Slowly, appeared the amazing phenomenon of the aurora borealis, or the northern lights! A vast moving curtain of light, in amazing colour was being drawn across the night sky and we were re-orientated and eventually made camp in Hofn village and food and a bed.

The aircraft and crew I had arrived with were able to return to Reykjavik in a couple of days, and an aircraft was to be sent for my return later. Unfortunately, the situation became very different, and for some days it was OK to take off from Reykjavik but not OK to land at Hofn beach and vice versa. Eventually a signal to me at Hofn said there was an Icelandic fishing boat bringing coal to Hofn (of all things, but it was needed), and would also return with RAF service men due for leave, probably local in Reykjavik, and would I be kind enough to accompany them? Yes, but little did I know the hold, usually for fish I suppose, and had last held coal, and had now been cleaned out, was to be their home for the 150-mile sea journey.

After assuring my charges, through the deck hatch, to the coal hole, sorry hold, (what am I thinking about) that all would go well, and I would wake them in the morning with a cup of tea, I said good night, and repaired, after invitation, to the galley (about the size of two telephone kiosks), enough room for two to stand, but only just, and that included a very small cooker. Cook was himself a big chap, so there was no room for me. He had asked me for a cup of tea, so here I was, 'Do you want milk'? 'Yes please,' he grabbed a tin of evaporated milk from the shelf, split the tin across the top with one well-aimed blow from a cleaver, and poured a lot into my mug, thank you very much. I then make my second mistake, my first was just being there, and looked at the sea, it was beginning to heave somewhat, and we were still in Hofn's small bay, so I decided, very quickly, that it was time to go to my bunk.

The bunk, by the way, was at the bottom of the short flight of steps down to the engine room, with no door between, and with a wood partition, on which was pinned, by one pin, a Reykjavik ship's chandlers calendar, which was moving gently with the increasing sea swell, and that was at the foot of my bunk. As we left the harbour the stench of the hot burning oil from the engine became extreme, the calendar swinging ceaselessly, from 3 to 6 o'clock, and vice versa, and my eyes swinging left to right, also vice versa. As the wind storm got stronger and stronger and the sea got higher and higher, I started to consider the possibility of going on the heaving and windswept area, one would laughingly call the deck, and then being 'Lost at sea', but only for a moment, as the Duke of Wellington said at Waterloo, 'It was a damn close run thing!' Funnily enough, and even with hindsight I cannot remember, all the time we were aboard, wanting to go to the toilet facilities. I don't even know if there were any, probably not, the ship wasn't big enough, although I did worry about how the airmen in the hold were getting on, under much worse conditions than me. But there was nothing anyone could do to help under these circumstances, and there were certainly no toilets down there. I had had nothing to eat since some hours before boarding, and amazingly I was not seasick, thank goodness, but was far from enjoying the trip, normally one day by sea, but this was Iceland, so wait a minute or two! I must have fallen asleep eventually. I woke to very calm sailing indeed. I went on deck to see how the airmen had managed in the hold, to find the vast expanse of the Reykjavik Bay a complete flat calm, like glass everywhere, and with only puffins with all their colour, quietly diving and emerging to feed, breaking the complete stillness. Unbelievable, but it's true ! The skipper said it was the worst passage he had ever made, or words to that effect, I got the tea for the airmen and they started their leave. All were as well as could be expected and I had breakfast at Camp Cook.

Having made some very good friends in Reykjavik on my earlier tour of duty, I was pleased to be able to renew my contacts with them, people like Ingolfur B. Gudmundsson, a building contractor who had been working for the RAF on the airport and also his very capable manager Knuter Johnsson, Godfried Bernholft, all older than me, and Larus Oskarsson, someone then of my age, and I hope still with us, I must check this. The father of Larus was named Oscar Larusson, and the son of Larus was named Oscar Larusson, and so it progressed in the Icelandic/Danish system, sensible isn't it? In the case of a girl in the family it becomes Oscar Dottir or Larus Dottir, ad infinitum, I suppose!

The US Army Engineers, and the USAAF, with whom I also had previous contacts, had increased in numbers, and as always were very cooperative to us – I have the set of Engineer Field Manuals War Department, Washington 1940, on communications, construction, and utilities, and engineer troops and operations, presented to me by one Staff Sergeant A. Hayden, USA who I also hope is still with us today.

On the relaxation side of my RAF service career, I was fortunate in my Icelandic and Norwegian friends, in being invited to accompany them on overland, mountain ski trips to the ski lodge in Josphdalue, which was accessed from the road, the Icelanders leaving their cars parked there for as long as it took. There were no 'yobs' in Iceland. The ski lodge was some miles from the road, much higher up the mountain, and snow all the way. We all had laden back packs, packed with various items if things went wrong and we were not able to return to the car, or in my case a Willy's Jeep this time, and we also each had Icelandic dry salted cod, dried on timber racks in the open air, a specialty worldwide today, but also commonplace there then, and light to carry, very sustaining and good to eat, uncooked! My first sight of the lodge was impressive, reinforced concrete, simple, good modern design, and larger than I expected, and I was even more impressed by the honours list plaque, listing the names of the club members, together with the number of hours they had spent working on the project. Remember, we were some miles from the road, on constantly rising, rough, snow-covered terrain, and in our case it was a good day. When they were building this refuge, club house, etc. they had to carry all the cement, aggregate, reinforcing steel, timber, roofing materials, all the tools, food, protective clothing, basic furniture, and all the other things you would need. The above paragraph is only part of the story: years before we occupied the country, they had built a timber ski lodge, or whatever they called it, by the same hard work, but unfortunately this had been destroyed by fire so, being intrepid Icelanders, they designed and built another one, probably larger, but certainly more fireproof, and here it now was with also the names of the 'timber builders' on an earlier plaque, side by side with the list I have already mentioned.

There were many remarkable aspects to life in Iceland at that time, for example, drink driving. Long before we in the so-called UK, tried to control it (and failed) a person driving a car, and who had a bottle of alcohol in the car, and was stopped by the police, was, not to coin a phrase, 'knicked', car impounded, put in a cell, no messing about with trials and such like expensive time wasters. They only at last remembered you were there, and wondered whether to release you, or go back to their chess game. No pubs or other licensed establishments, alcohol sales were controlled by the monopoly, government owned, and they dispensed it as they thought fit, and mainly including the locally produced 'brenavin', better known to the locals as 'black death,' and taken with Schnaps, together with shark meat that had been buried in the ground for a year, to marinate I suppose. Even the army, navy, and air force beer, spirits, etc., was distributed from, not by, the monopoly. At a guess, there were then probably more taxis in Reykjavik per head of population, than anywhere else in the world. If you were having a party, and were short of alcohol refreshment, you rang for a taxi, he kept a few bottles on board at a price. Bookshops were very much in evidence, all with good quality books, but not cheap. There were, and all of them very good, a university hospital, theatre, concert hall, churches and other public buildings. Icelanders at that time, after education, or also to extend it, went to America, England, or a few to Germany pre-war. Mr Gudmundsson went to America to work; there he met his wife, also an Icelander, and married, then they both came back to Iceland to have a fine family and a very good business.

My work continued with new steel framed aircraft hangar buildings and remarkably, a major new runway extending over the sea for which, in order to achieve, it was necessary to demolish a number of recently built good new houses, mainly single storey, that were in the way. It was not pleasant, to say the least, to have to bulldoze them down to complete the runway, the owners had been compensated of course. I was not responsible for the initial negotiations, prior to demolition. In lighter mood, I was present on the historic day of independence from Denmark, celebrated in the main square in Reykjavik, outside the Althing on one side and, the Hotel Borg at one end, bands playing, speeches, etc. I had also borrowed, especially for this occasion, a Leica SLR camera from the main photo shop in Rekyavik. The owner I knew, having dealt with him during my first tour, and since. So far so good, I took some, hopefully, first class shots for perhaps publication in the newspapers, to be developed and

66

trimmed etc. by my friend with the shop. Unfortunately, in my zeal I completely forgot to adjust the extending lens focusing, all 36 pictures on the reel were more than somewhat out of focus, not much, but somewhat!

My fellow officers at Camp Cook, with differing duties, were all cooperative and we all had our various additional responsibilities in the successful organisation of the station. They include F/Lt. Henson, ex. electricity department Nottingham, a particularly good friend of mine. F/Lt. Rosenvinge, he had been with me at Boston Spa, Yorkshire, where I was also responsible for a map reading and surveying course, for works officers, we had of course, as a group, our differences, but nothing serious. F/Lt. Dale, F/O. Jackson from Bradford, F/Lt. Newcombe, F/O. Burrows, F/Lt. Plumbe, and, checking a group photograph of the officers, total 13 including me, but another member may have been the photographer.

In due course, or as they say today to move on, I was ordered to return to the UK, on an aircraft arriving in a couple of hours at Reykjavik, then a short leave to see my wife and son again at Spinkwell Cottage, Jenkin Road, Horbury, then off to RAF 84 Group, Second TAF, (Tactical Air Force). Headquarters, BAFO, (British Air Forces of Occupation) at Celle, near Hanover, Germany. By air, land, sea and land again, this time, and to start with we were under canvas on Luneberg Heath. My duties were to take charge of a large group of German 'engineer troops', who were also prisoners of war (POWs) and comprised various trades in the engineering and construction fields of the German air force, the Luftwaffe, to be used in the reorganisation of the large Luftwaffe headquarters on the outskirts of Celle, North West Germany. The ex-German air force HQ, and now 84 Group HQ, had only been completed some 12 to 18 months earlier, and was constructed in 9 months, start to finish, according to the Celle towns-people, using slave labour, of course! The new HQ comprised a very large site area, with a formidable dado height brick and stone topped wall, and with substantial steel spiked fencing to approximately 9 feet total height all round the entire site. Access roads to all parts of the headquarters paved in granite setts, laid in interlocking fan shapes, and all dual carriageway width, with pavements for pedestrians, giving access to the HQ office block, barrack blocks, various workshops, storage blocks, transport garages, etc., and with the centrepiece to the whole, the semi classic officers mess building situated in the centre of the site, and very impressive, and well built. There were officers sleeping quarters across the lawns on the sides and rear of the main building. Internally, a formal entrance hall, main dining hall, with musicians gallery seating, with some hindsight, up to 100 officers, (including about 30 Canadian air force officers in the mess, 'attached' to 84 Group HQ), kitchens, food stores, sitting room, toilet facilities etc., and with officer accommodation, toilets etc., at first floor level – there was also a large basement area, bar, and other storage rooms, so you will see, for a change, we were at last reasonably well catered for!

By now, the surrender to Field Marshal Montgomery on May 5th 1945, on Luneberg Heath, had taken place, but there were huge problems for allied forces with the Russians in Berlin and German POWs loose all over the north western area of Germany, and the relief of the Nazi concentration camps in the area such as Belsen, north of Celle.

The AOC, (air officer commanding) Air Marshal Sir A. Coningham, KCB, DSO, MC, DFC, AFC, had his office, and his second in command, or ADC, was adjacent (who, by the way, was a lawyer from Wakefield), to my office, all on the first floor of the main office block, so I was in good company. I was the only officer from RAF airfield construction, at this time, to be with 84 Group HQ, and remained so until the time came for my demobilisation after over six years WWII service with the RAF. My initial responsibility was to organise the POW engineers and construction on various work around the HQ, and this I had already initiated but I was on the same floor as the AOC in C and ADC, so I was often called to one or the

My Jeep and tent, first night on Luneberg Heath

other, usually the other, for orders. I think the most unusual was that I was to be in charge of the Celle area prison, in addition to my present duties. This prison's most important guests were The Beast of Belsen, and his wife Irma Greasa, notorious for having lampshades made out of the tatooed skin of murdered prisoners of the concentration camp at Burgen Belsen. I inspected the prison and the prison staff on two separate occasions. However, the trial of the above mentioned guests was due, and I did not visit the prison again. I attended the beginning of the trial on either the first or second day, it was held in Luneberg, a few miles from Celle. I was in battledress, and I had a small Leica camera hung round my neck, by the usual lanyard or strap, and it was completely concealed. I always carried it whenever possible, it was like the proverbial second skin, this time I forgot it was there until I was at the end of a short queue of officers waiting to enter the court, with two Army MPs checking on entry, and too late for me to leave. I was next. Fortunately it was cursory, and he missed the camera. However, when I did decide to take a shot of the court scene, amid the usual discussions, etc., there suddenly was a deathly silence, coinciding with my pressing the shutter button, boing. Fortunately, we were seated high in the gallery, so I was lucky to get away with it. I probably never had the reel processed, there was too much happening at the time.

I was also allocated a few airfields to visit at intervals, which had airfield construction personnel working such as Wunsdorf, Gatow in Berlin, and Jever. The war in Europe now being over, I was of course waiting to be demobilised, and get back home to my dear wife and son Timothy, both of whom I had not seen, except for a very few short leaves in transit, since I joined the RAF, and continue my career in architecture, engineering and the many other subjects related thereto. However, whether it was my proximity to the very senior officers, and the fact that I was happy and enthusiastic with my work and position, and the war ending, I am not sure, but I was being tempted by some of these regular officers to continue my career in the RAF, and sign up – bags of promotion, early retirement, etc., good pension – even a suggestion that I would be RAF member in the organisation and development of the future Heathrow airport. No way, I do not like committees, in my opinion they should consist of you and me, and when we had a meeting, one of us to be off sick, then the other one can get something done. And of course, two seats only on the board!

Having got that bit dealt with, it is now later. Still at 84 Group HQ, and the AOC said he would like me to do something about the bar in the basement of the officers mess, to make it more presentable, for the

F/Lt Johnny Medworth

F/Lt Medworth and various officers

Officers' mess 84 Group HQ Celle

celebration of a victory party Europe, and the special guests, such as Field Marshal Montgomery, and the other senior commanders of the various services to be invited, and do it well, quickly. I did, and when it was done, and inspected by him, he was well pleased.

My good friend at 84 Group was F/Lt. Johnny Medworth, observer partner to the City of London Night Fighter Squadrons, Cats Eyes Cunningham, pilot, Battle of Britain. Johnny was always immaculate, and having completed his operational flying was now Flying Control Officer at 84 Group, for all the groups territory in Germany. At the request of the officers mess committee Johnny had organised an aircraft to fly to Ireland, for a suitable cargo of Guinness and another aircraft to fly to Chartres, France, for a suitable cargo of Champagne. Both, when mixed in the right amounts produce the very pleasant and sustaining Black Velvet, to be consumed free by all at this celebration!

Johnny and I went to the party, the bar now resplendent with gleaming brass foot rail, and other improvements here and there, and to regale ourselves on the aforementioned mixed cargoes. After a while, and much to my surprise and other assembled guests, Johnny, now standing on the foot rail, turned to all assembled and he addressed them thus: 'The PMC, (President of the Mess Committee) is a bastard,' and then turned back to more serious consideration of the Black Velvet. A short silence followed. You know my views on committees, I had no idea whether the PMC was, or was not, a bastard, and Johnny had never mentioned it before, he knew he was a group captain, and that was three ranks above Johnny and me. 'Calm down Johnny old boy, relax, take it easy,' say I, or something like that. Five or so minutes pass, again Johnny does his swiveling act on the rail, 'The PMC is a bastard,' a longer silence. The PMC comes over, puts his arm round my shoulder, 'Look after him, old boy,' or something like that. And, believe it or not (remember that?), Johnny again repeated his act and declaration. PMC came over. 'See him to his room, there's a good chap, will you please?'

A friend and I take Johnny, one on each side, up two floors and along the wide corridor to his room. Along the way we meet another officer he knows. Johnny decides to greet him. We wait and then continue to his room, he then wants to go to the toilet, good, we take him. Next morning he rolls in to breakfast, as usual, immaculate as ever, but he cannot remember a thing about the whole incident and the only thing that bothers him is that we had taken him to the toilet. Now there's thanks for you.

When I was eventually due to return to the UK for demobilisation, Johnny offered to arrange an aircraft to take me, and also the BMW drophead coupé I had acquired, back to the UK. He himself had decided never to fly again, he said he had done all his 'ops, and a few extra', and was not going to tempt providence. He did however drive me to Hanover station to meet the train, and see me off when I finally went back to the UK, and home. But at present that is a long way into the future, we are still at war with Japan, and no sign of victory there yet.

A visit to Gatow airfield, Berlin, was my next urgent item. Gatow, an ex German airfield, now occupied by RAF Transport Command with Wing Commander Stamford Tuck, distinguished Fighter Ace, Battle of Britain and now a no nonsense OC, on the outskirts of Berlin, and later to be one of the vital airfields for the Berlin Air Lift, the transport of vital supplies, food, clothing and importantly coal, when the Russian army blockaded the allied sector of Berlin.

Being a visiting officer, I was seated next to the CO, on his right, at the long dining table in the 30ft long room, with the mess bar at the other end and with a pair of doors, open, for access. Apparently the station was over-run by cats, the CO's pet hate. Suddenly, a cat walked past the open double door into the bar. The CO had his revolver from his hip fast, and a shot was fired, he missed. Fortunately no one was passing either! A couple of days later, having been guests of the Russian airforce, the Gatow officers were now reciprocating. I was of course a guest, the party lasted into the early hours of the next day – and a good time was being had by all, particularly the Russians! The barman was a German civilian and the barman's quarters were above the bar, one part of which came down over the bar serving area as a timber bulkhead exposed to the customers. Someone, I don't know who, Russian or RAF, said they could not get a drink, 'The Barman's gone to bed.'

'Gone to bed? I will soon wake the *expletive* up!' and the CO, reaching for a sub-machine gun lying on the adjacent bench seat – in case the Russian officers started to get obstreperous I suppose – sprayed the bulk head wall with bullets. Not unnaturally the barman came down forthwith!

This was the only RAF station I had been on, all during the war, where they had bananas, oranges and other more exotic fruits, and supplies on the table – it was, remember, a Transport Command airfield, their aircraft travelled the world on duty missions, no point in coming back empty, was there? On another visit to Gatow some Russian army soldiers were arrested by RAF MPs, while looting a bomb damaged factory in the area – they rang their Russian MP counterparts in the Russian zone to inform them, and request their collection. They rang them later to check, to be informed that, they had been shot! Sick joke or not?

The black market in Berlin was much in evidence, particularly in the large assembly area in front of the Reich Chancellery with the balcony from which Hitler had harangued his subjects. The area was packed with people, and some servicemen traded a little of 'this' for a lot of 'that'. I 'acquired' various pieces of Nazi swastika items from the interior rooms of the Chancellery, including the gold, blue and white cross award to mothers, *Der Deutschen Mutter*, engraved on the back with 16th December 1938, by Hitler (signature), and also the Bronze Cross, 1939, also with swastika, and red, white and black ribboned medal, for the German Forces. Not at that time to be recommended was a visit to the Russian zone, through the Brandenburg Gate. After the Russians had already, located their magnificent bronze groups of troops, in action, on the left side of the Unter Den Linden Strasse, for their well earned Victory Berlin parades, at least it was quieter now so we went, (there were two of us). Immediately we were confronted by massive posters of Stalin and his various generals etc., at the road and roundabout side, and Russian military police and troops much in evidence in the heavily bombed and destroyed areas of Berlin, which were many.

As a matter of fact, the conditions in the Berlin outskirts generally were to say the least a bit dicey. The Autobahn from Hanover to Berlin was pockmarked with aerial bomb holes, forming roundabout diversions at numerous intervals, meaning a slow crawl over makeshift road repairs. Groups of Russian deserters were in the woods, and other cover along the route, and they tried to stop anyone from other forces, particularly in one vehicle, and rob them of all weapons, the vehicle and its usual gerry can of fuel, food and any other possessions, personal or service. Hopefully they left you alive – sometimes not I am afraid!

At the Berlin end of the road, the 'Berlin Corridor' at intersections, there were on duty immaculately dressed Russian army police to wave you through, and as you passed he gave you a first class salute, as is correct if there is an officer on board. But on one run I was driven by an RAF sergeant driver (there was now a surplus of sergeants, pilot observers, rear gunners, wireless operators, so after two weeks' training as drivers in the UK, they were sent to Europe – to drive on the 'wrong' side of the road, in a foreign country, and officers were not allowed to drive themselves again)! In my case, and others, this was to have dangerous repercussions. Along with another officer, I was seated in the rear of a Humber staff car returning from an airfield south of Celle along a granite sett cambered country road, with trees every 15 to 20 feet, on each side of the road, and going too fast approaching a humpback, narrow, stone bridge over a stream. The sergeant got into a steering wheel 'wobble' and we were either going to crash into the trees or the stone bridge. More by luck than good management, I stood up in the swaying car, reached over, and grabbed the steering wheel. The 'angel on my shoulder' took over and we made it. Another 'near miss' for me (I am afraid I have forgotten which number) I was due to return to the UK for demob in about four days time!

However, life during any war is by no means all 'beer and skittles'. World War II was global, and also the most devastating and horrific in the history of the world, until the next one comes along, probably out of China. Hendrik Willem Van Loon – a truly remarkable man, Dr Van Loon, scholar, artist, observer, visionary, unique writer, and you have guessed, one of my favourite writers – said in one of his fascinating books, 'Man is an animal who every 25 years, has an overwhelming desire to destroy himself.' I am sure he would know, long before he died in 1940, that there were fewer than 25 years between the first and second world wars, and there are 'wars', or 'persecutions', or 'dictatorships', you name it, going on NOW! We never learn – no matter how many times we say 'lessons have been learned' perhaps, we don't live long enough to gain some wisdom – but then, elderly people are often no longer respected. They are despised, not 'with it' but 'past it', too many people on earth anyway – so lets have an annual culling and call it a 'just war'. Churchill said: – 'Jaw, jaw is better than war, war!'

I wrote the above in order to differentiate from my own 'nothing extra ordinary here' commonplace, life and wartime experiences – to peoples who, in their millions were, after years of torture, murdered, and thrown into mass graves at the whim of some magnificent dictator and his acolytes – and it still goes on NOW! Remember that please, and tell your children!

And now I was to meet some of the lucky ones, some of whom had survived, and some of whom had not survived the Holocaust at Belsen concentration camp, about 30 miles from Celle, and the one time 'home' of the aforementioned 'Beast of Belsen' and his 'lady'. I just don't know why I keep going on like this and, to my regret, there is nothing I can now do about it. I suppose it's what I think. I just wish I could have done more at the time – then, and I can't bear even to describe it now!

Myself and another officer from HQ, and both for different purposes, and I conveniently, forget for what purposes – me driving – we arrived in the afternoon, the last few miles along a country road, through continuous woodland with tall trees, as usual, along each side, with heavy foliage just

Army Guard   Chief Warder   J.M.W.

My Celle Prison Assistants

meeting at the top. The army, who had been responsible for the rescue of those prisoners still alive, but in a terrible emaciated state, were in charge, and had the exceedingly difficult and very unpleasant task of bringing some semblance of normality in an impossible situation, and burying the mass of dead bodies. Some prisoners, in small groups, in the early stages of their first sight of freedom, on release, and in abject fear of everyone, had rushed into the forests and were now causing problems to the local population, and service personnel in their marauding raids on both. We were warned not to stop, if we were attacked on our return journey – we were not. What did happen on our return journey in the early evening, and with daylight fading fast was, considering where we were just leaving, just something a little unusual. Service vehicles still had wartime black-out headlamp screens on, so we had to switch lights on, it was dark enough already under the tall trees. For about the first mile OK at reasonable speed, suddenly, all the lights packed up, and we were in real darkness. We stopped and did the usual checks all round, no joy – we had no alternative but to press on, me looking up at the gap in the tree tops over the road, and my passenger saying 'left a bit – right a bit' or 'a lot' as the conditions may be until after about three-quarters of our journey we came to lighted roads. But still no car lights, until we were turning into

HQ main entrance, and then they all came ON, and stayed on, until I switched them off in transport workshops! They say, funny things happened on the way to the Colosseum in Rome – this of course bears no comparison to that – just a funny, little thing!

Having, I hope you will agree, got out of describing, with my inadequate vocabulary, the completely *uncivilised* conditions that had been found at Belsen and at that time, and eventually, shown to the world in film, book, and other media, far superior to my abilities – I will try to continue with a less sickening occurrence.

Another officer and myself together, but for different duties, were to go to Jever, north Germany, where the RAF were occupying the former Luftwaffe airfield but with a very small unit of officers and airmen. The Jever small town area was awash with German, unarmed POWs walking the streets – there were so many at this stage, the army had nowhere to put them. We had the perhaps unique experience of having two or three German officer POWs, at the head of a contingent of German POWs, marching in column in the rear volunteering, to my travel companion and myself as the 'officers from HQ' to join with the RAF to continue the war

Unfit for service

76

to drive back the Russians, which they were convinced we, the allies, were going to do! NO chance.

Oh yes, and NOT by the way, I forgot to mention the atomic bomb had very recently been dropped on Hiroshima, Japan by the USAAF, and rather changed the situation, more than somewhat. We were invited by the few station officers to join them for a VJ, (Victory Japan) celebratory dinner at the local hotel, with the head chef from the famous Berlin Adlon Hotel doing the cooking – and it was very good indeed. I only remember the large baked Alaska he carried in, shoulder high, and flaming beautifully – the pudding! I still have a small sauce boat with the German airforce swastika and wings, from Jever's Nazi store rooms.

My colleague and I continued our journey via Hamburg to Copenhagen, Denmark, sleeping in the car, and arriving on the Lolland/ Falster Island and, about 75 miles further north to the capital on the coast with the famous bronze mermaid. Before that however, we had the very best bacon, eggs, sausages etc., breakfast I have ever had – including my dear mum's – in my life, and it still is.

Copenhagen, along with the nermaid is a fine city – it always was pre-war and more than maintained the highest patriotic standards during the Nazi occupation – as the people did, in my opinion, in all the Scandinavian nations. Again you have guessed, I am all for these countries – even, as an Englishman, including the Vikings! At that time the most obvious, but also to me most poignant, sight in the capital were the special markers, with flowers or a wreath inserted, and positioned immovable on walkways, roads, gardens and buildings, etc., wherever a patriot resistance fighter had fallen, murdered by the Nazi occupiers. Wherever they were positioned in the middle of the road, on private property, or on footpaths, and also in groups, pedestrians, transport, buses and other traffic walked or drove round them – no matter how inconvenient it may be. That is the Danes to me. Even the 'busby' headdress and Brigade of Guards uniform of the 'Child Regiment', on the famous Tivoli Gardens entertainment park main entrance, was back to as normal as possible, as was the hospitality of everyone we met but, as this was only a short as it may be called in the RAF today 'Rest and Refreshment' leave, we were soon on our way back to 84 Group HQ.

I had been informed earlier that my next posting was to be to the Far East – but that was not now to be, due to the capitulation of Japan after the two atomic bombs on Hiroshima and Nagasaki. So I could start looking at the, hopefully not too long, delay in my demobilisation. Johnny Medworth had decided to stay in the RAF, but I wanted to get back to my family and continue my architectural studies. However, I was still 'operational' as far as the RAF was concerned – with the usual urgency to perform, and changes to the programme.

As a side issue, out of the so-called 'blue,' an SS officer, in full uniform, was shown into my office – how and why he was on HQ site, and past the guard house, without supervision or attendant, I do not know – my 'flabber' was probably 'gasted' at the time. Smart walk to my desk, even smarter salute, and he introduced himself – he was an ex Bosch, engineer etc., and could he join RAF airfield construction mainly my POW group at this time. After some discussion, the answer was no and probably also *nein*. What happened after he was escorted out of my office, I am afraid I do not know, he should not have been allowed onto Group HQ site.

Since Adam was a lad, the females of the species, the girls, the ladies, the 'fair sex', from mothers to grandmothers, princesses, queens – since Eve was a lass, to Florence Nightingale, (who by the way, according to Isaac Asimov, 'The lady with lamp' wherever she went, and she went to the Crimea in 1854, carried a pet owl in her pocket) – to the first lady in space, the ladies always manage when they try, and not very much, to get what they want. I suppose you have noticed.

So, having had the usual invitation from the AO, C in C to attend, and make my presence felt, in his office, this I do, with speed and decorum Sir! and in this case also 'Mam.' The usual salute, the CO has a senior officer of the WRAF, (Women's RAF) in the office – seated – and I know, immediately, I am in the presence of inviolable and invincible and determined Forces, because that's how it is in such circumstances. A contingent of WRAF personnel along with officers and all necessary equipment are due to arrive at 84 Group HQ in the near future, and can I arrange to convert various buildings, designed for occupation by the male sex, to occupation by the female sex – sleeping quarters, toilet facilities, kitchen and dining, off duty facilities, etc., etc. How soon is the future, Sir? Oh, 14 days – so you had better get on with it, or words to that effect! The place had been built, allegedly as they say today, in 9 months, so this would be a 'piece of cake' in RAF parlance of the time.

You will recall my reference to my latest near miss with the sergeant driver, a little earlier. The time came for me to return to the UK for my demobilisation at Uxbridge, and not before time! My unit of mainly German POWs presented me with a pair of figured plywood 'suite' cases, leather handles, and with my name and rank on each case, and also a splendid hand carved and painted, (with a leaping dog handle) walking stick, one case to contain a large state of the art, 1943 or 4, 'Siemans–Halske' cabinet radio. This had been liberated by the Army from a cave stacked with them, and exchanged with other services for similarly acquired items. I still have both cases, the radio is long gone as Old Technology, although I still have one of the unique very small valves. The walking stick, long ago, went walkies I suppose!

There were the usual 'Parting is such sweet sorrow' sessions in the bar handing over of various duties, presents for civilian staff, barman, etc. with Johnny Medworth, waiting with the car for my kit and baggage, to take me down to Hanover Station, and the train to the coast, and then Dover, and the last farewell to Johnny. For some years afterwards, I continued to receive requests from his solicitors to give him a reference and vouch for him for various properties that he was either renting or buying, but I regret that he never phoned or wrote to me, and I had no idea where he was – I sincerely hope he is still with us.

I can't remember whether I embarked from France or Belgium. What I do remember is the ferry was packed with troops – on the decks, lying with their kit bags as pillows, or hanging over the rail being sick – mainly being sick, and the ferry being unable to enter Dover harbour, and having to stand off for some hours to wait for the heavy seas to abate. The captain said it was the worst crossing he had ever experienced, before we were able to enter the harbour and disembark, then train to London and Uxbridge, RAF officers demob centre.

My Certificate of Service and Release from Air Ministry London WC2 shows that I enlisted in Royal Air Force Volunteer Reserve on the 6th November 1940 (also, later, to be my son's birthday in 1942), Last day of Service 9th September 1946, Adverse Reports NIL.

My Leaving Certificate – Officers also has pages for Income Tax, claims for Disability Pension, Medical treatment after leaving dispersal centre, and finally Conditions of Release – this contained, among other instructions, that my commission is not terminated, and I am liable to recall to duty, until my 'commission is terminated or relinquished', after which 'a communication will be issued at the end of the Emergency', – to this day I have never received such 'communication' – and I am also to 'preserve' my uniform in good condition in case of recall to duty. I suppose it's all too late now, or, as they say 'at this moment in time' which is daft, when one can say 'now!'

I received the various items of civilian clothing issued, suit, overcoat, etc., and after all the usual formalities I was on my way to Kings Cross railway station and the Yorkshire Pullman – and, to the amazing surprise I mentioned very much earlier in this conversation, I was in good time for the Pullman, and soon to my favourite corner seat in an empty first class compartment. Officers travelled first class in those never to be forgotten days, but I wouldn't bet on it these days – and I was, properly dressed, as I should be, in uniform.

As the train began to move slowly out on the journey north, an elderly gentleman came into the compartment, and sat diagonally opposite me in the corridor corner, with the usual nods by both of us. I do not remember who remembered who first, I had of course, after 10 years, a tremendous 'load' of things on my mind – not least having with me, in its box on the luggage rack, the latest Hornby Dublo electric train set, cajoled out of the kind lady assistant at Hamleys toy shop in Regent Street, an hour earlier, 'the last one they had', probably of two at that time, a gift for my four-year-old son, and as something for his father to play with. The gentleman on the Pullman said, 'I remember you, – you are now I see, a very smartly dressed, handsome, intelligent looking Royal Air Force Officer, who used to run my factory,' or, as I may have said before, words to that effect. Then I remembered – he said, 'I am Duncan Bailey' (OBE, MIMECHE) Chairman, Charles Roberts & Co, – and I was able to say, 'I thought I recognised you on entry, Sir.'

I am not a betting person, I only bet when I have rock solid, pre-information, and can't lose, which is not often – but what odds would you give me to have this happen even after one year, – not 10 – 1000 – 2000 – 10,000 to one?

We did, of course, have a most interesting discussion on the way to Wakefield, and he invited me to have lunch with his fellow directors at the next board meeting in about two weeks at the 'works' in Horbury and, there and then, entered this in his diary – but not me, I had not had a diary since my schooldays at Crossleys, and perhaps only then as a Christmas gift diary. I didn't need one – I could remember, I had been doing it for the last six years, easy, but I failed to appreciate that I was at long last to be at home with my wife and son and my mind full of many, many, things in the future and even more in the present. I completely forgot the invitation, not very bright to say the least! I was later informed that Duncan Bailey was going to invite me to design a new office block for the works etc. I would have been delighted to do so, but I was already committed to continuing with my School of Architecture studies, which is a seven year full time study course – with bus travel, summer and winter, daily, and carrying $42'' \times 27'' \times \frac{3}{4}''$, thick drawing boards with instruments, and mahogany T-square, etc., etc. I could not at this stage afford to get a car – so you will appreciate it was not going to be all beer and skittles, by any means. So it was back to the LSA (Leeds School of Architecture), and the pleasure of reuniting with various ex service friends from six years earlier – but regrettably some no longer resuming where, some of us left off – so it was a very mixed pleasure.

Architecture is not only the longest study course in advanced education, with its 'knowledge of the various arts and sciences connected therewith' (Royal Institute of British Architects Certificate) but is the only one where there is required, from years one to seven, the virtually continuous presentation of design and working drawings, calculations, 'esquisse' drawings, structural design drawings, theses, presentation drawings, surveying, lectures, examinations, and two years professional practice. You can only be accepted for interview, prior to acceptance to year one, if you also have certain specified subjects in your list of school examination passes, and they also have a place for you in the usually over-subscribed, application list! Fortunately, you will recall, I had been there and done that.

The five day County bus, single deck, previously mentioned, to and from Horbury and Leeds, daily, lugging home my drawing board etc., each weekend, was a right bind (as we would have said at Crossleys), but was in fact enlivened by being joined at Ossett (as a small boy at Sandal I could not believe that there was anywhere a place with a name with two SSs and two TTs and only six letters, as the tram from Sandal to Ossett had on its destination board – sorry about that, thought you might be interested) by my friend Charles Moss, a fellow student at LSA, with his drawing board. We were both avid readers of our favourite author, Damon Runyon, of previous mention, as you should recall if you have managed to get this far and are paying attention. Runyon was the USA's top sports columnist, and also mainly humorous writer and playwright of the rise and fall of gangsters during the prohibition period. 'Runyon on Broadway', Guys and Dolls, 'Runyon a la carte', 'Take it easy', and of course, as I hope by now you know, more than somewhat – or else!

With hindsight, on my postwar return to LSA, my problem was that some of my original contempories as students were either unfortunately no longer with us, or long since graduated. Fortunately there were still some in the 4th and 5th year. A friend/pupil, although at that time he was in the 4th year but worked in our studio, was P.A. Boyes. I was to learn some years later that he was one of the sons of the chain of Boyes Stores in Yorkshire, based at Scarborough – and by whom I, together with my dear wife and son, were to be hailed, across the Scarborough shop's large, open floor, as a long lost friend, or something like that, and invited to lunch with him in their restaurant on the floor above – in the early fifties. I still occasionally visit their unique stores, in various towns in Yorkshire.

I had, along with a good number of fellow students, volunteered to join HM forces in 1940, and at some time in the 6 years since then the LSA had temporarily moved the senior students from their old site adjacent to the College of Commerce and College of Art to an even more central area of Leeds, near the Town Hall. With staff shortages and the two final design and thesis years I found myself in the position of tutor unpaid, but I hope appreciated, and so my more or less daily attendances were taken up by requests to give students advice, and general help, on their various schemes, which was fine, but I too was also supposed to be submitting a final thesis and a large number of design drawings of the various buildings, perspective drawings, all of which take an awful lot of time to create and present, and even before all that need a lot of very important decisions, which are continually changing and improving, hopefully trying to ensure that all decisions are the right ones. Today, some students, (and architects), can download academic written theses, along with design and working drawings, perspectives, and quantities etc., of probably every type of building in the world, via the computer, and world wide from the Internet, and World Wide Web.

Maria and Timothy

82

Another friend, who I again regret to say I have not seen or heard from since we both graduated, is J. Donald Eastwood, who at that time I think lived in Pannal Ash area of Harrogate. Donald attended daily, usually late morning, with his roll of design drawings, and spread them out on his drawing table, and requested my opinion or advice on various problems. Nearing the time for final submission, he breezed in as usual, greeted me with cheerful hellos, and said, 'I've finished – how are you getting on?' After what used to be called a pregnant pause, I admitted I hadn't even started yet. 'Well you had better get on with it!' he said. How considerate – he was indeed, however, right – so I did.

Getting on with it had its problems. It was mid May, not historically my best month, since, and for many years later, the most unhappy week of my life was the first week in May, when I first went as a boarder to Crossleys and was homesick. Things that could go wrong seemed to have a habit of doing so – my work room, with my drawing board, on its fold-up, adjustable stand (one you will recall, I made earlier) was on the first floor, with a large window overlooking the lawn and gardens at Spinkwell, Jenkin Road, Horbury – where my wife Maria and our son Timothy enjoyed themselves having fun before my very eyes, very pleasant but very distracting. Spinkwell was my wife's family home (where my son was born, and where we lived until the time when I was able to do something about a home of our own) together with her father Frank J. Baines and her mother Alice – both of whom, I am glad to say, did not want us to leave.

Time again was of the essence. I had four weeks to do a year's work, before submission, and I had frittered time away doing interesting things with my family and students, and possibly doing a lot of thinking – but not much doing.

My design project was a development for the small seaside town of Filey, on Yorkshire's east coast – and a very pleasant place indeed, also the last resting place of Emily Brontë, fishing cobles, RNLI lifeboat, large wide bay – with, at one time, racing car races, on the fine long sands from the Brigg – a long rock promontory used by the Romans as a landing pier, a 'listed' Railway station, golf course, to the huge cliffs of Flamborough Head and the seabirds nesting at the south side of the bay, not to mention one of the first Butlins holiday camps, beyond Primrose Valley, further south. Now, having written in praise of Filey, I am reminded that the same sands at the south end were the scene of yet another 'near miss', not only for me, but this time also for my dear wife Maria, and son Timothy (age 6). We had taken the car, at this time a Jowett twin cylinder, made in Bradford, onto the beach. It was evening, late autumn and deserted, we stopped in the centre of the bay. Tim wanted to go to the south end – at that time what Tim wanted, as far as Maria was concerned, Tim got. I was just the chauffeur, 2 to 1. I got my orders, 'orf we jolly well went – and ran into quick-sands, soon up to our axles. I desperately tried to turn back, and it was a fast incoming tide – and no one about! I looked up and there, on the edge of the cliff, was a farm tractor, heading towards the sloping side of the Hunmandby Gap valley, to end his day ploughing. I frantically waved my arms, and, thank the Lord, he saw us and turned at the bottom of the valley onto the beach towards the car, hooked up, and pulled out the car and the lucky near miss occupants!

My scheme proposed a multi-purpose concert hall/cinema, restaurant, etc., with all mod cons of the day, landscaped parkland areas, and on an extended foreshore promenade area, south side of the town, a pier and entertainment pavilion. Since the end of the war my wife and I had first rented a timber house in Primrose Valley for holidays at Filey – a long time favourite place. I had also photographed the area – as probably our friend, the aforementioned Dr John Stoker would say – too comprehensibly to include photos in my written thesis.

Cometh the day, maketh the man, I hope, and with a few, off breaks, for tea and cakes, and the play wrestle on the lawn, or a game of cricket, I did my best to get on with it. Towards the end it was on occasion necessary to work through the night to the early hours, but at least it was quiet.

Came the day, Presentation Day, with all the schemes pinned up for exhibition and inspection by the examining board – and the handing in of thesis also, to be examined by our peers, and await the publication of the successful entrants' names.

THE LEEDS COLLEGE OF ART
THE LEEDS SCHOOL OF ARCHITECTURE
DIPLOMA IN ARCHITECTURE
With Distinction
WE HEREBY CERTIFY that
JEFFREY WALTON
Having attended approved courses of study in the college and
having satisfied the examiners was awarded this diploma by
resolution of the Board of Governors
ON THE First DAY OF July 1949
Chairman   Chairman, Architectural Advisory Committee.
Principal Head of School & Director of Education.

'With Distinction' was the real surprise, the gilt on the gingerbread, or my friend on my shoulder, I will never know, but as they say it springs eternal so I can at least hope!

Approximately five months later, on 30th November I received the following certificate:

THIS IS TO CERTIFY THAT
JEFFREY WALTON, DIP. ARCH. (DIST.) (LEEDS),
'Spinkwell,' Jenkin Road, Horbury, Near Wakefield, Yorkshire,
Having passed the Qualifying Examination established in 1882,
was elected on the twenty-ninth day of November, 1949,

ASSOCIATE
OF THE ROYAL INSTITUTE OF BRITISH ARCHITECTS,
Founded in the year of Our Lord, One thousand eight hundred and thirty-four, and afterwards constituted, under Royal Charters granted by King William the Fourth, Queen Victoria, King Edward the Seventh, and King George the Fifth, a Body Politic and Corporate for the general advancement of Architecture, and for promoting and facilitating the acquirement of the knowledge of the various arts and sciences connected therewith.

IN WITNESS whereof, the Common Seal has been
hereunto affixed, at a Meeting of the Council, held at
No. 66, Portland Place, London, this third day of January 1950.

(signed)	Chairman of the Meeting
"	Member of Council
"	Member of Council
"	Honorary Secretary
"	The Secretary of the Royal Institute

So now I can exercise my profession, practice. No, not like some of the 'professional' football players of today – bought for millions of pounds, then paid up to 5 million pounds a year wages, where did I go wrong? The most famous footballer of his day, and perhaps still, Stanley Matthews, now the late Sir Stanley Matthews, was paid £24 a week, and had to work as a joiner to, as they would say then, 'make ends meet'. Times change, but we still have to move with them, so they, say, so I continued to practice – I still do – but only for some old friends, although I am still technically consultant to my practice, JWHA (Jeffrey Walton, Horsfall and Associates) now at Shelley, near Huddersfield, but thank goodness they have never, so far, and it's a long far, called on me to consult. If they did, knowing them, it would mean trouble, and they are well able, by now, to deal with that themselves.

My dear wife, always having my best interests at heart, and I suppose not wanting me to get bored, presented me with an advertisement, in the education section of the press, for the position of Head of the Department of Architecture in the then Huddersfield College of Technology, School of Art. I duly applied, late 1949, and was eventually interviewed by Dr W.E. Scott, Principal of the College and members of the board of governors. The interview went well, but I insisted that I was not interested in being appointed to the post if I could not continue with my private practice. In my opinion, it is no good preaching the things you don't practice, sorry about 'adjusting' a well known phrase, and also a few other observations for improvement of present practices in the schools of architecture, and I suppose, in spite of my rocking the boat, more than somewhat, I was offered the post, and I accepted.

I commenced my appointment, for the enrolment period at the college, and the new term, with some forebodings, to say the least. I was very soon to realise that the whole ethos of the provision, of even the basic needs, for adult students to study for any occupation was a shambles, in every constituent, accommodation, staff, equipment, books, library, to name a few.

Now may I make one thing clear, at the outset, please, in my opinion schools of architecture are made by their students, and these come in many shapes, sizes, personality, abilities, gender, and, so help me, political opinions. They also uniquely hand down, to those following behind, from year one to year seven, a *tradition*, due to the fact that they are in contact, physically with each other for seven years. I know that this can continue even after they have retired, it has even with me, and above all, they are all *different* – thank goodness or, the Lord, or whatever deity you fancy.

Back to the so-called shambles, and, again, at that time all places of learning, large or small, rich or poor, had suffered deprivation of most kinds for at least ten years, but nothing like the so-called 'lack of resources' after the 'Education, education, education' of recent years when billions of taxpayers' money has been squandered, since the 1997 election of Tony Blair's government. Things now are, in practically all departments, worse than they ever have been.

In 1949, the only Architecture Studio, was on the ground floor of the main Victorian building of the College of Technology, with no external windows, except with roof lights over most of the area, but practically, they were inaccessible to clean on the outside, with the three storey building that surrounded the roof – the Studio was corridor accessed, one on each long side and, two opposite doors, with three small office rooms, also on the long wall, one of which was my office, together with a stack of good quality books, but mainly Victorian, or older – all, probably, a 'Bequest' to the Library from a past student, I was never able to find out – but I am afraid, not even properly stacked, no shelves, dusty, and some damaged – and it took a long time to get them, I hope, properly housed – you can't ask a librarian if they have been, can you?

So my first job, obviously, was to get the basics right, and this was not going to make me popular with the establishment, but had to be done – somehow.

Question: What was the curriculum? I am afraid there wasn't one, at least for an RIBA School of Architecture – students had been occupied, by weekly visits to other departments of the college, Painting and Decorating, Building Trades Department, cast and life drawing classes in the School of Art – and even a foundation course in English for the first year students. The RIBA entry stage required a list of GC of E, or Baccalaureate, etc., subjects of study which *must* include English and Mathematics as compulsory and, due to the lack of information on the previous studies curriculum, I was only to discover these anomalies when the person in charge of the English Foundation course rang me to complain how poor was a first year student in English, one Harry Noble who, after graduating was to become Chief Architect to Barnsley Borough Corporation in 1960, or thereabouts. He had produced an essay on a Yorkshire subject, in broad Yorkshire composition, not an easy task. The poor lady had not even appreciated he was taking the mickey, and that was the end of the foundation course for my students.

The date, today, now, is Thursday, June 14th 2007 and my *Daily Mail* has just arrived. I also take the *Times*, but this is now changing somewhat, since Mr Murdoch of SKY took over, but fortunately, he still keeps Scarfe the brilliant Cartoonist. My long time favourite in the *Mail* is columnist, playwright, writer, Yorkshireman, Keith Waterhouse.

Mr Keith Waterhouse and I, according to the various items of information on his personal life and activities that he has written about over many years, have some things in common. We are both roughly of the same generation, both Yorkshiremen. He was very probably studying at the adjacent College of Commerce at the same time as I was, at the

Leeds School of Architecture and perhaps, having started working in the offices of *The Yorkshire Post* and *Yorkshire Evening News*, also has a copy of the new edition of the *Modern English Dictionary*, published in 1924, when, at best, Mr Waterhouse would be, like me, four years old, and he probably had his by the age of sixteen – I wish now I had read mine before I started this project at the beginning of this year, 2007 – particularly the chapter Principles of Grammar, of which you will know the four main divisions, Orthography, Etymology, Syntax and Prosody, including his favourite, the 'itinerant apostrophe'. I wish I could meet him any time, perhaps when he comes to Leeds.

I had been appointed to follow the only architect in the entire college, Mr Norman Culley, FRIBA, a gentleman of the old school of architects, of the late Victorian period, a very good period. Huddersfield was Norman's home town. He published two excellent sketch books of the main buildings in the town, and adjacent villages like Aspley and Almonbury, all renderings in pencil, and in all of them, while he was sat in a car, he always placed a similar small car parked, on appropriate sketches, during the 1930s. He very kindly presented me with copies, and next to them, on my bookshelves is also another slim volume by James Walton BSc, FSA on 'Early Timbered Buildings of the Huddersfield District' published by the Huddersfield Tolson Memorial Museum, 1955 – he wrote the preface when he was in Basutoland, April 30, 1953, he returned on six months' leave to complete this book. I never met him so I do not know whether we are related.

Norman and I shared the aforementioned office but he only attended on two half days per week, (when he was able) for some months to complete his contract. Norman was a small slight person, who had been at one time President of the West Yorkshire Society of Architects, based in Leeds and also editor of our journal, and he was now in his sixties at least, smoked a pipe – as I also did then. He would regale me, without provocation, with jokes and stories which was fine on the first, or even second time, or even third time, but he seemed to forget he had told them before, and would sit, leaning back in his chair, with his eyes closed completely, and repeat, in exact detail, every word from the previous renditions. No matter how many times you suggested, Yes Norman, or Mr Culley, you have told us that before, he never stopped. I don't know how he got on with students, as he did not spend much time with them, in fact he reprimanded me on two or three occasions (probably forgot he had told me before), 'Why did I tell them my design secrets, when I was asked by a student to discuss his drawing board drawings?' or words to that effect.

Norman had his office in Byram Court Chambers Huddersfield and, some years later, on two occasions, asked me if I would look after some of his remaining contracts, which I did and they were successfully completed. He was not in the best of health and retired, regrettably, and some time later I attended his funeral, together with some of my students who knew him. A very likeable man, and knowing him, I think he also had a very enjoyable life.

The enrolment days enabled me to see the present students, and to interview prospective new students, both full time and part time, where necessary, in order to get to know them as much as possible, as early as possible, and of course, for them to know me, likewise. I had two first year full time students, Alwyn Hull, and Paul White, and there were also new part time students who were articled pupils to architects in Huddersfield, Bradford, Wakefield, Halifax etc. One local architect, Gordon Berry, MC, ARIBA, World War II tank commander, always accompanied his pupils, to his credit, to every enrolment session for some years.

My priorities were better accommodation and more architectural staff. Other than Mr Culley, and Harold Morris ARIBA, both part time, and the periods to occupy them in other departments, previously mentioned, it was me, day and sometimes evenings. I let those who had no facilities at home or in lodgings work on in the studio, and these arrangements continued for at least a year, and unfortunately also me doing my best not to get into the principal Dr Scot's bad books, as well as the caretaker's black looks, on turning us out at 9 pm, 'closing time'.

When raining, the studio drips were going from bad to worse. We had various receptacles catching the drips, and moved drawing boards around to avoid them, but enough was enough, and I decided to mark every drip with white on the timber boarded studio floor. I invited Dr Scot to call in to see us, as soon as convenient – which he did, and I am pleased to say he fully appreciated the problem and said he would do his best – or again, words to that effect. The 'drips' by the way numbered over sixty! What I was hoping to achieve was to get the school out of the rather depressing environment of the Victorian college building, and more light and space to enable both students and staff, including me, to develop to their full potential away from the schoolmaster attitude of the technical college – with the exception of the music, art, and engineering departments.

Chronic shortage of space together with large numbers of junior pupils, coming out and going in, morning, noon and night, with limited facilities, including toilet, classrooms etc., and, including some peace and quiet. We had to have more accommodation, on our own, and with staff always available, even if it was only one or two. Students are doing hard work over a long period and don't want to have constant interruptions.

Rationing of almost everything, from food to all materials for building construction and structural engineering etc. etc., was in force, and so continued until about 1953, so we needed to find something now, not waiting for a building to be built. We were offered two buildings, both belonging to the corporation, one a fire station, possibly built just before the war, and if we had use of all of it would have been most suitable, and the Corporation Transport Headquarters – office block and canteen, (but use of only part) and of similar vintage to the fire station, both on the side of the Colne river. In the case of the latter, the main stone wall (two storeys) came out of the river and they were within a mile of the fire station, and a mile and a half from the transport HQ, and from the town centre and the college. The fire station became unavailable to us and decided to move to Longroyd Bridge transport depot, before anyone else changed their minds!

The School of Architecture at Longroyd I allocated to be, entrance hall, with open staircase to first floor, lecture room, library, model workshop and Sin Bin, and my office – first floor main studio, staff room, two senior studios (each, two person), toilets, etc. Outside there was the large forecourt for buses to enter and leave, but mainly for the mass of transport workers who started to assemble on the 25-yard wide door line ten minutes before 5 pm finishing time, daily, and then rushed out en masse, past the few cars parked on the forecourt. At that time there were not so many cars on the roads, now everybody has a car, and haven't you noticed they are all sparkling new cars, you rarely ever see a used or old car on the roads now, and only very few, well looked after and maintained, vintage cars, of quality. 'Too easy come by these days,' as my good friend Margery, who is as I write, using my Apple – G.4 computer and PC Microsoft 'Word' – has just explained to me, with a rider that, 'Even those on benefits, can get a car these days!'

I took the opportunity of the new broom, and designed drawing tables for students, long enough for a double elephant drawing board and a similar length at the side for a DE sheet, or stack, of drawings for reference, and these were supplied by the Education Department during the summer vacation, for students by now in increasing numbers to make a new start in a better environment.

Naturally, the School of Architecture was a department of the School of Art, after all it is the Mother of the Arts – in ancient Egypt the architect was the next, as you may know, in authority to the Pharaoh he was designing the pyramid for, and to be so engaged when the Pharaoh died he was, on occasion, buried alongside him, to ensure that he could not give away the secrets of the pyramid – and of course, perhaps, so that he would know the way out when the time came.

A.D.S. Sugden was headmaster of the School of Art, according to the principal's report of 1958–1959, when he apparently resigned, I don't know why. He seemed a nice chap to me, when we very occasionally met, never saw any of his Artwork either, but I never even met his successor of 1959 – B.G. Cope, as headmaster, and I was there for the next fourteen years!

Another of my lesser known phrases or sayings is that 'The country is over populated with schoolmasters – but there aren't many teachers about.' I hasten to add, I am an architect, I hope I can prove that, who I hope teaches – I can't prove that, I am afraid – what I do know, is that at the end of WWII the then Labour government allowed ex service personnel to train as teachers for a six month (approx) period, as distinct from a three year period, with one year's teacher training, as in my brother's case, and he also did a full course at Carnegie Hall Physical Teacher Training School, at the same time.

This inadequate training of schoolmasters who, in some cases, were to pass through the education system, not getting any better, except in schoolmastering, and many, eventually, headmastering to both less fortunate colleges, innocent pupils, of all school ages, and possibly some probable – teachers – if they hadn't already been disillusioned. This situation, like the sins of the fathers, handed down at least to the last retirement of the last headmaster, and we, the taxpayers, are allowed a head of the school. As you can see, to me words mean things – wish I could put them together better for you.

Even more important were qualified staff. At this time I still had only Mr Culley, who would retire soon, Geoffrey Rowe, who had been a student with me pre-war at Leeds, and Ralph Hudson, all local architects and one day only, part time. We needed full time staff to deal with all the subjects in the RIBA curriculum and these we eventually appointed, not at the same time or order of appointment – Geoffrey Whittlestone ARIBA, G. Gordon Furness, ARIBA, John Midgely, ARIBA, R.J. Oetgen (Australian) AAIA.

As I was able to appoint part time staff, without the bureaucracy involved, and because in my experience these volunteers, as usual, do it because they want to do it, not because they get paid, and they are a great help, a new face and attitude to students, and again, in architecture, usually stay friends for life. I appointed at various times, Harold B. Morris, ARIBA, Geoffrey B. Bray, structural engineer, with Abbey Hanson Rowe, a successful architectural practice in Huddersfield. I regret that Geoffrey Rowe, on retirement, went to live in Australia with his family, and unfortunately passed away a few years ago, a charming fellow. Thinking of Australia, I will at this convenient point mention two artists I appointed at different times and for different periods, as artist in residence: David Blackburn and Ian Henderson – David was a Huddersfield artist who went to Australia as artist in residence at one of the Universities down under, Sydney I think, but I am not sure. I bought some of his very good modern land and seascapes of Australia. Also my very long time friend, W.F.G. Sutcliffe, gave me a crayon rendering of the small town of Meltham near Huddersfield executed in 1969 for one of my birthdays, with a note attached saying, if I wanted to change it, the artist had other examples of his work. I did, but under the circumstances, I couldn't – but it is still very good. I hope to be able to include W.F.G., more fully, later. Ian Henderson is also a very enthusiastic artist, with a strong interest in architectural schools. A letter from him, April 27th 1972:

Today I have been in the Adelaide Institute of Technology School of Architecture. Funnily enough I made an appointment to go in and have a chat with one of the Senior Lecturers and it so happened, (wait for it), – that she knows you (of old). Pauline Moss (nee Pauline Peters) was at the Leeds School with you and I believe Chas. Moss is an old friend of yours any way, you could have knocked me down with a feather, after coming, two and a half months ago to Australia I met someone who knew you – do let us know how things are going at (Your) School of Architecture at the Poly. I expect fun and games are still carrying on!

As you will, I hope, read later, you can say that again, and again, in fact a few more, more than Somewhats!
A second letter, May 10th 1972 two weeks later:

Yes do please become a National member of the R.I.B.A. Council – that would give me a big kick, I am sure you would work wonders with them – as I was leaving for Australia I was interested to learn of the various directors – with a small 'd' I received an offer of a job from compatriot, Armstrong – he's one Australian well off where he is … I will let you know how I get on at the University of Newcastle School of Architecture – remembering your maxim: It's not what you call a thing that counts, it's what it is that matters!

Having taken the opportunity to fast forward to the early seventies, I will get back to the fifties and sixties, and do my utmost to include at least some of the things we managed to achieve – but I must warn you, they may be, perhaps, out of time sequence. I would have to be Methusellah,' at my age now, to put in everything, and I reckon I am only half way through, so now is your chance to return the book and get your money back, if it is ever published.

Even back at the very beginning of being in charge of the department of architecture in the technical college in December 1949 with the leaking roof, I tried to make sure, at the beginning of the day to speak to every student there, using their Christian names. 'Good morning John, any problems?' and always I dealt with it to the best of my ability, and subsequently, when we were at Longroyd Bridge, the RIBA sent to me qualified architects for teacher training, each one of whom, amazingly to me, asked me how was I able, when asked by a student, to go up to his drawing board, and immediately start answering his questions and criticise his work? I had to say, 'I don't know, but that is what I hope is called Teaching,' not having been trained at a teacher training college to be an 'expert' or a 'professional' teacher – or am I being too cynical?

Being at last free from the classroom atmosphere of the College of Technology and having some staffing improvements including Dr Arnold Pacey PhD (Physics) a senior lecturer at Manchester University who was invaluable to all years 1 to 5, the artists in residence I have already mentioned, and also invited architects, such as Grenfell Baines, Geoffrey Rowe, and others to discuss architectural subjects, present prizes, etc., over the years. We also made visits to various buildings of note, in first year for purposes of measured drawings, sketching, surveying etc., and later I started something of a tradition in visits to factories, famous buildings, Blenheim Palace, Oxford and Cambridge Universities, I.C.I. Billingham – I suppose carrying on the tradition of my old school Crossleys at Halifax, also Huddersfield's near neighbour – and from which I had some students at H.S.A. Longroyd Bridge, but they had been day boys.

Having mentioned these places which I visited, I am reminded of Pilkington Glass, St Helens, Lancashire, the world famous glass manufacturers, which we visited on a number of occasions over the years.

On one occasion in the early fifties I took a coach party. I had a rather hurried breakfast of cornflakes and a boiled egg and drove to the HAS which, as you may know, is on the site of the headquarters of the Luddite uprising against the pay and conditions in the mills in the north of England. I was in a bit of a rush and, by the time we arrived at Pilkingtons, I was not feeling very well. I put it down to indigestion (having rushed my breakfast) the journey to the School and the bumpy coach journey to St Helens.

Fortunately, Pilkington's is a large, first class company and at that time had its own medical centre with a full-time doctor in attendance. I was in no condition to argue when he insisted I take a bed in his 'Casualty Ward' to be on the 'safe side'. As the time went on to 5 pm with only slight improvement on my part, he was worried about my condition and advised that I should go into hospital. In my opinion, there is no substitute for good professional advice; I try to give it and I always take it. He offered me two choices: a general hospital and one which was staffed by nuns. Both would have been OK but I decided on the General and was driven there by ambulance. I arrived without bag or baggage and was issued a very 'sturdy' pair of pyjamas and was given a bed in the large Surgical Ward which had beds down each long side and a wide space between them in the middle. As with going to the dentist with life threatening toothache, by the time I got there I was much improved. I was thinking about arranging transport to take me home when I was accosted by three medics who examined me, one at a time, and discussed things generally with each other, such as the availability of theatre space the following day. Not conducive to a food night's sleep, and it got worse; the patient opposite me died, the patient on my right was starting to recover from his operation and making his presence felt in no mean manner and the patient on my left, although apparently sleeping, was making a good deal of noise.

If this was not enough for this poor Yorkshire boy on 'foreign' Lancashire soil (when his home in Sandal Magna is a few hundred yards away from Sandal Castle, site of the battle of Wakefield, where the Duke of York was beheaded and his head taken and hung on Mickelgate Bar so that 'York could overlook York') in walked a Salvation Army Brass Band, complete with lady members. They formed a circle at the foot of my bed and played and sang a number of hymns prior to the ensuing sermon, all before a final march round complete with euphonium accompaniment!

Before 'lights out' I rang my life-long friend, Edward Hanscombe Neal, 'Ted' Neal (FFF), genuine expert in most engineering fields, to come and collect me the next day in his Riley car and take me back to Spinkwell, Horbury where we were still living before Tree Garden was built. I also rang my doctor, John Brandon Stoker (FFF), who informed me that I had jaundice – and that it was serious. I was in bed for between two and three weeks and was visited every day by J.B.S. (not like today) and it was very painful. As you have read, I have some small connection with HRH The Duke of Edinburgh; we both suffered the same disease at the same time, he in London and me in Yorkshire. In my case it was yet another near miss but neither of us can ever give blood. I wish both him and the Queen a long and happy life. I know what you are thinking: all three of us have not done so bad! 'God save the Queen' and you can, as they say, 'stuff your presidents!'

I have been putting it off – it brings back so many memories. I had more or less decided not to include any more information than I already have, earlier, in this life story, my dear son Timothy Baines Walton – my family, the most precious blessing of all in my life – and also our friends. Fortunately only two and a half enemies – but these two were world class – bottom of the heap – and they were to have a satanic effect on my life and my family, for over 25 years of our lives – including dear daughter in law, Sandra Elizabeth Walton, of Crofton near Wakefield and my partner, Mrs Sheila M. Jackson, and of course, some of my friends. I said satanic not titanic, earlier, – just to try to keep a sense of proportion!

I may have said this before, among my BKPOS I don't think I have, but here it is, 'if you can count the names of your friends' – and I mean real friends, people you can run to, when you are in real trouble, and they will really help you – 'on the fingers of ONE hand, and use ALL five fingers, you are a very fortunate person!' Try it now, and you will see what I mean. When I last tried it, probably when I coined or thought I had coined it, I was indeed a very fortunate person. Since then, I am sorry to say, time like an ever rolling stream – you know the rest, except the 'forgotten' bit, in my case, I call them my five finger friends, (FFF) – you met some of them earlier, I hope you will meet more as we go along.

You may have guessed, I am not a desperately gregarious person, more, a private person – don't like gossip – but I have to suffer it, sometimes, for peace and quiet, don't we all?

I mentioned, during my WWII meanderings, my marriage to Maria and the birth of my son Timothy, and my return to civvy street – hopefully, with your approval, I will continue with more on family and friends, and personal, to today October 11th 2007 – or thereabouts.

I started building my house, 'Tree Garden' at Sandal Magna,

Wakefield, in 1950 – Maria wanted a house that was private, had a good garden area, with possibly some trees, and with medical, hospital, local and town shopping etc., also it had to have a PINK bathroom – reason, Maria was a sparkling readhead, therefore Maria could not wear pink, and Maria always knew what she wanted – and usually achieved her objective. But as teenagers, why did Maria want me? After Wakefield Girls High School, and with Wakefield Grammar School, (my brother's old school) only a few hundred yards away, she had plenty to choose from, but then you already know what happened. My brother was already well and truly 'booked' by another Mary, also a teacher at his school, where he was head teacher. At that time, Mary had to leave before they could marry! How different now!

Finding a suitable site was not easy, and I had also one or two other things to attend to, you may remember, as well. However, I happened to be driving through Sandal Magna, my birthplace, along Barnsley road into Wakefield and there was an estate agent's board sticking out, over a high stone wall, on a line of trees, advertising seven house sites, shown on a cul-de-sac layout plan. I drove on to the office of the agent, whom I knew, and was fortunate in being able to put an option on all but one of the sites – which due to a line of fine beech trees you would not get planning permission to build on. This too, you will find, was to later have interesting connotations.

The land was approximately half of the estate of Milnthorpe House built in the 1700s, and originally the home of the Ellis Family – my wife's great grandfather had married an Ellis daughter, and her grandfather was named Joseph Ellis Baines, so, you will see there was remarkable coincidence and connection, for some 150 years (approx). Believe it or not, there is Angus Ellis, Architect (ex-HSA student) in my office – and he was born in Milnthorpe House, 200 yards from where I am writing this now.

The site initially comprised of a grass tennis court with cast iron line markers and cast iron net sockets, bolted to buried blocks of stone, and they are still here – a neglected orchard of only three apple trees, two pear, and one mulberry tree – which unfortunately had to be removed. There are now eight apples, three pear, one Greengage, eight plum, 10×30 feet raspberry cage, blackberry bushes, a fig tree, and at least 35 different genus of trees, potting shed, 12×8 feet greenhouse, Cold Frames, and 30×14 feet barn on a second entrance and right of way from Milnthorpe Lane which leads to the barn and a car park area adjacent to the garden which is walled or high fenced throughout. Trees all round, lawns, mixed plant borders etc.

The land was being sold by Mr W.S. des Forges who also was town clerk of the City of Wakefield. We met at his very spacious and mahogany panelled office in the Town Hall to sign and seal the deeds etc. He was a very pleasant person – and we both agreed that no trees were to be cut down without prior approval. As you will have gathered, if there is one thing I am all for it is trees. One of my original sayings is 'a good reputation is the hardest thing to get and the easiest thing to lose'. A tree is likewise the easiest thing to saw down – but it's a hell of a thing to stand back *up*, if you have made a mistake – or change your mind – so I was all for that – but as sometimes is the case, things can change.

The builder was Mr Eric Nicholson, a conscientious, honest, and competent person, who was local and undertook one or two contracts at the most, at the same time. He soon had the overall reinforced concrete raft laid on the tennis court area, which was partly on rock, and made an entrance through the stone wall from the Barnsley Road side of the house and a ramped driveway, (due to level difference). I did consider a turntable for cars, but couldn't afford it. Things continued to progress. Some time later when my workshop and garage was due to be built, which necessitated the Mulberry Tree being removed, I decided to ring Mr des Forges and offer to buy the portion of land I had originally not included. He was very sorry he had just sold it, so that was that, and I could not save the mulberry!

About a month later I had a phone call from a person telling me he had bought the site next to mine, and could he connect to my sewer system, and if so, could he have a copy of my layout? He had not said who he was, or ever asked who I was, but you know what a kind, and helpful chap I am, so I said OK, who am I speaking to, and what is your address? He said its Mr Sykes. I said what are your initials? He said L.D.F. SYKES. I am not very good at names, but there are some I can't forget. L.D.F. Sykes was a good violinist and he was wont to practice in the studio at lunchtime in the early days at the HSA at the technical college – in between the rain storms. So I felt I must warn him that the large beech trees, one in my garden and three in his garden, were not to be cut down – and the trees were so large they would have to be removed to enable even a small house to be built. He thanked me, we had a chat, and he said he would have to see about that. I wonder what he meant?

In my garden, the two large pear trees, one situated near the far brick, 8 feet high wall, were OK, but half way between it and our living room window and terrace was an even bigger pear tree, which Maria had already said must unfortunately go! I had said, don't worry I will in due

97

course approach Mr des Forges on the matter, and perhaps give him the money I hadn't had for the turntable. I arrived one morning to deal with anything that may need dealing with, only to find my very old friends the Earnshaws, timber merchants, sawmill owners, tree surgeons etc., in attendance next door with bulldozers, tearing out the trees by the roots, to protect the beech trunk to be sawn at their sawmill, undamaged. You will, I hope, remember Wing Commander Earnshaw my CO at Reykjavik, on my second posting there, he was a regular officer and his, I believe, younger brother, was in charge. They were friends – I later designed a house near their premises at Midgley, Wakefield. I asked them to remove, forthwith, the offending pear tree in my garden – they did, there and then.

As expected, I duly received a polite letter from the town hall, would I please call in to Mr des Forges Office etc. I did, and reminded him of our agreement, and that it works both ways. It ended amicably, but he was a lawyer – he had the set of law books, all solicitors have, with it all in. Only my beech tree left, and they were all protected trees – only to be removed with local authority approval, which I had to get, just 3 years ago, to remove my huge beech tree which had become dangerous due to fungus growth attacking the main roots. I now have a 3 foot stump at ground level, still being attacked by fungus!

There was one other incident, which was to have answers a few years later. In my garden there were some 20 long established, large, peony plants along one border. I arrive after the weekend break on Monday to find every plant missing and only large deep holes left – it must have taken a lot of effort to steal them, and load them on a large truck etc. It was some years later that Geoffrey Whittlestone, architect, a long time member of my HSA staff – he also lived only a short distance away in Sandal – said to me, 'I have solved the mystery of your peonies.' He had the same contractor doing work for him, who had built Mr Sykes's house, and had asked him to work on a Saturday. Sorry, his truck driver never worked at weekends, except only once, when he had pinched my peonies!

Since those days, 56 years ago, many things have happened, and I have just finished day dreaming, trying to remember them all, and even put them in the right sequence. That's only here at home, and I realise all the other things, events, Gerald Sutcliffe, office, works, life and death, friends and enemies, to name a few – am I wasting my time? Should I just be more cryptic, and just enumerate the events in a list and get it over – or I can't see me finishing, why was I daft enough to have started in the first place?

April, 1964, spring. Gerald had a good idea, why don't we take a holiday, go touring on the continent and down through the Simplon tunnel and Italy (this was before the disastrous fire in the tunnel, killing many people). We would use his Bentley, as usual I would drive, Maria insisted. His patience, driving, was virtually non-existent, (he had driven another Bentley off the road, earlier) and as I have suggested to all my visitors, for years, 'Arrive alive'. After all, there is no point in going, and not coming back!

Our route would take us through France, Switzerland, through the Simplon tunnel, and visiting Milano and in Italy, zig-zagging some-what, to Venice, Florence, Siena, Rome, etc., and returning along the Mediterranean coast line to Livorno, Pisa, La Spezia, Genova, Niece, Nîmes, and points north etc., and on to Calais and Dover. In Paris there is one of the most remarkable memorials to the thousands of French people, Jewish, and other races, that I had ever seen – it is situated on the narrowing peninsula of land at the choir and transept end of Notre Dame cathedral, on the Seine. The first thing one sees is a very long, low, four-foot high, white, hammered concrete slab which has a narrow vertical slit doorway to enter, down stone steps to a very small prison cell, and alongside is a long circular, tapering tunnel with thousands of small light bulbs on to the very end, all round – or so it seems, to a larger light in the centre of a circular end wall, and one for *each person killed*, in concentration camp prisons – very memorable, even after nearly 50 years.

Chartres cathedral 1194–1260, (of which I did a Chinese ink rendering, that's stick ink, and jet black, you have to rub it for hours in water to get the subtle shades) has the most wonderful stained glass, even in France, in its 130 windows.

Rheims cathedral, 1212–1300, the coronation church of the kings of France and also some of the finest champagne in the world.

Ronchamp, (The Saône), – Chapelle de Notre-Dame du Haut, architect Le Corbusier. This most unusual chapel, built after WWII, a modern pilgrimage place, well worth a visit – but when we were there the immediate countryside area was a complete derelict mess. However, it's an architectural icon! I took a good few photographs – the interiors are very interesting.

Switzerland, Basel, Bern, Lugarno, wonderful mountain scenery, snow topped, and everything spotlessly clean, particularly the hotels, with superb food. I was doing all the driving – Maria, looking after the 'chat', when there were any language problems – she is good at Italian, French and Spanish. Gerald, due to his regular business travels, is better than me.

On through the Simplon tunnel to Italy and to Milano – Milano cathedral and La Scala, opera house, all the magnificent, and top quality fashion and expensive jewellery, restaurants, cafés and other shops and services etc., in the fine arched multi storied arcade in the town centre.

Continuing on our way to Venice we stopped at a large busy petrol station to refuel. This having been completed, I started to leave, passing a line of vehicles on my left, fortunately at a slow speed, suddenly a woman with a camper van opened her door, as I was passing, and the sharp lower door corner tore into the door panel of the Bentley. We were stuck with it until we were back in Britain – only packing tape and a hammer for immediate surgery.

Venice – what can I say? By this time, I suppose, you have all been a few times to Venice, and as they say, got the T shirt to prove it. It is of course 'paradise' for architects, and what a history. Bit wet, getting about – I have a snapshot taken on the Grand Canal of a gondola, packed with people, all standing up, with umbrellas up, in pouring rain, going to the office I suppose. The Canal is also packed with a variety of water transport, vapporetti, and private speed boats. Our hotel had a magnificent view across the wide expanse of water at the mouth of canal and the Golfo di Venezia, flanked on both sides by the most beautiful, magnificent, buildings. It would take a lifetime, and more, to do justice to all of them, and the city was built virtually on timber piles into sea water, centuries ago, and requires constant monitoring and protection from the sea, it is in the centre of a partially protected, island strewn lake over 30 miles long, with the small island of Murano a few miles away, world famous for its glass-making skills – well worth a visit.

Florence – Our hotel was in Fiesole, overlooking the city with all its wonders, including Florence cathedral and the famous renaissance dome, architect Brunelleschi as result of a competition, a truly amazing feat of design – which you may have seen explained on TV, two or three years ago – 138′ 6″, to be likewise precise, in diameter!

The baptistry, with the bronze, north doors, – 'the Doorway to Heaven' – designed in competition, also with Brunelleschi, competing with other sculptors, as he then, was, and later to study architecture in Rome, but sculptor Lorenzo Ghiberti, was the winner. The Ponte Vecchio 1345 on the river Arno, with small shops along each side of roadway – the goldsmiths quarter, Michelangelo's statue of David.

Siena, the walled city in central Italy – I nearly got the Bentley wedged in the narrow streets, even with my rear mirrors folded flat.

Rome for Easter – Cathedral of St Peter – Piazza of St Peter, width 650 feet, oval on plan, and the Bernini colonnade, Michelangelo's wonderful sculpture, the pietà, in the cathedral, and his colossal Moses – in the adjacent Sistine Chapel his chief work is the amazing ceiling and last supper, and he was architect of St Peters from 1546 – an Everest of the art world!

The Colosseum, building commenced AD 70 and it was 12 years to completion in AD 82 – the plan is a vast ellipse, 620 ft. by 513 ft. – and the external façade is 157′ 6″ high – staggering!

The Pantheon is a magnificent building and the best preserved of all the ancient buildings in Rome, and dates AD 120–124. The dome is a hemi-sphere, the thinnest part of which is four feet thick and the central 'eye', in the crown of the dome, an unglazed 27 ft. diameter opening, providing the ONLY lighting, amazingly, round the rotunda's circular interior diameter, and height, both, of 142 ft. six inches. The concrete walls are 20 feet thick lined with marble and porphyry, ornamental granites, supported on a travertine podium, and a huge entrance portico with monolithic marble columns 4′ 11½″ diameter at the base, and 46′ 5″ from floor level to top of Corinthian capitals – 19 of them. Portico overall height to roof ridge 80 ft.

Then there was the Forum Romanum, baths of, or thermae of, Caracalla, AD 211–217, now in ruins – where you will recall the three tenors, Pavarotti, Domingo, and Carreras, celebrated Italy's success in the soccer world cup, with conductor Zubin Mehta, and shown worldwide on TV.

The central building, used entirely for bathing 1600 bathers, was 750 feet by 380 feet, covering an area of 285,000 sq. ft., equal to the area of the Houses of Parliament, Westminster Palace, and that's even more than somewhat! How did they design and build it all so very well? Slaves, etc., I know – but look at all the magnificent, overall skill in conception, detail design, planning, management, and superb artistry – well over 2000 years ago!

Having experienced Easter in Rome at St Peters, time was, as usual, counting, and our two weeks plus tour of Italy was at an end, and we still had to get back to the UK. We decided to return via the Mediterranean coast line, from Rome to Genova and through the south of France, Monaco, Nice, Cannes and taking in Arles, Aix-en-Provence, Nîmes and then onto the N7, and eventually Calais.

Pisa and the world famous leaning tower, campanile, (AD 1174), 52 feet external 24 feet internal, in diameter, rising in eight storeys of encircling arcades, and was leaning nearly 14 feet out of perpendicular, top to base, and had been very unstable, for a very long time. At the top, and only added in 1350, was the belfry – which can't have improved matters, the problem was subsidence in the foundations. I say was, because, in the later part of the twentieth century, British architects and engineers did, hopefully, a very good job in making stable the foundations, laid about 900 years ago, not bad is it? We will hope they last as long again.

The campanile is only part of what is called the 'Pisan Group' and was only added later to Pisa cathedral (1063–92) and the adjacent baptistry (1153–1278), designed by Dioti Salvi, and Campo Sonto, together are one of the famous building groups in the world.

Out of Italy, into south of France, via Cannes, and digressing to see the Pont du Gard, Nîmes (150), which forms part of a remarkable aqueduct 25 miles long, built by the Romans, to bring water to Nîmes from the Uzès area. It is 900 feet long crossing the valley 180 feet above the river Gard, and formed of three tiers of arches. The masonry was laid dry, without mortar, and supported the 'specus,' water channel, above, and all is still standing today.

I now (2008) have a few Italian friends – one is even a Five Finger Friend, Mrs Angelina Smith-Shakleton. A friend for many years, she was born near Benevento, in the mountains, 40 miles inland from Naples in a small village, was a member of Benito Mussolini's 'Youth' organisation as a young girl, and she had trained with a top class Italian couturier, from being at school, who designed for the proverbial Italian cognoscenti. After the Italians had changed sides, and the allies had occupied the country, along came a Yorkshire army sergeant who, in spite of her three brothers acting as chaperones – and meaning it as Italians do in such circumstances – they were married in Italy, Sgt. Walter Smith to Angelina Carboni, and became Mr and Mrs Smith. As you will be aware, there are quite a few Smiths in the UK – the number of Smiths in the world is, as I have possibly said much earlier before – 'a matter for some conjecture'.

However, Walter was demobilised in the UK, and Angelina could then rejoin him in Sheffield, South Yorkshire and, both, full of hope and enthusiasm, lived happily ever after. Walter became manager of the furniture department of the best multi departmental store in Sheffield, and Angelina, even before that, was welcomed at her tender age as the really bright one, in the 'world of fashion department' very gifted indeed. Walter in due course took an even better job as furniture department manager at an even better store, Brown and Muffs, Bradford, West Yorkshire and they then bought a house at Wyke, on the outskirts of Bradford.

Sheffield was the world leader in most types of steel, and had also been for centuries, in silver and gold (Essay Office) articles: cutlery, silver plate, etc. Bradford, along with Halifax, Leeds, Wakefield, Huddersfield and numerous smaller towns, produced, and still does produce, some of the finest cloth in the world. Our forebears in England invented the various weaving and spinning machines for mass production, and then sent the older ones to India and Pakistan as new and improved models were invented here.

The happy couple then begat, as they used to say, two sons Peter and John Smith, (more still), who were not exactly St John and St Peter, but both very bright lads indeed. John, trained as a motor mechanic, which was to stand him in very good stead when as a young man he was to take multi-wheeled, pantechnicon trucks to the continent and particularly Italy. Angelina, 'rode shotgun' on occasions – and to make sure he behaved himself, the trucks had bunks. John now has his own business in the used car trade, shop, for allied products, fuel, and car cleaning etc., along with two lively daughters having a whale of a time as the Misses Smith. More still for Angelina to do since they were children, designing and making fabulous dresses etc., and even still more fabulous dresses now they are grown up, and want her to alter and restyle the rubbish called 'designer' these days. Angelina still smiles, and bears it.

Peter, on leaving school, and younger than brother John, also went into the burgeoning motor car business, but more into the sales and management side – and was soon to be one of the German, VW manufacturers blue eyed boys, regularly winning the Salesman of the Year award, and being invited to Wolfsburg, or some place like that, to be wined and dined, and presented with an award certificate. He seemed to make it an annual event – and in no time, it seems, doesn't time fly, he was a director of the main Halifax area VW suppliers, at nearby Lightcliff Motors – large new premises and all. My partner Sheila has one of his VWs in her garage here, and very obligingly he collects it for servicing, MOT, etc., and leaves his own VW here and returns the same day, and then drives to his new home in the small village of Wooley, a very select area about five miles away. His house, along with three or four others, the developers had the temerity to erect in an older building's high walled garden, complete with locked gates, which may be a small deterrent in these crime ridden times. Thirty years earlier, I had built a house on the large grassed field area of land adjacent, with an access road between, and the main entrance gates 100 yards further along the main village road – but as I told Peter, my client had made no objection to the developer's planning application, as they had at least not been allowed to take the high wall down, and spoil my client's view!

After some years as a widow, and grandmother to her son's children, Angelina married Mr Arnold Shackleton, a retired junior school headmaster, and they live today in Angelina's house, he helping her with her pride and joy, her garden, and brewing gallons of elderberry, rhubarb, and other wines, which he stores under the timber suspended floors of their bungalow – to the amusement of John and Peter's children – some of whom may in a few years be flying the coup, John with two daughters and Peter with a son and daughter. All of them in my opinion owe Angelina a very big debt – which, after all that lasagna and other delectable Italian dishes, they surely will.

Having managed I hope craftily, if not very skilfully, to have changed the subject, to relieve you of the monotony of showing off my architectural interests while on our 1964 tour and, hopefully, getting you back, dear reader into some sort of chronological reality (some hope), I will try to finish quickly, our 1964 European tour. From Nîmes, continuing on the N7 to Avignon, taking our time, at the towns we had not visited before and I have forgotten how many overnight stops we made, or where, now, Boulogne, Calais, Dover, and home – quick enough for you?

At that time, things I have mentioned earlier, like the formation of the two companies, Speeduct Ltd., and Hobbimate Ltd. and the subsequent two factories at Skelmanthorpe and Scissett, the successes and failures – the later being 'mine', and former being 'our' – pale into insignificance with some of the happenings that were to come – at least as far as my real personal interest in life was concerned. That is why I have delayed having to address them until this late stage.

Then, it was rather different. We were somewhat younger, Maria, and I, and Timothy was now married and to Sandra, and I wasn't sitting on my hands doing nothing. Maria, and I were, within a few weeks, of the same age, and born in the same month, December, she a Sagittarius, and me a Capricorn. Up to our sixth, (approx) birthdays, we actually lived about 100 yards from each other on Benton Hill, Horbury, and remarkably, it only now occurs to me we could have met, and probably did, and we were too young at the time to remember, as we were late teenagers when we did meet.

Apart from visits to and from our friends, Doctor & Mrs Stoker, the elder, socially, and visits to me, already mentioned, Maria always seemed to manage her colds and headaches and other minor ailments herself. In fact, at that time, neither of us had a doctor, in the present method of GPs, under the NHS regime, where they now seem to be mandatory. Unfortunately, shortly after our golden wedding anniversary in 1991, she was obviously not well and I insisted on calling the doctor (we were by now on the panel of a very good practice of doctors a mile away.) He came immediately, and after he had made his examination in our living room, I pointed to a William Thomson, 1958, large portrait of Maria, seated, and said, never having realised, or said it before, 'The last time she had a doctor was when Timothy was born, and the time before that, was when she was born.' He replied, 'Don't worry, she will look like that again, in a couple of months' and arranged for a consultant specialist to see her, who later rang me to ask if she would mind, if he brought his attendant student doctor trainee, with him as he was a friend of ours – cardiologist John Stoker's son. Maria said of course not, after which he arranged for Maria to go the Meltham BUPA hospital, about 5 miles away. I drove her there, and the consultant said she was very dehydrated. She was there about a fortnight or three weeks, during which I visited her daily, with her most of the day. Timothy and Sandra together visited her in the evenings and, during that time, the matron was on holiday. The dietitian was a young lady, I assume, just out of college, who asked me what things Maria liked as she wasn't eating much. I suggested one of her favourites, crème caramel, she preferred the sweets. She informed me the cook couldn't make that, and she would have to go to the shops to buy some – oh dear. My wife also had an antique gold bangle, that I had bought her years ago, and which she never removed. She was in an en suite room, which she had never left, since she was admitted, but the bangle disappeared. The matron returned just before Maria was due to leave, and I acquainted her with all these, and more, shortcomings. When I said the food was worse than an army cook – she replied, well he is an army cook! – and she didn't do any better with the rest of my complaints.

The day before Maria was due to leave BUPA, she was taken by ambulance, to the tubular complete body scanner unit of Pindarfields Hospital, Wakefield, for a heart scan check, which we were informed everything was fine with the scan, etc. I brought Maria home the next day from Methley to Tree Garden to convalesce and we spent the early weeks of a fine August, having occasional picnics in the near countryside, and Maria was recovering.

Maria passed away at 4 am on August 28th, 1992, and the lives of Timothy, Sandra and me would never be the same again, ever.

In 1972, or 73, I can't remember which, I happened to be in Huddersfield, probably doing a bit of shopping or whatever, and noticed that demolition work was starting on a building in a street area between the town hall and the polytechnic which was a theatre or meeting hall or possibly now even unoccupied, perhaps a cinema at that time – I just don't know. I had never been in the place – all I did know was that this building had a fine 'classical' frontage of the Victorian era. And having spent much of my life building things, and as with trees, as I say, 'easy to saw down, but it is a hell of a job making them stand up again, if you have made a mistake' – so it is with buildings, and this one had a fine stone ashlar frontage, in good condition. Gerald Suttcliffe's birthday was coming up and he also had a long driveway, with land on both sides and a house that, Nicholas Pevsner credited to the wrong century, in one of his books, when he had visited the house, Badsworth Grange. The date of the house, believe it or not, is carved in large letters over the main entrance!

I phoned Gerald, and he was very appreciative of my proposal, so it transpired, and the now carefully removed stonework of the frontage was transported to Badsworth and deposited at the side of the driveway to be erected in due course. Unfortunately, this was never to happen as Gerald's health over the next few years began to deteriorate and along with problems with some of his brothers, and business problems, and differences at Richard Suttcliffe Ltd., etc., things were not looking good, even though he was still chairman and he was staying at Tree Garden or we were staying at Badsworth, when able, and going on short visits together, as I was still driving.

Shortly before Christmas, 1979, Gerald's birthday, Lois his sister-in-law now living in Huddersfield invited the three of us for dinner there. Unfortunately, Gerald was really in no condition to be going anywhere, but it was his birthday and he really wanted to go, so we went, and as it turned out he was happy. But due to circumstances, Lois, Maria and I sat in the farmhouse kitchen for the excellent meal. Gerald asked to be suitably ensconced beside the interconnected servicing hatch in the dining room, where we eventually joined him and he obviously enjoyed the celebration of his birthday. Then we went back to Badsworth. Sadly this would be the last time, after all these years, I would drive Gerald anywhere again.

Regrettably, the time came when we were going virtually daily, to help his housekeeper Mrs Pickering to look after him, and me joining them in the evenings and at weekends. The cancer, halted for so long by Professor Gollacher's operation, had returned and after a month or two it was agonising for us to have Mrs Pickering, show visiting friends into his study (for his and Mrs Pickering's convenience, she had to go up and down, two high floors otherwise) and to see them recoil in shock at the first sight of his condition, getting worse each day. At last there was a glimmer of hope, in that there was a Swedish doctor at a London hospital – I forget which it is 38 years ago – with a 'new' treatment and Gerald was advised to be treated by him. Arrangements were made for Gerald to be taken down to London by Mike Dawson, director and financial secretary of Tunstall Telecom Limited, who was to take him by car, the next day, my commitments not allowing me to do so, unfortunately. Maria then went down to London to stay with a friend of ours, at that time Rodger and Anne Batt, she a British Airways hostess, and he a first class, hons. PhD., mathematics at Cambridge. We were guests at their wedding in Wakefield, Anne was related to the Skidmores – they now live in Monaco.

After a few days I followed Maria to London, but after a further few days Gerald passed away, and we had now to return home to Tree Garden, to arrange for his funeral.

Over the last few years Gerald had not been on good terms with his brother Dermod, who was married to Helen, his half Italian wife, who I may have mentioned before, along with their daughter, who had a number of times visited us at Tree Garden. Of course we had been together at Badsworth, and also at Christmas and New Year at their home in Pontefract, for drinks and light refreshments – never anything more, or less, acceptable for Gerald and his brothers, and Maria and me, who all fully provided for them. Dermod and Helen had also had a house built in the very small Badsworth village, without mentioning it to Gerald, but that was earlier, and by this time, Dermod had passed away, and was buried in Badsworth's small cemetery. Gerald's brother Edward, barrister and high court judge and Maria were his executors. He had left me in no doubt whatsoever, that he was not to be buried in Badsworth cemetery, should he not survive his present illness, and his executors, Edward and Maria, also knew this, so things were now up to me as usual. Quickly, if I can now say the word fortunately, the Hobbimate factory I had bought at Scissett was previously owned by the area's main joiner and undertaker, now retired, who lived close by the works, and nearly opposite the fine parish church, with the cemetery, less than a mile away – along with the joinery works – with machinery and a large store, ventilated and stocked with timber and other buildings and wide stream running beautifully along the valley. I also had, alongside the stream, the chapel of rest – Gerald would have been delighted.

The undertaker made all the arrangements for the transfer of Gerald's body from London to the chapel of rest, and for his grave in the cemetery, etc. The service in the church was very well attended, and Lois's school boy, youngest son – she had married a Mr Mike Smith, road engineer, so was no longer a Suttcliffe – asked me, could he go back to Badsworth with me in my Jaguar, which he did. The same car I had last driven Gerald

107

in, from his above mentioned birthday dinner and from which I changed, reluctantly, to a German car, BMW 7i series, some few weeks later. Gerald died in 1979, sixty years of age. On his gravestone is inscribed, 'A Yorkshire Gentleman', which he was, but not born – RIP.

Timothy and Sandra had many friends and, as I must have said before, but to make sure, I will say it again, everyone, since he was born, liked Timothy. When I left my office in the capable hands of John Horsefall, Russell Lumb, and the other appreciated members of my staff, including Peter France, Timothy eventually took the opportunity offered by his longtime friend and fellow railway enthusiast Stewart Pichforth, to be joint partner in a Wakefield plastic windows, doors, conservatories etc., company, and worked together – and this he thoroughly enjoyed. It also reduced his travel commitment to Huddersfield each day – six miles a day longer than mine – and his honest personality would become a real asset to a firm producing quality products, in an industry that some companies had a very poor reputation selling windows etc., of inferior quality and design. As we were architects, surveyors and valuers for banks and building societies, I had a number of times pointed out to additional mortgage applicants, did they realise, that they were paying more for changing their windows, than they had paid for their house? – and the existing windows were in a good condition as well.

Maria had for some years suffered from an ailment that various doctors, at that time in the UK, said did not exist – it was a form of depression due in her opinion to lack of sunshine and in her case was very debilitating, and she loved sunlight, even though she came out in freckles. As usual, unknown to me, she had done her homework, and found out that some American doctors were researching that very thing, saying they had discovered that the treatment for this disease was a special light treatment – so for a couple of years I was doing my best to get this type of light, without success. It was not until a lady by the name of Clare Francis, who had also done her homework to enable her to be the first woman to sail round the world single handed, and following on the heels of the first man, map publisher, Francis Chichester, to achieve this amazing feat. Doesn't it make you proud to be English? It should. Clare, was diagnosed as having this very ailment, and so it got, by chance, some publicity and became accepted, but unfortunately too late for my dearest Maria. RIP.

In consequence of the foregoing, Sandra and Timothy were taking over the upkeep of the Primrose Valley house at Filey – except when something was very wrong. One winter the water system had not been drained off correctly, and a very small leak, from the main cylinder tank

108

continuously sprayed water over the lounge ceiling until it collapsed, and the carpet below was floating, etc. We had the usual, 'independent' loss adjuster – when I asked, who was paying him, as I was not, he didn't have an answer. Funny, it is not.

Maria and I occasionally went for the day for a 'run out', but otherwise they kept the house and garden in very good order and spent many happy times there and Sandra, and her good friend Christine, still do.

Timothy and Sandra were born in the same year, 1942, and throughout their marriage they both lived for each other, were inseparable, they also had a hands on love of animals, and always had a dog of character – selected together, after careful search of RSPCA kennels, at the poignant time of the end of the devoted dog's life, and at least two, three or four cats. Over the years they have spent the proverbial fortune, on the best veterinary surgeons, for all of them when needed. Timothy's house had a very long separate garage, up to three in line cars originally; he suitably equipped it as an aquarium and fish hatchery – on entering it was like stepping into an oven, and together with the number of light bulbs – I am sure he must have made them switch on another generator at Ferry Bridge power station! He reared 'deadly' piranha fish etc., and enthusiasts came from miles away as customers – so he must have at least have broken even!

Eventually in 1966 they had their silver wedding anniversary and they both continued to work, Sandra with her hairdressing and beauty parlour and Tim at my office – and again, things were all sweetness and light – reasonably everywhere – with the occasional, and inevitable, unfortunate experiences suffered by everybody. That is until, February 1991. They had been at Filey for the weekend and were due to return on Sunday, but before lunch time, Sunday, Timothy was not feeling well, apparently, and Sandra suggested he have a lie down and they could return a bit later. This they did, but Timothy was still not OK, and Sandra drove home, and it was not until much later on, the next day that she phoned me to inform me and of course Maria, of their present predicament – as you will have noted – we were not there with them. I am only repeating what she said to me at that time. She went on to say that when Timothy woke next day, he was still unwell, and was taken by a friend to the doctor's surgery in their village and the result was that Timothy was taken more or less at once into Wakefield's main hospital, Pinderfields, and was now in the cardiology wing, under intensive care! Immediately, Maria, who was herself not well, and was lying on the sitting room settee and could hear both sides of the foregoing conversation, said ring John! – which I did immediately. He was at his holiday home at the Kyle of Lochalsh, Scotland, and I gave him what information I had. His, also immediate, request was, 'Who is the consultant?' and I hadn't got the slightest clue. I did not think Sandra in her position would know either, but thank the Lord, she did know, and I rang John back at once. His reply was, 'Don't worry, we will soon change that – I will ring you back in about half an hour when I have had the prognosis.' Which he duly did, and after my obvious query, 'How bad is it?' he said, 'Well, I am afraid the prognosis is not good, but remember, "a creaking gate".' I can't remember at all what was said after that – all I knew, was that at least there was some hope, and if he does read this, as he will, God willing, (as I said at the start, he would 'like a copy')'

At the other end of my property, Milnthorpe Lane, Milnthorpe House, and a couple of cottages, things were to become somewhat different – in fact much more than 'more than, somewhat' as you realise. I have decided to continue getting on with it, as is my stupid wont!

Life was quiet, peaceful, placid, nice people, nice area – Mr and Mrs Des Forges eventually left, when he retired to live in a smaller property – a lodge on the Nostel Priory estate, with the large lake and grounds and the magnificent stately home I mentioned earlier. Major Marwood, ex Army Regular Officer, WWII who had been made redundant along with many others – officers, NCO's and other ranks also made redundant in the 1950s by a Labour government, with Navy and RAF personnel. They were a delightful family, his three children, stood to attention and called him 'Sir' whenever he addressed them. I let them have the run of my right of way, entrance and car park area, including pony riding. All sweetness and light. Major Marwood sold his old kitchen garden, as was, to a Mr and Mrs Skidmore, Reginald and Eileen, on which to build a single storey house – Geoffrey Whittlestone was to be their architect, and Reg Skidmore had his brother, a solicitor, living just across the road, who also acted for him on the land purchase, etc. – all grouped together, and nice and cosy. In fact due to high walls, I was not aware, until the house was built, of any of the foregoing, and I was not to meet Reg and Eileen until – but that's another story.

Major Marwood had also sold to me the right of way and the land, barn, and car park area, giving me a separate second entrance to my property in the event of any road widening etc., to the now very busy Barnsley road, A61, a year or two after he came to Milnthorpe House to live. Subsequently when he was selling his house – again, a complete and 'unwelcome,' surprise to me, he was going to live in Northallerton, North Yorkshire – he came to me to remind me, again, I had completely forgotten, that he had agreed to ratify the sale deeds if he ever sold his property – this was to prove to be crucial, and, thankfully, shows you the type of person Major Marwood was.

A.G. Hughes was of not easily forgotten memory by a large number of honest people, some fortunately, still alive, but many regrettably no longer with us. I am only recording this quite unbelievable episode in all our lives, in fond memory of Eileen and Reg Skidmore, who suffered most of all, along with many others, for over 20 years, daily – I wouldn't waste my time on such trash, otherwise.

My first innocent connection with this saga (with my apologies to all my Icelandic friends) was on opening my Milnthorpe Lane entrance gates. There were, at that time, no gates on the public road end of the 100 yard long driveway– in fact, what were the original, well made, timber gates, were in my barn, having been removed to allow cars easier access, for parking off the road, by Mr Marwood, as with car users in most houses everywhere, due to the massive increase in the number of cars, have been forced to do. In my case I am fortunate, I have two entrances, each with garages and parking space, one off the Barnsley Road, and one from Milnthorpe Lane – by courtesy of Major Marwood, when he sold me the right of way to my property, the land and barn, lock, stock – and gates. Having opened the gates, I easily noticed a painter busily painting the barn – the colour was what I would have specified, white. He had not done much, and there was a lot still to do, and he was suitably dressed, not a graffiti yob, and you may say I should have him continue – but I think you may know by now, perhaps I am not that type. I started to express my gratitude but, then I saw a woman approaching, she said she was Mrs Hughes, and who was I and what was I doing, and what did I do. I of course had no idea who she was or where she lived at that time, and politely gave her answers to all her questions ending with, I am an architect. She said 'Oh, my husband is an architect,' and then I saw a smaller man approaching . He was, I assumed, the architect husband – we come in all shapes and sizes – but he was somehow different, and we talked, this and that, and then it came back to me. 'I have met you before haven't I?'

'Yes, I enrolled at the Huddersfield School of Architecture,' (HSA, if you are still listening) and then I remembered, that was years before, and after enrolment I always checked – the registrar didn't always – that his CV was correct. His wasn't, it was faked, and I had to dismiss him, but that is all my knowledge of him at that time, and for about a year I did not meet any of the Hughes family or know anything about them, or the Skidmores. Their house was literally on his kitchen doorstep, with driveway in common, also my ROW, but neither Maria nor I used this entry, we had two garages in Tree Garden, off Barnsley Road. Only my son Timothy, Gerald Sutcliffe, and other friends used my parking area – that was until one day my telephone rang – it very often did. 'Hello, Mr Walton.' She went on to say that Hughes, (and from now on his name is the Yob) had installed some old, open metal gates on the driveway entrance – and had told her they were to be kept closed at all times.Could I help? We met and I was soon to learn a lot, and it was not funny.

When the Yob, his wife and three children first took over the house and two cottages, the Skidmores had provided them with sheets and blankets, etc. – they had not sufficient. Later, during the week, the YOB and his wife were out all day – the children came home to a locked house, from school with no parents or food for hours – the Skidmores looked after them, fed them, Mrs S. knitted clothes for them etc. and they also worked on their neglected garden – they had no gardening tools etc. That was happening unknown to me, for a year, since they came. Major Marwood told me that when he sold his house to the YOB, (for £6,000 – then), the YOB who took up residence before he had paid for it, deducted £800 saying he had had Rentokil in, and they wanted that sum to treat the beetles and rot etc. The house was in a poor state generally, but he never had Rentokil or anyone else in to treat it. Only a few weeks before this I had some ReadyMix concrete delivered to cover the earthen floor of the old potting shed, along with a new roof – of corrugated asbestos cement sheets. It had been a hen house for years, and I was practising what I preach – the tradesman's part – I had some concrete left. The YOB came up my ROW and asked could he have it. 'Of course you can,' said I, little knowing he was to become a full time YOB.

Mr and Mrs Skidmore were a quiet, gentle, couple, she a very small person, with firm, traditional opinions, he more dour, but equally determined. Reg had apparently studied at Wakefield Technical College, they were both locals and with family members on both sides, and just before WWII, he had joined BP in Bahrain or Kuwait, I forget which. He was apparently an engineer, but he never discussed any branch of engineering with me – his main interest was cricket – he had been scorer for the other British expats in the compound, all the time he was there – and subsequently spent all his lovely warm summer days in Sandal in their curtain drawn, living room, watching cricket on TV here. But, so what? They were content with each other, and wouldn't hurt the proverbial fly. We were soon to realise they were also very punctilious in their domestic and personal time keeping, as this mad ridiculous saga unfolded.

From the time Reg had moved into their new home, and for a few years after the YOB arrived as their next door neighbours, Reg had an 'office' job with a Wakefield engineering company, he went to work exactly on time, he came home to lunch exactly on time, went back to work from lunch exactly on time, and he came home from work, exactly on time. You of course get my message, – I do mean exactly! They always went out shopping, went to church, etc., on exactly the same days, at exactly the same time every week – you will gather, they were people of habit – more than somewhat. And through thick and thin, they never deviated in this habit – and it suited the YOB's designs on them to perfection. In previous years the YOB had worked for a time in the WRCC Planning Department, Wakefield – and of course, had information on land purchases, building approvals etc., and other matters of interest to doubtful people, for financial gain – as in the Poulson and T. Dan Smith in Newcastle, and elsewhere, affair – need I say more. The YOB had acquired land and property, set himself up as a property entrepreneur in the area and with Milnthorpe House, a very old dilapidated house – but with a good garden and old cottages etc., all of which could be demolished and, of course, he could easily get, and even possibly had already obtained, planning permission for the site. The first problem was the Skidmores, and getting this defenceless pair out. To begin with, he was able to get copies of Geoffrey Whittlestone's site and construction plans – I wonder where he managed to get those from?

There was also a strip of site most unusually only three feet wide, across the strip of land from the entrance door and the garage doors – coloured in red. The YOB claimed this was the end of their land, and they must not leave their car parked outside their garage – ever – although this large area, originally from coach and horses, and had been common usage land – and his own garage was immediately alongside theirs along the front inline. He then erected a wall of very old battered doors, in various colours – hideous about 30 feet long like 'shanty town' – and two cars, one an old clapped out Bentley, at the far end. At that time there was a huge beech tree, which cars could drive round, to turn round – this now stopped that possibility, and in any case, he had banned the Skidmores from driving anywhere except straight in and out of their garage without stopping – necessitating, on entry, Mrs S. opening the always closed gates, walking over 50 yards to open the garage doors, walking back to the entrance gates, after Mr Skidmore had driven through, and then walking back, yet again. Believe it or not, Reg was not allowed to stop and wait for her to close the gates, and for her to get into the car! I know, you don't believe me, I think I told you so – you think it's me that's mad, yes, maybe I am mad, deciding to take on, at this late stage in my life, having this conversation with you.

The YOB then built, with old stone blocks, a 2 feet high stone wall alongside my ROW, but not on it, for about 30 feet, from the 3 foot boundary line of the Skidmore's property, making it very difficult for Mr S. to reverse out of his garage without damaging his car rear end on the wall as he was required to do. He also installed so called 'sleeping policemen' at regular intervals down my ROW, consisting of timber railway line sleepers, projecting 4 inches above road level and at 8 feet intervals along its length. So I too, although it had been obvious since he started on the Skidmores, was to suffer from his paranoia, but not like Reg and Eileen suffered. They were at his mercy day and night, all day and night!

The YOB, knowing their exact routine all day, always came out at their set times and would close the gates and harass them, whatever they were doing – or trying to do – particularly when either was alone, going to the post box or local shop – walking very close to them, all the way, taunting, with filthy vilification, all the time, every day. Why didn't you do something about it, you may say. Of course I did something about it! I did something about it for 20 years, until the YOB rejoined Satan in hell. Doing something about it entailed me instructing my solicitor, John Balmforth, partner in a Leeds firm of good standing.

The hearing was at Wakefield, West Riding County Court and was a complete disaster. After the first day's hearing, starting about 10 am, and finishing at 4 pm, having had lunch in between, the judge announced to the entire court, and the media, that he would visit the site, together with legal advisors, etc. The next day, morning, say about 10 am, court time.

Next morning, like a miniature procession, down a miniature mall, to Walton's Palace – along my ROW progressed his honour, two legal teams of lawyers, and their clerks, BBC and ITV camera teams, reporters, from many of the West Yorks newspapers, and a gaggle of Sandal's society gossips bringing up the rear. Weeks later, the court reconvened. His honour, after serious deliberation and consideration, in depth, of all aspects of this case, said he had come to the conclusion that this was simply a domestic problem, on private property, and the protagonists, he would propose, should meet, preferably over a cup of tea to peruse the problem and prognosticate, or some words to that effect. He also awarded one penny to each protagonist, with each to pay their own costs. He was on his way to the high court, Eileen, Reg and I were on our way. The publicity during and after this case ended was not what we needed, but in some ways

114

it did help, in that I received many phone calls from people sympathising with our predicament, having had the YOB living near them or had dealings with him, none of them pleasant. These court cases were to continue for many years, some instigated by Skidmores, some by me. The YOB was never able to reciprocate and was always the defendant, and in fact three different judges, for three separate case hearings, said the same thing about him, 'Mr Hughes, you are a real Jekyll and Hyde, aren't you!'

Again, I am reminded of an appalling session, of my attending as a potential witness, in one of the Skidmores' cases – you will recall, they were both with BP in the Kuwait area, and Mrs S. gave birth to a baby girl who unfortunately had spina bifida which they understood was fatal. In order to get the very best professional attention they returned to the UK, unfortunately the baby died. In court, towards the very end of the session, 4 pm, the YOB, retaliating to a question from Edward Williams, their solicitor, said that they 'kept the body of their baby in a box on their sideboard, in their living room'. Poor little Eileen was completely shattered. I was sitting near to Edward, and reached over to tell him that she had not got a sideboard in her living room, and never had one, ever. At which point, and immediately (at 4 pm), the judge adjourned the hearing for 6 months! Well, it was summer, and he may have Booked his hols.

At the continuation of the hearing, I reminded Edward of the importance of explaining, verbatim, in detail, the YOB's statement at the adjournment – and this time make him look the liar he was, and force him to reply. I regret to say he never ever mentioned a word of it. Edward was profuse in apologies, he was sorry he completely forgot – solicitors!

Over the years, due mainly to the publicity generated, and numbers of people who had been involved, and getting more numerous – I was often asked such questions as 'What was the full story'. My response, after asking if they were really serious, 'Well, have you got a week to spare?' – and, after some laughter I would say, 'It would take that long to tell all', although, I assure you, I have omitted far more from this part of my life, in an effort to avoid any further boredom, to you, dear reader. You will I hope appreciate, it is by far the longest, most time wasting, and dangerous, for the many people involved, there lives, and in particular the Skidmores and their family and friends.

From the very beginning of this nightmare situation for the trapped Skidmores, year 2, their lives became intolerable – their pleas to the police were met by 'it's on private property, just a neighbours' quarrel' every time – no help, their friends stopped visiting, their relatives were made to leave their cars on Milnthorpe Lane. To allow their friends and relatives to visit, and more importantly Mr and Mrs Skidmore, to leave and return to their property without threats, insults, and assault. I had installed a door into the 10 foot high brick wall, between my ROW and parking area, and their house. This meant they had a 150 yard walk from their house, through the parking area, and then across my lawned garden area to my entrance drive gates and the Barnsley Road, A61, and of course the return 'journey', day and night, winter and summer, rain or shine, frost and snow, for TWENTY YEARS, and getting worse, particularly for the Skidmores.

The solicitors, Reg's and mine, were involved at this stage, more Reg's. They recommended they keep a diary, as this could be useful as evidence – they always let me know what was going on – meticulously. I had a Blundell Spence, Paint Manufacturers, Hull, leather, gold edge, page-a-day diary, so I let them have it, and I continued, each year, until the YOB died, to give them, exactly the same diary, presented to me by the firm, and Eileen filled every page with her neat handwriting, all of them, and I dearly wish I had them now, they would be a great help. Remember, I was away all day, every day Monday to Saturday, Maria and Eileen were alone, in their homes and Maria always, every day, at least four times a day, went and watched until Reg had gone to work, been and gone back from lunch, and returned in the evening, for TWENTY YEARS. Each time they had to change their solicitor (at least three times) the new one asked Eileen to let him have the diaries, all of them, to date – they charged for doing so, but court proceedings, later, proved they had not done so. The attacks continued on property and people – Gerald Sutcliffe, who was 6 feet tall, but was just recently, at last, home in Badsworth Grange after being a patient of Professor Gollacher, in the Brotherton Wing of Leeds General Hospital, and who was convalescent and still fragile, and was delivering some items to the Skidmores, before continuing up to my parking area – the YOB dashed out from behind his grotty wall of doors, bashed him on the head with a club of some sort, and dashed back inside again! Blood streaming down Gerald's face, the Skidmores brought him to us, for first aid, and rang the police – wasn't life wonderful!

A police inspector came, in due course, to discuss the situation with Gerald and me. He had also briefed his solicitor, and showing the file to the inspector, said, 'I have already got a file this size.' The inspector sitting in an easy chair, raising his hand 18 inches from floor level, replied, 'Mr Sutcliffe, we have files this high on the man.' The Skidmores regularly had human and animal excreta put through their letter box. Earlier they had been advised by their solicitor, to employ a private detective to be able to witness the YOB's demented actions, and the solicitor arranged this for them. He was an ex policeman, in his forties, I would guess. He came to see me one evening, after being at the Skidmores during the afternoon, and he had, naturally, entered from the Milnthorpe end to their house, and the YOB had seen him. Was there anyway I could arrange for him to arrive, they had told him I would help. Hence his call on me, he had gone away from them the way he arrived, so was able to visit me from my Barnsley road entrance, unseen. Very early in our discussion he said he was sorry to have to trouble me with his problem, but, after the time he had spent with Eileen, he was fairly sure she was exaggerating, she must be. I probably said, 'Well, we will see how it goes.' I then explained how he could put my ladder against my 10 feet high boundary wall, at a point where the YOB could not possibly see him, and another ladder on the other side for a safe landing, and both left in place for his safe, unseen return after the day's observation. He came next morning. I had everything ready for him – even, and inclusive, having converted the Skidmores' garage into a rather large, Kodak box brownie, 'pinhole' camera, like I made in my early Crossley days, with pricked holes in concealed places, very small, in the garage door – there were no other windows, doors etc., on that entrance side to observe any other way. He came to see me, as requested, on this, his first full day – he said he could not believe it, never ever seen anything like it before, Hughes was mad, (we already knew that!) and much more! After a few days he had more than enough on his 'dossier' but no normal person would believe it!

The assaults continued, my gardener. Walter, age 72, and who had lived on Milnthorpe Lane all his life, always carried a hammer, up his coat sleeve, in case the YOB tried to attack him again – he later gave evidence in court on our behalf, twice. Eileen's niece Anne Willows, Wakefield Girls High School, head girl, together with her school friend came to see Eileen and Reg and Maria and myself. In Maria's case, on the usual girls' things, she was a young Old High School Girl herself – I think I may have mentioned that before – and in my case to borrow books, I have a few, and ask my advice on her career etc. She, in her car was blocked in and assaulted, on a number of occasions after parking here, by the YOB putting his old car on the walled-in end of the ROW. In Anne's case, this was soon dealt with, by Harry Willows, her father, and Eileen's brother in law, who had also been blocked in by the YOB. Harry Willows was a boxing champion, in HM Royal Navy, WWII and did not like his daughter assaulted. The YOB's blocking in was able to continue because he could, immediately a visitor had driven in, drive in behind them, lock his car, and run into his house, lock the door, and to all intents and purposes no one was in – even to the police and they could do nothing. Remember, it was all on private property and we were continually ordered by the police, not to 'take matters into our own hands'. The Skidmores were not capable of that if they could, and Eileen and Maria, were home alone, all day.

Maria, a true redhead, lived for sunshine, enjoyed sunbathing, although she always came out in a mass of freckles. Her favourite place in summer or any time, if the sun was out, was on the lawn, in front of the terrace, on the south frontage of Tree Garden, very private, and she was not of course overdressed and may have on occasion gone to sleep. I had my hearing damaged in WWII (bombs and explosives), Maria could hear a pin drop at a hundred yards, or so it seemed to me, but not on a lawn, and the relatives and friends were walking on 100 yards of lawn, in procession, as they often did going to and fro, to visit Eileen and Reg – not a safe, or relaxed situation, particularly, alone, and for so many years.

From the beginning I had wondered if I had done the right thing, in providing facilities for Eileen and Reg to live in peace, and they would, possibly, have decided to sell up in 6 months, to avoid the hassle – we did not know then, how long it was going to last. After probably the first month or two, I put this proposition to them, as delicately as possible, the response was immediate. 'In no way, we don't intend to be driven out of our own home, by any one, no matter how long it takes.' They never ever wavered in that resolve. I then installed a telephone line from our house to theirs, through the Bramley seedling apple tree, over the wall and into theirs, for immediate communication and safety, and it was to continue in use for well past the YOB's demise. His wife, and some of his family are still there.

When finally, all the tumult and the shouting had died down, and I retired from being head of the school of architecture at Huddersfield Polytechnic, December 31st 1971, my wife and I, were formally invited to a dinner dance and presentation, at the George Hotel, in St George's square, Huddersfield, – the largest and best hotel in the town, by the students of HSA. Unfortunately, as you may recall, I was still banned from the HSA, and also not yet recovered from whatever it was afflicting me – it was not pleasant – but as usual I had to be there. Everything was organised and booked for Friday 3rd December 1971, 7:30 for 8:00 pm– 2:00 am, dancing to the White Eagles Jazz Band (the card says). I of course had no idea of the scale of what had been going on – even though some of the culprits turned out to be from my own office. My secretary at HSA was responsible for letters to past and present students, and the artwork was perpetrated by Russell J. Lumb – no one better, together, they were responsible for the $4' \times 2'$ cartoon, framed, with my big head, as the sun, with a little red book in my left hand, with THE THOUGHTS OF CHAIRMAN WAL, on the cover, and SONS OF LONGROYD circled around my head with sunray lines extending from the 'sun', and with the signatures of staff and students, etc., along one side of each of the 34 lines, 196 names in all. I hope that's right, as I have only now, and for the very first time, counted them today, October 29th 2007.

The presentation consisted of six items: (1) a gold framed, hand lettered, in red and black, on parchment, the presentation scroll herewith … the Latin tag of the last line is to me the best thing I have ever had said to me – translated it reads, 'A mind conscious of the right.' (2) The above mentioned cartoon, with all those student signatures! (3) A mahogany veneered casket, $13'' \times 9'' \times 9''$ stopped dovetailed, which was made in the woodwork department of the Polytechnic by students. I now take this opportunity to thank them for their excellent efforts, and I hope they also enjoyed the dance at the time. Inside the casket is a superb William IV silver teapot by Crespin Fuller, London Silver Hallmark 1832. I have just copied this accreditation from an even more exquisite hand lettered, in pure white, on matt black card, executed, along with all the other hand written gifts I received at the presentation by my late, very good friend, Joe Carruthers, a master of his art, and lecturer in calligraphy and lettering and printing. He was also a first class photographer and had his own studio in St George's Square, Huddersfield. He also took Shirley Bassey's publicity photographs, at the famous Batley Variety Club, from a seat in the audience, as an ordinary, paying spectator. Miss Bassey asked him for copies, and she always used them, for theatre billboards publicity, for years afterwards, and she never paid him a penny! Joe was a dedicated man.

(4) is two silver wine cups, four assay markings, makers mark, BES Co, assays anchor and lion passant, and date Letter W – this letter was only used seven times between 1423 and 1834, the dates when the City of York were granted individual 'touches' and assay mark used from mid sixteenth century to 1776 – and the City of York was granted assay powers, to commemorate York's 1000 years of history. Hence these two goblets, especially made and sold by the council – my good friend the late John Midgley ARIBA, being an architectural historian, would know the coincidence of the W – he was the person who ferreted out not only these wine cups, but also the silver teapot, and (5) a silver salver to use with the silver wine cups, I suppose. John Midgley, you will recall, was a member of my HSA staff for some years until this presentation. I had visited him at his home in the Dales, bought paintings from him, some are at present

hanging in Tree Garden – he and his wife had an antiques shop in Settle, North Yorkshire, in later years, and it was John who, when he was trying to persuade me to put forward my name for election to the RIBA Council, said I had been a thorn in the side of the RIBA for 20 years, and it was time I was a thorn in their backside. This was referring to the fact that I had proved that RIBA examinations, for listed schools (London, Liverpool, Huddersfield, etc.), held twice-a-year, in HSAs case, for the last 21 years, were a competition, not, an examination, in that the results for the past 42 examinations, the Pass rate was 20 per cent (approx), of the total entrants for each examination, a competition, or of course, they may like *Readers Digest*, have drawn names out of a hat! Or a barrrel, there were few PCs then, to do the 'fiddling'.

Very regrettably, a couple of years ago, and after some years of previous attempts to find John and his wife – but this determination on my part is a two-way thing – he had not contacted me since I left HSA. He also left soon after, and perhaps, he has been just as busy as I was. I rang the tourist information centre at Settle and enquired if they could help – mentioning that Mrs Midgley at one time had an antiques business in Settle. The lady in charge said that oh yes, they were friends of hers, but unfortunately John had died of cancer, she had been to his funeral only last week. I rang his wife to offer my condolences and we had an interesting chat, reminiscing.

To finish on a happier note, I will mention the various other gifts I was presented with by students, usually after their return from summer vacation.

(1) A bottle of Greek 7 star brandy (no less) from Greek General Argyropoulos, father of Stavros Evangelos. I still have half bottle left, as a conversation piece, I prefer Scottish single Malt – but I am not a spirits drinker.

(2) A hand carved Chinese chess set with carved carrying case with two drawers, black and white chess figures, and decorative tile, chess board presented to me by Willy Tji, a Chinese Student at HSA – I was also a guest at his Huddersfield Catholic Church wedding to his Chinese wife. I had also lent him, either £300 or £500, I can't remember now which – probably £300 because he had problems meeting his house mortgage payments – I still have his 'IOU' in my files somewhere. Unfortunately, some time later I was asked by the Halifax Building Society (we were surveyors and valuers to HBS, they were also clients) to value a property where the mortgagee had

120

absconded – it turned out to be Wily Tji and his wife. Ah well, it was nice knowing them, at chess you win some and lose some! However, Willy had some two years earlier brought me back a genuine Chinese teapot with tea bowls and saucers – they all knew my penchant for a good cup of tea!

(3) An Indian ivory pedestal, columnar, stand, 6″ high, and a 2″ diameter, amazingly intricately carved, ball, of, at one time, solid ivory, comprising two outer globes with two dragons, black-eyed, writhing across the globe and internally attached to a second globe and then with seven successively smaller, all internally free to revolve globes all with smaller holes in them, and there is also an ivory needle 2 mm thick and with a very small elephant at one end, and pointed at the other end – the idea is to pass the needle through all nine globes – how about that, then? – and I cannot remember the name of the Indian student who presented it to me, sorry.

(4) A very smart black briefcase, presented to me at an al fresco buffet meal in the students union rooms in the Poly, along with a bouquet of flowers for Maria. The briefcase had been specially prepared with metal block capital initials and internal fittings – all this to wish me every success in the future, after my twenty-first year as head, HSA and two years before the student sit in, at the Poly, you have read about earlier.

(5) My first year curriculum – once I had got to know the lecturers in other disciplines, in the school of art, and other departments of the technical college and later polytechnic – provided for students in first year to attend weekly periods with Joe Carruthers, on lettering, and associated, font design and production etc., and periods on cast drawing, sculpture, and pottery design, and hand throwing, in the school of art. In consequence I now have a number of various original pieces including vases, inlaid natural leaf trays (one as a small change tray I use daily) and sculptured pieces dotted about the house to remind me of the students, who produced and presented them to me over the years, with pride, and which I display, with equal pleasure – not dissimilar to my own efforts at Crossleys, for dear old Rucks, and Hadrian's Wall, Mr Tolson, and his collapsible canoe boat and Mr Umpleby, and his oak furniture on getting married!

Still in my School of Architecture days, I had many invitations, some to lecture at universities and schools, various civic societies Rotary Clubs, etc., and I can't now forget my worst ever effort, at my childhood favourite place, next door to Horbury – Ossett, a place I have for some years now, visited, weekly, a lecture, or speech, to the Ossett Civic Society, booked some months before. When the time came, (during the sit-in at the polytechnic, and banned from the HSA) I was ill, stress I suppose, but I was also under doctor's order, the doctor, whose practice was down the road at Sowood House, Ossett, 300 yards from the Civic Society Rooms, was my friend from pre WWII days, the late Dr John Brandon Stoker, father of Dr J.B. Stoker, cardiologist, I have mentioned earlier and hopefully will again. I had not been able to prepare anything, so I was only able to muddle through with an obvious, shortish, off the cuff, very, dis-ertation, on Ossett's town centre – and I now take this opportunity to apologise to the Civic Society members. Very sorry indeed – will try to do better next time, but it's a bit late now!

The most unique invitation I ever received, truly a one off, never ever to be repeated, was one ultimately from, the Shah, of the most ancient country (probably) of the ancient world, Persia, via a senior member of his cabinet. This was to celebrate, with the Shah the 7000 year existence of his country, Persia, and for which an entire town was to be erected in the desert, to provide for the guests for this unique celebration.

At that time students from countries like Persia and Iraq, etc. came to the UK to study architecture on oil scholarships – in short, being in oil producing areas, they were financed by governments – at HSA. I had a few, and if I remember correctly, it was Houshang Mojar (a student in second or third year) whose father was a member of the Shah's government doing the inviting. Unfortunately, I had by now, as you will have gathered, a number of more compelling things to occupy my time, and I was reluctantly obliged to thank Mr Mojar, and respectfully decline his much appreciated invitation.

To be honest, there was also another reason – but again, please let me make one or two things clear – I thoroughly enjoy seeing things, going to places, being there, meeting people and I have been to a good few places in various countries, but I am a northern hemisphere person, prefer north of the equator to south of it. I find it easy to keep warm – next to my underpants and shirt, is just me, summer and winter – unlike my wife who said of winter, ' I am as far north at Tree Garden, and perhaps parts of Scotland, as I am going to go.' She loved relaxing in the sun, summer and winter, so she was at home when the post delivered a traditional sack (for potatoes, coal, etc.,) to the door, she immediately rang me saying she 'was sure it was a snake' and she was leaving it outside for me to open, and come home quick. When I did arrive home, I admit, it did feel a bit queer – but it duly appeared, as a superb Persian rug, from Mr Mojar, in consolation, and it was December, both Christmas and my birthday month – and a second one arrived a year later, same month.

Another piece I received was from an Indian student was a metal plate, the centre bowl area engraved and embossed with an Indian orchestra playing all over, and with the raised outer rim of the plate profusely decorated with pierced small areas between engraved flowers, and all silver plated and very historically traditional. And here endeth the presentation and gifts lesson.

Have just received a letter, today, 10/11/2007 from my dentist, Mr Julian A. Brain BChD, Dental Surgeon, Headingly, Leeds – an excellent dentist, and person. I remind him of his initials – but only occasionally! I visited him for my 6 monthly check up, two days ago – saying 'It was good to see you again. Hope the memoirs are going well!' – followed by 'If you have any problems before your next visit, do not hesitate to get in touch with me' – with kind regards, yours sincerely. I have been going to this practice for 50 years. Some years ago I sat in the waiting room adjacent to another person I was sure I knew. I said 'I am sorry, but I am sure we have met before.'

'Yes,' he said, 'I used to be your dentist Mr Platt.' He had been very ill, but I am delighted to say he is still with us, retired!

As you will have long since noticed, I can be at times somewhat a little speculative about exact times, dates, full names, places, etc., in our conversations. What I do know, is where I was, when I got the idea of what I think is the best invention I have made – I was in the bath at home! No, I did not do my Pythagoras display! – Eureka – Eureka. I was just lying back in a nice hot bath and reached up, extended my index finger, and drew with it, in the condensation on the wall tiles, and thought, what a good idea – if no one else had thought of it, and, as it turned out, no one had. In the bath, I named it 'Speeduct'!

Only yesterday evening, I was delving into my filing cabinet, and it is packed! So I lifted out two wads of large, legal type, brown envelopes, long by narrow, and just put them on my desk, and left them. Now, I have very recently written the above paragraph, and decided to tidy up my desk, I turn over the two packs and find they are from my Patent Agents, Abel & Imray, Northumberland House, 303 to 306, High Holburn, London W.C.1, one of the oldest patent agents in the country, in fact, they were the company involved in the actual formation of the patent system, along with others, that exists now world wide.

My solicitor at that time was John Balmforth, Park Lane, Leeds, and he arranged a first meeting with Abel and Imray in 1966 – it was very early days as regards to Speeduct, but in the patent business, it is better to get the bad news, earlier rather than later. So, John Balmforth, John Horsfall, and I were sitting on the visitors side of a very fine, large desk, in a large, fine, hardwood panelled office, with the head of A and I, Mr Pike, seated opposite (waiting to Strike, like the voracious fish). All I had actually got to show was the very first, somewhat hastily prepared, booklet on the system! Picture the scene, as it actually happened. The usual pleasantries, I then quickly explain why we are there, and hand over, with apologies, the booklet. From then on, silence, and still more silence, and yet more, still silence, and then a pause, and then only six words: 'This is a very good idea.' I don't know if he says it to all the girls, but then, I am not always there!

And that is why I have one elastic banded wad of A&I Letters Patent, in red, dated, 7/9/67 – 29/12/67, 25/9/72 – 4/3/75, 26/5/75 – 26/5/78 and one USA 29/9/81, all with title of Invention. Improvements in or relating to electrical conduit, and A&I address, also in red, on each envelope. I won't bore you with the second wad, and, I don't know if this is unique, my solicitor John Balmforth, a very competent fellow, invited John and me to lunch at the famous Wig and Pen pub and restaurant, watering hole for generations of legal eagles and newspaper reporters, columnists, and those of similar ilk, and that made up for him not saying much at the meeting!

Mr Pike, and Abel and Imray, continued to prepare all my patent applications, and after about a year he rang me to ask if he could come up to my office at Huddersfield, where he knew I had a room showing various invention prototypes and applications. Of course, I invited him, and he was very impressed, and asked me if he could buy into the Hobbimate Company. Until this visit he had not seen any of our drawings, presentations, booklets, instructions, publicity, and he was even more impressed – A&I drawings were for a different patenting purpose, and not in the same league as ours, which of course we both appreciated. I still have all of them.

GEC, General Electric Company, was one of if not the largest electrical products company in the country, with the chairman of the company being at that time Sir Arnold Weinstock. GEC had sent to my office in Wakefield a rather splendid catalogue, with cardboard covers in sparkling, and very shining silver, to advertise and promote their brand-new product 'Silvaduct'. A few days later my then broadsheet copy of *The Times* was also delivered to the office, which on opening I found a blank page or nearly so, in the centre of which were the words, in Times Roman text size font: Silvaduct speeds work on site. Only this, as you will know, is a well-worn trick to get your attention, it certainly got mine! I decided, there and then, to decorate the entire page, except the Silvaduct slogan, with multi-coloured felt pens, listing the superior advantages of Speeduct, over Silvaduct (which was exactly the same as other ducting of that time, except it was made in aluminium) and also included drawings giving details. That same day I sent the sheet by HM Post Office, addressed to Sir Arnold, at GEC headquarters in London. By return of post, that was 2 days then, not like the present pathetic excuse for a once great British Postal Service they invited me to their London offices, ASAP.

John Horsfall and I duly presented ourselves at GEC HQ to be met by three managers of the marketing and production departments, and an overall general manager who acted as chairman. We still had only the original booklet, but we had now managed to produce more copies, so that each person could follow my explanation, page by page. On completion and without any further discussion, the marketing man said, 'This is a really good marketing product.' The production man said, 'We can start making that in a week.' The chairman said, 'We are all very impressed, but of course we have to report to the board of directors, so we will get back to you as soon as possible,' or words to that effect.

Again, in due course, and very reasonable time, I had a letter back from the chairman, Sir Arnold Weinstock, thanking me for my visit, and saying that they had decided that, as they had already invested in tooling, aluminium stock, and marketing etc., they were obliged to continue with Silvaduct, 'but if anyone else manufactured Speeduct,' they would have to! Or, as usual, words to that effect.

The architectural practice at Huddersfield and, to a lesser degree, at Wakefield, but also my daily visits there, and to the two Hobbimate works, with staff increases at all four – we now had our own quantity surveyors and a resident structural engineer at the office – and the ongoing development of the Speeduct system kept the indispensable and loyal Russell Lumb and myself out, of mischief. Then one morning, on arrival at the office, Russell greeted me with had I seen BBCs 'Tomorrow's World' last night? This was, if you are old enough, a science/invention/and similar future developments, TV programme, with an ex WWII, RAF fighter pilot, Raymond Baxter, as principal presenter, an all round nice chap. No – I hadn't, I rarely got home in time, anyway, and probably had the lawn to cut before dinner, much to dear Maria's, objections.

'Well, there was a competition announced, for the best invention, sponsored by the East Kilbride Development Corporation. Prize, a factory unit on the development site for 2 years, free rental, and £10,000 – why don't you enter Speeduct?'

My secretary wrote to the Corporation requesting application forms etc., to be addressed to my Wakefield office. They arrived, and were duly returned with all the drawings, now also with new developments etc. I must admit, I forgot all about the competition, from then on, and as I had also let the ground and second floors to a branch of the National Union of Mine Workers, but retained, for my own use, the top, third floor, with separate mail box in the main hall entrance doors, so there was less mail to collect. I am afraid I did this sporadically, I had a few other things to take care of.

Some six to eight weeks later, I called to collect the mail. I was still in oblivion about the competition – a few catalogues, circulars, junk mail – and I was just about to tear in half one thin, ordinary envelope, but happened to turn it over for one last check, when I saw a small stamp: East Kilbride Development Corporation. By chance, I was reasonably awake, stopped mid-tear and opened the letter. It was, let's say, Friday 15th August, I haven't got the letter, it's not of any consequence now. Dear Mr Walton, and then the following: 'I am very pleased to inform you that the adjudicators consider your entry in the competition to be one of the best received and would be obliged if you will kindly answer the following questions,' and then followed a list of five or six questions, which I actually answered as I read them, no problem, and then the letter continued 'and I would be obliged if you will kindly reply before Tuesday 11th August, which is the last and FINAL meeting of the adjudicators – Yours sincerely' – or words to that effect! So, that's that then.

Arriving at the office about ten o'clock, I asked my secretary to ring the secretary of the corporation, intending to make my apologies, and express my regrets. She rang. He was sorry, he was in a meeting and would ring back later. Lunch time and my secretary and some of the staff had gone for lunch, and I had my usual cup of tea at my desk and decided to ring him again, lifted the phone, forgetting I had no secretary, and said 'Hello,' and found I was talking to him. He had had the same idea, so I started to explain my dilemma. 'Oh, don't worry about that! You are one of the five finalists, and you are invited, along with the other finalists, to be interviewed by Sir Monty Fineston, Chairman of the Adjudicators, and representatives of the BBC, at the Caledonia Club in London to select the winner!' Or again, words to that effect. So much for deadlines and competition rules and conditions.

John Horsfall and I arrived at the Caledonia Club in the West End, and were shown into a waiting room with three other persons waiting. We were informed that we were being seen in alphabetical order, so being a W, I was last as usual. After the good morning greeting, almost immediately – the first person left to be interviewed and in 15–20 minutes it was our turn. We never saw any of them, until Tomorrow's World was broadcast at 7.30 pm, and then only one!

We were then invited to meet the panel – John was equipped to be a wall, as would be my request to him when I demonstrated the invention – namely a 4–5 foot × 4 × 2½ inch length of industrial HD plastic trunking or ducting which, being white plastic, was pretty obvious to say the least! We were ushered in, and the door closed behind us, to a very fine, large, banqueting hall, with a coffered ceiling and a very large desk for the five or six panel members, seated at the far end of the room. It reminded me at once, of Hitler's office in the Berlin Chancellery, which I have also been in – no, he wasn't there – the Russians were and I have medals to prove it.

Sir Monty Fineston followed by the panel, immediately started to walk down to us, still just in the room, to greet and thereby surround us, as he said, 'And what have you got there then?' So, again, there and then, I said, 'Be a wall John, please' and I told them that I could insert a cable into Speeduct as fast as a man could walk down the factory, or run if he was feeling energetic without taking off screws, bolts, covers or clips and he could continue *filling* the duct with cable, using a Speedmouse. That was years before Steve Jobs and 'Wozzy' of Apple Computers, the best, invented the Mouse (must get round to suing them sometime!). Again, immediately, 'That's amazing! And I am a member of the Magic Circle,' (he actually was!) and then again, immediately, he said 'you see gentlemen,' looking up at the coffered ceiling, and pointing, 'we could install lights up there,' (we had small section Speeduct, in a bundle with us) 'and it would not be seen!' Sir Monty was the only person ever, and I have demonstrated Speeduct to a lot of people over many years, to appreciate at once how it worked – but then he knew a thing or two about engineering, factories, production, marketing etc., and he was in fact chairman of British Steel, again the best – until it was sold off to a foreign company, how stupid can we get?

We all then walked up to the desk end and we were seated opposite the panel, and discussions began in a very good atmosphere. The BBC, Tomorrow's World producer, and his colleague, were very enthusiastic and asked if we could design a full scale demonstration stand, using the actual Speeduct product. I agreed to this, and the discussion continued for over an hour. It was obvious by this time – they had already taken more time with John and me, than the three others together – that we were the winners – and we then went on to discuss the prize details. The prize consisted of a factory unit, on the East Kilbride Development Site, for 2 years, free of charge, and £10,000. Fine, I had only entered the competition for the priceless publicity it would generate – if I won. The £10,000, would of course, be acceptable also – but, I already had two factories in West Yorkshire at Scissett and Skelmanthorpe, both close to the crossing point of the M1 and M62, at Junction 29/42, roughly the centre of the UK, north to south, and east to west. Being an architect, I knew that an employer could get factory space on an industrial development site free for 1 or 2 years, to improve employment in the area and rent prospects etc., in the long run and the last thing I needed, at that time, was another factory not even in Scotland, one of my favourite places to visit if I had time. Full stop, consternation in the panel. The factory space was the main, integral, part of the prize, and a condition, they were very sorry. Obvious, when you think about it, the corporation were sponsors – but it had not been mentioned before in the conditions of entry! The BBC people, once things had settled down, asked if I would agree to them showing the system on the programme, by now I realised they probably would not have a programme, as published on the date, without Speeduct, and the stand they were to provide and I was to design using Speeduct products in a couple of weeks' time. Publicity, particularly of such world wide quality that, I could in no way afford, was, remember, on my part the object of the exercise, on my entry to the competition, so I agreed, and all this was later, on the day of the transmission, to be fully corroborated.

John and I together drove down to our hotel in London a day or two before, in my Jaguar XJ6, packed with the Speeduct bits and pieces, and the design, that we would be assembling on the basic stand provided by the BBC at their TV HQ, at Shepherds Bush, and in their largest No 1 studio. We also had with us one of four plywood suitcase boxes I had designed for an electrical company, interested in Speeduct, to enable their reps to demonstrate the system, as a market research programme, on a desk top. I had made all four in my own workshop at Tree Garden – as I also made all Speeduct and Hobbimate prototype products. We arrived at BBC Shepherds Bush, at 8 am, having done a recce of the place the day before, and parked in the VIP area. Then, escorted to No 1 Studio, by staff taking our entire tools, boxes, and Speeduct components etc., into this vast main studio, very long and wide and high – at least three storeys –

and cables all over the place, floor, walls, ceiling – a prime customer for Speeduct, in all its forms. Raymond Baxter, came and introduced himself and other members of the presentation team, male and female and then we were taken up a floor, to the main control room with observation windows flush with the studio wall along part of one side, the entrance side. But something was wrong in the main studio, there was obviously some altercation going on between them and the control room. Staff explained to us it was a storm in a teacup between a new young presenter wanting more presenting I suppose – in place, perhaps, of Raymond Baxter, I don't know, but it was obviously very disrupting to all the people on different sets – including John and me – working to get everything ready for 7.30 pm. Tomorrow's World went on air live, more often than not.

We were working on our set, which was a full size open part of an office or house room, with entrance door, skirting boards, architraves, and cornices, all using Speeduct. Once we had these in place, Raymond came for me to demonstrate, and describe the set-up – and continued to repeat the process, about every half hour, or so, until he was satisfied with his rehearsals. However, typically I suppose, he praised the product to the BBC electricians, and, unknown to us, how good he thought the system was – and we were interrupted at regular intervals for the rest of the afternoon by electricians and others wanting to see how it worked. Fortunately, the suitcase was designed to turn into a half full size set up of a similar room – and between John and me we managed to get them thinking and they were very impressed. Despite all the interruptions we managed to have everything operational by transmission time 7.30, and as the programme was going out live, everyone at the various sets, at 7 pm, were taken to a special VIP room, in our case by Raymond Baxter, where there was comfortable seating, refreshments and a bar, and of course a large TV screen to see the programmes. On the way he was most complementary on Speeduct, and said that, had I not agreed to let them show the system there would have been no programme – or words to that effect. During his presentation he did in fact make only one mistake, but superbly covered it – John said he didn't even see it – and after the show was over, and he came to have a drink and escort us back to collect our bits and pieces in the studio, he reiterated his previous observations and said it was one of the best ideas the programme had shown, again, or words to that effect!

The winner now was, believe it or not, a motorway cone, with a half hemisphere base and the usual cone size – like a children's dolly or skittle that always erects itself, by being heavily weighted in the base, the rest was plastic, like the present ones. As John said as we were driving back on the M1 to Yorkshire, with his usual dry wit, 'Get one of those stuck in your oil sump on the motorway, and you would be in a fine fix!'

Gerald Sutcliffe, of previous mention, was recording the programme, with the first video recorder for home use on the market, made by Philips, and later improved on by Sony. I still have the programme, and I later transposed it from one system to the other. Then came the aftermath. Monday morning, telephone calls, to arrange meetings, and press interviews, by 'Prufrock' of *The Times* to virtually the front page of *The Huddersfield Examiner*, broadsheet, emblazoned with capital headlines: 'The Wonders of Walton', *Building Design*, the Rank Organisation, central marketing to name a few. I had chairmen's Rolls Royces parked on the main road, outside my office – and other, similarly impressive vehicles – on a weekly basis. One of these, in particular, was the chairman or MD, forget which – along with his technical director and marketing director all passengers in the chauffeur driven Rolls parked outside – and from the probably largest manufacturing company of ducting, in all its bits and pieces in the country. I demonstrated, and described, the many different applications of the Speeduct system, and towards the latter end of my spiel he kept interrupting me, the poor Yorkshire boy, with only the latest Jaguar XJ6 outside and no chauffeur. He was a prime example of what I call an Habut Man: Habut, what about this, and Habut, what about that, without sounding the H – as a lot of us do in Yorkshire. This, I am pleased to say, was the first and last Habut Man I encountered when promoting Speeduct systems. In this case the chairman, eventually somewhat exasperated, said to his technical director, 'Jack!, for the Lord's sake, shut UP, you're only sorry you didn't think of it yourself!'

The Burma Oil Company – who are quite different, they don't only do oil, they also do about everything else in the construction world, airports, ports, oil fields etc. – were very interested in Speeduct, and would we join them at their London HQ, directors' meeting, and could we be there for 9 am? They were out on the west side of London, and, at that time the M25 was under construction, as were other major connecting roads on our route! However, we always made a point of arriving on time, from experience, I wish everyone else did – always a reason. So, we were up early. The chairman said they had a lot on today, so could we manage to be 'through by 10 o'clock.' We said we would try our best. The meeting started, and I asked John to be a wall, and he was, and one of the nine directors said, after I had first demonstrated, how fast and simple it was to insert cables, and, this time it is all verbatim, 'Mr Walton will you do that again, I didn't see it that time.' No, it was not the director secretary, it was the technical director, and after I had explained to the chairman that, no, I had not, given him a backhander to say that, I also, immediately, did it again. After a pause, he said, verbatim, 'It's bloody marvellous, I think I want to applaud!' As I said to John later, as we drove home, 'Well, if all else fails I may still have a chance on the stage.'

The meeting went on very amicably and the chairman told me that they had asked the general works manager for their various factories to be available for the meeting, and would I mind if they asked him to attend. I said of course not, in this case, hoping against hope, he would not be so soon my second, Habut Man. He entered in his pristine white warehouse coat – like I wore in my engineering years, at C.R. & Co – and he wasn't the second. He was most impressed, and all in favour of the potential of the various systems and my heavy duty types, for motorways, docks, roadways, carrying water, electric, gas, and oil pipelines, in one, pre-cast, or metal or moulded unit sections, etc. There were discussions between the member's lunch, afternoon tea, and refreshments, during which, the chairman, at least three times, said to us, that they were interested in all applications of the system. Continuing the meeting, he proposed a certain member of the board, who was due to retire that year, to organise the business for them with us. After a meeting that they only wanted to last from 9 to 10 am, we left at 6.30 to 7 pm. And we never heard from the member, or Burma Oil Company, in any shape or form again! Maybe they each thought someone else was 'handling the matter,' or the chap retired, soon after, or they went, together, on a jet aircraft to Burma, and they crashed in the Andes mountains by mistake. Or maybe, they all just forgot. But one must draw a line somewhere, and this meeting, as with most of them, gave me more experience and insight into the higher echelons of large business organisations as with ICI and GEC and others.

The Rank Organisation was another very impressive group – and not only in the movie world, by any means. Here again, we were invited to their London HQ in Mayfair, well placed between the Grosvenor House Hotel and the Dorchester Hotel – and off Park Lane. We were to arrive at 10 am, we arrived at 9.50 am, approached the large black door, similar to No 10, but larger, and it was locked! There was no bell to ring, we decided it may have been time locked – particularly in such a 'deprived' neighbourhood, so came back at 10 am – no problem, it opened on well oiled hinges, into a predominantly black, but immaculate, small hall and an even smaller, black, lift in which two people would feel crowded. It did then manage to whisk us up, I don't remember how many, but at least four floors, to a much more spacious area of well lit, landings, offices, etc., and into the office of the director secretary, I assumed then. Now, as you will see by their letter to me, from Mr John H. Etheridge, JHE/jd, circulation or typist? – he might have been chairman Sir John Davis, perish the thought. I did not address him with due deference, and respect! However, I am a bit late now as I see the date is 7th June 1973 – 35 years too late!

The meeting went very well in either case – and the director informed me that I was right about the entrance security, and also that the building was once a palace for a queen! He also informed me that they received hundreds of inventions a month – I still think he must have made a mistake when what he actually said was three hundred, or I'd misheard which is also possible. What he did say was that it was the best idea he had ever seen, and he would so present it to the board in a few weeks' time. The subsequent meeting with Mr John Etheridge, of Central Marketing, was arranged by phone a few days later followed by the aforementioned letter:

THE RANK ORGANISATION
38 South Street London W1A 4OU telephone 01–629 7454 telex 263549
CENTRAL MARKETING

JHE/jd   7th June 1973

J.M. Walton, esq.,
Jeffrey Walton and Associates,
Chartered Architects, Surveyors & Valuers,
New North road,
HUDDERSFIELD.

Dear Mr Walton,

I must apologize for not writing to you earlier to thank you for all the precious time you gave me when I visited Huddersfield, not to mention your kind hospitality.
Thank you also for your letter which dots the i's and crosses the t's.

Whether Speeduct is for us or not is something which we hope to settle fairly quickly. But whatever the outcome, it still remains the best new idea to be presented to us for a long time.

Yours sincerely,

John H. Etheridge

This was followed by another letter from Mr Etheridge, after the board meeting, informing me that, after a very close vote of their 16 board members, it was decided not to enter this new field (they were considering building a new factory to manufacture Speeduct). One of the boards members, was HM the Queen's cousin, the now Angus Ogilvy. He also said he had been looking forward to working with me, I had been looking forward to working with him, he was a very well informed, competent and knowledgeable person.

You will of course appreciate, that along with Speeduct systems we were also fully involved with, at the same time, Hobbimate and its two works, and the architectural practice at New North Road, very ably assisted by our staff including ex-students of mine at HSA, (I don't know why). I also did the same thing in Barnstaple, Devon – and with outposts in Spain, or so I am told. Peter France, who I inherited from the late Gordon Berry on taking over his practice, and our two, at different times, chief quantity surveyors, and both unfortunately no longer with us, and partners John S.J. Horsfall, and now Russell John Lumb, 'Meccano Boy' as I first named him – to begin with he always or nearly, turned up at the office in red pullovers, like the boy on the Meccano box for those, like me, old enough to have had one. Although, he was further to the left than Ghenghis Khan at the time – I don't know how he stands now. I, by the way, am not, never have been, a member of any Party. Parties can easily become dictatorships, e.g. Communist Party, Nazi Party – and they don't have Boy Scouts, they have Hitler Youth, and between them, these two parties, have murdered more people, most of them their own people, than anyone else in the history of mankind: *millions more*!

To say we were hoist by our own petard, is an understatement of the situation. Tomorrow's World caused me to be simply inundated, by meetings, requests for meetings, time spent visiting, and demonstrating, to top companies, and some of them had been making ducting for years, the same old type. Like GEC's, Sir Arnold Weinstock, said, they also said, 'If anyone else makes it, we will have to.' Which doesn't get us very far, does it? It was my time and money that was being spent – and some of them certainly did not even appreciate the range of applications involved – and that was only Speeduct. The Hobbimate products were in a similar situation. I had a request to visit a large multi-product company, situated midway between Wakefield and London for them to see my various inventions, which at that time were all in full size model form, all made by me, in my workshop at my home in my spare time, believe it or not – in order that all of them were there to see, in my office and also in the room above my office, where they were on display, with me to explain, and a similar set of items small enough to fit into the current Jaguar XJ6, to be quickly reassembled whenever needed, as now. We set up the items – they were very impressed – we met again at a hotel, midway between their office and mine to reduce travel time – arranged, at their request, for the sales director to come and see all the actual and prototype products at my office in 3 days' time – he came, and asked if they could have some of them, particularly the Hobbimate multipurpose table range (all Patented) for further 'evaluation by customers' suggesting a sum of £6,000 for the privilege, which I agreed to. Two days later a van arrived with a sales manager who had then taken them on to a 'designer' firm in London, to see if they could design the same things, without infringement of patent, so I was told, by the sales director, when he phoned me a couple of weeks later. He had sacked the sales manager and was very sorry etc., and could they continue the discussions? No way – and what about my £6,000? 'Sorry, they hadn't signed anything yet'! My fault, and, as with our present government, lessons have been learned. Yes, but what about trust and honour – in both cases. There were others, but not so blatant as the latter, time wasters, but you have to meet to find out, you never know, until you meet them!

'Miss Yorkshire', Eric Kenworthy's daughter, in winter!

134

The Hobbimate contract with the Roller Cloche was going along fine, and they had also asked me to design a sales and display stand, using the Clipstick system, to market my Clipstick double glazing system, to be issued, to their multitude of shops selling ICI products. This I had done, they had seen the actual, finished stand, complete, not prototype, and were well pleased, and we had a range of other products they were interested in marketing. The number of units required by ICI would be huge nationwide, and that's not counting their customers overseas. That's just the stands, each one was to be stocked, fully, with the Clipstick double glazing system components. At this stage and they could easily, and economically, be extended. Following a requested visit to the ICI Research and Development HQ, where the main block, which is large, high, and rectangular, on plan, with solid walls all round – to a height of approx 16 feet – with above, fixed glass for a further 10 feet, to the flat roof. The building was air conditioned, and with only one entrance. We were asked to supply and install Hobbimate Clipstik 'Melinex' Glazing – all round. Only a few people would know about it, or even see it – they never have, even installed on my own glass entrance doors 7'6" × 7'0", and it has been there for over 40 years!

We would need more staff at Hobbimate, factory, space, storage etc., but that would be no problem, they were both available locally – our problem had been, since day one, the lack of a marketing organisation. We could invent the product, and make it, but advertising for mail order, was very expensive – and then ICI had come along with marketing expertise as good as the best, and they also produced *all* our raw materials, as a bonus, and delivered them, and took away our product, to distribute to their customers, along with the tins of Dulux paints, fertilisers, chemicals etc., from their various separate companies that were all part of the ICI group. In our case, it was the one already mentioned, dealing with garden, household, agricultural, horticultural, products etc., and they were all very capable people we dealt with and things ran very smoothly.

And then came disaster! For the very first time in their history, ICI made a loss on the year's trading – a 50 million pound loss, (if it had been today it would probably have been at least trebled) but the amount is incidental, I suppose to ICI. It's the disgrace, and that also would have to be rectified! And it was, it hasn't happened again, unless I am mistaken. What did happen, then, was that ICI decided to concentrate on their main companies and close down others, and one of these was the company we had been working for. With them went their chance, and mine, to make the odd million or two, each – believe it or not – or possibly more for

'Growsticks' winter

Roller Cloche
winter

them! In came Mr Harvey Jones, ex naval officer, to be ICI managing director to put things right. I don't know whether or not he succeeded, he was a likeable chap, and I hope still is – you may remember, he later went on to have a TV programme where he advised some well known firms, how to improve their own businesses. I remember one was at the Morgan Car Co., one of the very early car makers, with the Morgan three wheeler and of course at that time still doing all right, with their hand built Morgan sports car. Unfortunately he was not very kind to them, as I remember, and his proposals were a little dire – like going into liquidation. Harvey Jones was also noted for his flamboyant silk ties on TV which were just coming into vogue but were soon to be obsolete with the advent of jeans, (cloth 'de Nîmes') worn for years by working men in America. But the flamboyant tie is making a comeback, along with Hong Kong made but Savile Row labelled black lounge suits, worn by our multi-millionaire professional footballers. Turn in your grave, Stanley Matthews!

But in no way does all this mitigate our Speeduct and Hobbimate predicament, in that all of us, directors, had other basic professional

136

commitments. John Horsfall and I were both architects with a practice and staff to keep in employment, and produce the very best for our clients. Eric Kenworthy, accountant, was our practice accountant, but also earned his living with a large firm in Huddersfield and they were also our accountants for the two main invention products – Hobbimate and Speeduct. We, along with my son Timothy, who also worked in my office, were the only shareholders – none of us ever were paid a dividend!

I hope you will appreciate, from all my conversation in the many previous pages, that my sole object was to find good companies, with all the production facilities, transport, marketing, finance, and work force, who knew far more about running a large successful company than I did – a great deal more – and were prepared to buy the rights to manufacture my inventions and/or pay royalties. At least you have seen how near I came – and we did produce all the products of Hobbimate, and the domestic and commercial, and architectural Speeduct components, the heavy duty Speeduct, for use for example in laying, say, a fibre optic cable from London to Leeds, at tractor speed, on the M1, without obstruction of transport on any of the traffic lanes – or for that matter, in any roads, towns or city. You are able also to fill the duct with domestic electric, telecommunications cables, street lighting cables (CCTV-Prohibited) but these are now radio wavelength operated, anyway.

During my commitment to the formation of HSA, on a proper staff and standing, during the fifties, my private practice was a one man band, having to refuse some commissions. However, my practice with staff progressed with my first office at 14A, Bond Street, Wakefield, a Georgian building of three floors and kitchen basement floor with wine and food cellars with Yorkshire range with spit turner and a 5′ 0″ stone sink, coal delivery via pavement grate, to coal cellar below. The building was Grade 2 listed and with stone slate pitched roof, etc., and with garage, and garden off Laburnum Road, at the rear, and with the West Riding County Police HQ opposite, and the National Union of Mineworkers, annually, assembled on the road between us, for their official parade to Clarence Park, with flags and banners hoisted, and flying. The famous Grimethorpe Colliery Band playing, drums beating, and President Arthur Scargill leading the parade, eventually, and in the long process, closing the centre of Wakefield to all and sundry, but it was a very good for the pubs – until next day! We were also kept busy with work from the Richard Sutcliffe Company Ltd., and its subsidiary companies, Sutcliffe Rubber Company, Ossett, Yorks, Factory Extensions etc. – this was in the days when the Hoover tub and twin tub were on the market and very popular, to such extent that Sutcliffe Rubber Co. had some thousands of rubber rollers to retread every week!

One of our projects was for the West Riding County Library and Book Distribution Store in the centre of Maltby on the main street. At the same time we were building much smaller West Riding CC Library at Ripponden Yorks, both projects were to lead to other commissions in the two areas. At Maltby we were asked to design a civic centre for Maltby Urban District Council.

Maltby is a coal mining town as are many towns in Yorkshire, north, south, east and west. At that time they were all nationalised, (NCB) including Maltby main colliery (I had designed 'rolling stock' items for them in my pre-WWII days in engineering, at CR Co – remember?). Nearly all of them are now closed, including the very modern well designed, architecturally, Selby coal field, built after the war. Maltby main is still going strong, under private company ownership – and unless I miss my guess, we will be opening them again in this century – China is opening three collieries a week, every week!

Maltby council offices also at this time were situated in a larger domestic property, at the entrance to the town, and totally inadequate for council purposes. The chairman of the council, Labour Party of course, was Mr Jack Layden, ballroom dancing champion, accomplished brass band trumpet player, ex miner, and all round hard worker for the good of community. Along with the then town clerk, Mr Bert Ellis (there goes that Ellis name again) the two brains of the council par excellence, Jack Layden was, without question, one of my nature's gentlemen – a group I may have mentioned before. Over the years to come, one of my little earners was having bets with him on the outcome of various elections – national, local, and constituancy – and he never won, although I told him every time that I only laid bets when I knew I could not lose. J.L. was some years later to become chairman of Rotherham Metropolitan Borough Council, and subsequently chairman of the Metropolitan councils themselves, and eventually H.M. the Queen conferred a knighthood on Sir Jack Layden, for public services, in my humble opinion, very well deserved. Regrettably, Sir Jack retired at the same time, and some 6 or 7 weeks later, while walking I understand, had a heart attack and died, a very great loss to the community and particularly Lady Layden and his family.

Having got that sad part off my chest, I can go back to the Maltby civic centre building, when J.L. was there. The building was built by Messrs Dixon of Doncaster, a very competent company of builders who did other

138

projects for us and the building was duly completed on time. I had managed to persuade the council to allow me to rent, for the official opening of the building, original paintings of quality, to be displayed in rooms throughout the building, on a monthly payment basis, with option to purchase for a set price that included the monthly rental. This I arranged with a well known art dealer in York, Mr Austin Hayes, from his gallery in The Shambles. The civic centre was duly opened by the Right Honourable Lord Robens of Woldingham, PC, DCL (details below, Lord Robens was also chairman of the NCB, appropriately):

The Chairman

and Members of the Urban District Council of Maltby
request the pleasure of the company of

Mr J.M. Walton,

on the occasion of the formal opening of the

Civic Centre

by
The Right Honourable Lord Robens of Woldingham, P.C., D.C.L.

on Wednesday 19th July 1967
Reception at the Maltby Grammar School at 11–00 am.
for the formal opening at 11–30 am.
R.S.V.P. to The Clerk of the Council, Civic Centre, Maltby

On the pre-luncheon tour of the centre, Lord Robens was particularly appreciative of the pictures I had chosen for the various rooms, being a collector himself – as were the council's own department heads, in their jealous attempts, to switch my choice for their offices. What they did after the opening would be their own business – what I had done was on behalf of the council and stayed my way!

In his address, Lord Robens said he had been in many public buildings in his experience but this civic centre was the most satisfying and pleasing he had ever been in! I assume he meant except the Houses of Parliament!

We were also architects for Kiveton Rural District Council civic centre and council offices, some few miles south of Maltby. This building, comprising council chamber and offices, on the site of previous domestic offices, was officially opened by the Right Honourable Harold Wilson, OBE, FRS, MP, and Mrs Mary Wilson. The contractors were S & A Parsons Ltd., Killamarch, Sheffield. Perhaps two years after Maltby civic centre, the council commissioned us to build, on the same large site area, Maltby sports centre. As you will be aware, there are today centres for just about anything, including hand loom weaving, and media studies – at degree level, in that case. In this case the Maltby main colliery area was forecast to subside by at least 3 feet under our site during the next 18 months – and we were to provide two swimming pools, one for adults with high diving platforms etc., and one for children, I am pleased to say both pools, are still there, in full use.

I am not pleased to say that one month before opening, the Chief Fire Officer of Sheffield, who was responsible for supplying his detailed requirements for fire safety to the architects, which he had done 12 months earlier, and also approved our designs when they were submitted, and which we'd already installed, complete, was superseded by a new chief, who apparently unilaterally decided to alter all the finished provisions, approved and required by his predecessors. The council, against their wishes, were obliged to accept, and a month's hard, unnecessary extra work by the builders and ourselves. For what reason, again, I do not know.

We were also architects for a variety of housing projects in the Rotherham Metropolitan Council, and Maltby Council areas – Maltby UDC, aged persons housing, and a larger mixed housing development at Flanderwell, for Rotherham MC. In other parts of Yorkshire we designed housing schemes for Ripponden UDC, aged persons housing development, Denby Dale UDC, housing development, at Upper Cumberworth, etc.

The National Coal Board had a department called the Coal Industry Social Welfare Organisation, CISWO, for short, and we were responsible for architectural projects in the large Yorkshire coalfield area. We were asked to design the Maltby Miners Welfare Club twice, first a general refurbishment, much improved, then out of the blue a serious fire destroyed the steward's family first floor accommodation, and part of the club. Then we were asked to design and build a new single storey house alongside the large bowling green – Chairman, Jack Laydon, of previous mention, and Mr Jack McKening Head of CISWO, who along with, I think, the Mansfield Brewery Company, both our clients – I still have a pint glass, the only one left unbroken in the debris of the fire and rescued by me to present to Mr Laydon, as he was then, when all was sweetness and light, but never got the opportunity to do so, unfortunately.

Again, after a year or more, and a few miles away from Maltby at Dinnington, where Dinnington main was the NCB colliery, history repeated itself, as is it's wont. The circumstances were similar. Dinnington Colliery Institute was in a pre WWI, brick built school, with playground and steward's family house attached and long since superseded, by a post WWII, school locally. We were asked by CISWO to do internal designs for the institute, and generally refurbish. This we did, and had them accepted by all concerned. Unfortunately, while the steward and his wife and family were on holiday, the institute caught fire, and necessitated the provision of a new building on the extensive site, adjacent bowling green. This we duly accomplished, and due to my periodic site meetings and institute committee meetings I usually found myself having to oblige the no longer young and huge chairman of the institute, by driving him home in my, then, Jaguar. He was a reputed something like 20 pints a day man, so it was a struggle getting him into the car to start with, and I was on tenterhooks lest he was to have a heart attack or something, en route, so I made a point of getting him home rather sharpish! Then I had the problem of getting him out of the car safely.

I was asked by Maltby UDC, after the official opening of the civic centre, to design a suitable presentation piece enclosing, the very first piece of coal to come out of the Maltby mine. Very unusual, but very interesting, to be presented to the Right Honourable The Earl of Scarborough, whose stately home and estates are at Sandbeck Park, near Maltby, Rotherham MBC. His Lordship invited me to Sandbeck Park in September 1974, a most interesting visit as he personally showed the home and estates, including the bills submitted to his forebears, by Capability Brown, for work done by Mr Brown on the estates. I can only wish Capability would come and help me keep my garden in order, at the same price!

Still in the coal mining field (and pre Mrs Thatcher) the president of the National Union of Mine Workers (NUM), Mr Arthur Scargill, who, I had met on a number of occasions previously, at our Bond Street offices in Wakefield, invited us to enter, as one of three architectural practices selected a competition, to design a new NUM HQ building in the centre of Sheffield. The other two practices, one in Manchester, and one in Sheffield, were much larger in staff numbers, been practising much longer, and consequently better known, and were also very good indeed –

in fact, the principals of the Manchester firm I have already mentioned, as I had previously invited them to present prizes, lecture, etc., at HSA on various occasions.

After a very great deal of work by all concerned, including our quantity surveying staff, etc., having completed project summaries of elemental costs, estimated at £2,500,00, not including professional fees, in addition to all the project design drawings, site surveys and presentation perspectives, etc., we managed to complete within the competition time. I went to London by rail to avoid any risk of accident – as far as possible to deliver our submission to Mr Scargill's office. It was just a matter of depositing on time, he was not there – and certainly was in need of better offices. I now had time to spare before being at Kings Cross at 6 pm for the return Yorkshire pullman, so as usual I took a London cab to the West End, Harrods. The taxi driver was a very pleasant chap who, when I asked why he wasn't going the usual way, apologised, saying the way he was going was quicker, due to roadworks and so it turned out. We started chatting about this and that, people he had had as passengers, and the fact that he would like a change of job. He had, prior to getting The Knowledge been in the building trade, etc. He asked me what was my job, and at that time I was of course involved also with Hobbimate and Clipstick double glazing system and other products. I was also considering, somehow, organising a franchise business particularly for the double glazing system, which he was very interested in. We arrived outside Harrods, sat talking for some minutes in spite of the looks he was getting from the commissionaire, he paid me some nice compliments about people he had driven in his cab, and further amazed me by absolutely refusing to accept my fare and that was that.

A quite different attitude was exposed by the president of the NUM – he had all the drawings etc. put on display to the public in Sheffield and we three firms of architect competitors met at the opening together, with no suggestion of the eventual winner being announced. But both the other firms said that we had produced the best proposals, which of course was typical of my profession, and in this matter, again, that was that – or so I assumed. Remember, back in my Crossley School days, the Irish Sick Room Maid, in my Autograph Album – 'Thy Friend has a Friend, and they Friend's Friend has a Friend – so be discreet.'

The three competitors were to discover that Mr President Scargill had a Friend, and they in their earlier days lived next but one to each other, and he happened now to be an architect, and he was not typical of architects. They would have refused to act, but this friend had, for his final years, been a part time student, and very sporadic attender, at the HSA in the 70s and had no time for other students, but tried to monopolise staff members. He was also unusual, in having one eye blue, and the other brown, the only such person I have ever met. However, President Scargill gave him the project to design, without any further consultation with the three practices who for some weeks had made available three excellent complete schemes for contemplation, and copy – and to hell with the copyright laws. All to no avail, the times they were a-changing – cheaper coal from abroad and Mrs Margaret Thatcher taking on the unions including the NUM. The HQ building, was in fact built and was also copied from the three schemes exhibited, in planning and design, although with reduced accommodation and facilities.

There were of course many other buildings we designed during the continued progress of my practice, and also in taking over the Gordon Berry practice, Huddersfield. For some time this was to be a problem and, as I suggested to John Horsfall, now my partner, the first one, I had not bought goodwill, but I am afraid much badwill as well. For example, on day one we were to find that a project, just down the road, in Huddersfield town centre was contracted to commence in just one week's time. All the construction drawings, including some detail drawings, were completed for the Bradford and Bingley Building Society's new building – site cleared, etc., and on checking the drawings they showed the structural steelwork in the basement, with staff cloakrooms, toilets, etc., with $24' \times 6''$ steel universal beams to support the building, in a position giving only 5 feet 6 inches headroom! There were also problems with the fire safety provisions so it was all hands to the pumps – revised drawings, but quickly please – like today, Baxendale!

The list goes on, as does my life, along with it – electronics laboratories for British Aerospace at Brough, Humberside, telecommunications factory for Tunstall Telecom Group, PLC Social Services day care centre for the physically handicapped, Dewsbury, for Kirklees Metropolitan Council Batley Central Club, phased reconstruction, East Dene, social club, Mexborough Athletic Club, Pilling and Sons, Jewellers, Huddersfield. I still have a Bulova Accutron, gold watch I bought from Mr Pilling some years before we designed his very smart corner shop in the centre of Huddersfield. Unfortunately, about a couple of years later, a large multiple shop jewellery & watch company 'made him an offer they told him he had to accept' or they would buy a shop on each side of his – and close him down! That's what some people call business.

Naturally, we had our difficult times – one of the problems in architectural practice is that we are at the forefront of the building industry, and therefore the first to suffer in times of recession, political problems, and government mismanagement, stock market runs, etc. In my case I carried the financial can on a number of occasions, but I am very pleased to say that on none of the occasions did I have to make redundant any staff. Hopefully, it's that long suffering angel on my shoulder I have to thank. Eventually, in 1986, I was reluctantly able to retire, and become consultant to the practice (knowing that I would in all probability, only be consulted in the event of disaster, thankfully one never arose).

After retirement, I only visited the office very occasionally, not wanting to give any impression of interfering in any way – and they all knew more about everything now, than I did anyway – so I referred potential clients and had phone calls with them etc. Then a couple of years ago John Horsfall retired, and 3 months ago Russell Lumb and his wife came to dinner, and informed me of his intention to retire in July 2008. I sincerely hope they both have a long and happy retirement.

Going back to 1986, my files and my memory took me a little further back to 1983, and the motor cars, Bugatti, Vauxhall, Austin 7, of my pre-WWII days, and my post-WWII Riley Kestrel, Citroen 15. Jowett, and another Riley saloon I left at my dear old friend Ted Neal's, to put in one of his garages, for later sale, at Horbury – which I never got around to, and it stood immaculate in his yard for some years, still my property, until regrettably Ted passed away, and his wife Jessie sold all their property, land etc., and moved to Brighton to be with her sister (we kept in contact, and they both lived to be 100, I am pleased to say). The Riley saloon, which I admit I forgot all about for some years before the sale, I had taken delivery of my first Jaguar (about 1960) I left. As you will know, I had a few things to keep me otherwise occupied – so I hope the person who bought it enjoyed having it, even though it wasn't the vintage Kestrel – but haven't you noticed, except for the London to Brighton run, on TV, most people haven't seen a vintage car these days. They are now all highly polished, brand new cars, millions of them, and there are thousands more of the same, in car dealers' showrooms, and second hand, but looking brand new, on the showroom forecourt!

Sorry, back again to January 1983 – I received a letter from Mr R.G. Putnam, Director (UK Sales) Jaguar Cars Limited, Browns Lane, Coventry, inviting me to test drive their 1983 model Jaguar, on the occasion of their sixtieth anniversary. The car duly arrived at 9 o'clock, and was parked behind my then BMW 7 series, on the opposite side of New North Road, Huddersfield, both, visible from my office window. I

144

regret to say, I completely forgot about it until 5 o'clock, when staff were leaving, dashed outside, drove the Jaguar a mile up to the next junction of the M62 to turn round and eventually arrived back at my office and sat in the car making notes etc., until the driver arrived to return the car.

I subsequently wrote to Mr Putnam, and quote the second and third paragraphs below – I also in the letter listed 14 points requiring attention, in my opinion, and some days later received his reply, which follows my comments:

It came as some little surprise to me to realise that I have been driving Jaguar cars for going up to half the 60 years! ... having had 12 new Jaguars, since 1968 all XJ6 models either Jaguar or Daimler, in that period.

I last changed my car in August 1981 and for the first time, with very great reluctance, bought the Flagship of the BMW models a 735i special equipment car. The reason for this was the continuing decline in my previous two new Jaguars, that is before Mr Egan took over as Managing Director.

Dear Mr Walton

Thank you for your letter of 7th January and comprehensive comments regarding the car you test drove following our 60 years of Jaguar promotion.

I have circulated copies of your letter to the relevant parties who are involved in formulating product policy as I am sure they will find them of interest. However, I can assure you that the car we produce for America with the exception of certain safety items and exhaust emission controls is identical to our British specification.

In closing may I take this opportunity of inviting you to visit us here at Browns Lane in the event that you are in the area, so that you can see at first hand our efforts to recreate the spirit of Jaguar once again. My sincere thanks for the time and trouble you have taken to put together your letter.

Yours sincerely

R G Putnam
Director, UK Sales Operations

I was later invited to visit the factory and lunch with the directors. I was taken round the factory in the morning, and soon found that my test report had been photocopied to each relevant department – oh dear. But all my suggestions were accepted with approval by the various foremen, craftsmen, etc., and in the process I was shown their top secret, literally under wraps, new model, which in fact did not go on the market for some years later. Like British Leyland, Jaguar had problems with people like Red Robbo, a union leader, eventually being taken over by Ford.

There were also three very large, high-bodied, Daimler saloons being finished off in one side bay, painted black, and impressive, for use by H.M. Queen Elizabeth the Queen Mother. No E-Types about, but all very interesting. So far, so good! After luncheon, talking round the table, and answering or asking many questions, I mentioned that I had devised various pieces or improvements for my needs in my previous and present cars, such as tables for front and rear passenger use, easily removable modifications to front sun screens and rear window blinds etc., which I already had installed myself. They were interested and asked if they could see them. Of course they could, so the group of us left the dining room, and walked down to the visitors car park, just outside, in line abreast. As we got closer it dawned on me that I wasn't in my Jaguar – but in my first BMW 7 Series! My experience with Jaguar cars goes back to the Series 3, pre-Inspector Morse and up to the XJ6 Series, very impressive, when I had one of the first in the north from Appleyards, Leeds. It was only a month old when I was returning from a site visit in South Yorkshire, via Barnsley, and leaving the town on the Wakefield, A61, side, through the centre of a large council housing estate the XJ6, pride of Jaguar Cars Ltd, came to a very quiet, full stop, and for no apparent reason. I rang Barnsley Jaguar dealership, they arrived with a van with no lifting rig, and driver with no idea of methods of towing automatic gearbox cars, unbelievably. By now the two local schools' children were out, and surrounding my car. 'What's up Mister?' – 'Posh car!' – 'Never seen one like this before,' – 'Won't it go?' I phoned Appleyards Leeds, Jaguar, Rolls Royce, Morris dealers, 20 miles away. They arrived with a suitable large van with eight orange lights flashing and with sirens wailing. They must have been told it was an accident. The kids were still all around, it was better than going to a film show. The Jaguar was suitably hooked up and I was dropped off en route, at my home – time wasted, actions delayed, the usual problems of an incident with cars these days, as you will, I am sure appreciate. The car was returned in a couple of days – cylinder head gasket shim failure, I was informed – and it could well have been, but should not have been, in a new car, and a Jaguar.

The same type of thing happened in my next XJ6 two years later. I left home on my way to the Hobbimate and Speeduct works, and then the Huddersfield office – yes I did these visits, daily. I had stopped at my usual small garage repair and filling station for petrol, filled up with fuel, pressed the engine starter, nothing happened – I rang Appleyards, Leeds 15 miles away. Someone arrived an hour later, this time it was a contact switch, value £2, that was hidden, with no indication in the book, under the gear lever casing, necessitating the removal of half the front passenger floor! The switch was made in France, Spain, or Germany, I can't remember which, but it was not made in the UK., in a Jaguar! Completely ruined my day's agenda. I can hear you say, what is he banging on about cars for? Is he just showing off or what? No, I am not just showing off, I am not that type, believe it or not. You will recall that in my school days I was fascinated by cars, motor bikes, cycles and any machinery, including motor mowers, even, but after being knocked down by a motor bike, outside Nettletons furniture showroom in Horbury, they were not at the top of my wish list – too fast, no protection, would dawn on me a few years later. But cars were a different proposition, protected, comfortable, and four wheels, and you don't get wet, but by the time I was old enough, and had some cash for a secondhand car (Riley, Kestrel, for example), it had also dawned on me that all that really mattered was not how much it cost, how posh it was, or how fast it was, but how safe it was, particularly for my nearest and dearest and I now had this last item, – my family. The important thing, above all, if you must have an accident, – is that all the passengers *walk away* from the smashed car; it is only metal, not your flesh and blood – and if you have any sense it is insured. And remember, about two million drivers, coming along behind you, or towards you, worse still, are not insured. Sorry, I know *you* know all about driving, we all do, it's always the other 'chap', person, or idiot. So, in an effort not to be one of the latter, I commend to you this simple mantra, saved me many times: Right position on road, right gear, right speed, and most important, IF YOU CAN'T SEE, DON'T GO! All of course, assuming you are sober!

Still banging on about cars, another, again Jaguar XJ6, and new, I tested the seat belts (manufactured by the firm that made them for the RAF) and found them to be inoperative, so much for Appleyards' pre-delivery preparation – the third time, or was it the manufacturer's fault, possibly both. Since the end of WWII, I had refused to contemplate anything German in the transport field, or items not made in the UK, and then I saw in *The Times*, a full page, colour advertisement, showing the then first

BMW 'Seven Series' going down a mountain road, in winter, at night and raining, brake lights on, car coming up narrow road – nothing else, except along the bottom margin of the page, in small Times Roman Font, 'This is the new BMW Seven Series with the electronic brake control system invented by Bosch and BMW', that instantly, whether one wheel is on gravel, the rest are on ice, takes over, and automatically allows you to steer safely – that is, so long as you are keeping to the laws of physics, and not going too fast! Similar amusing, full page ads, continued for 6–8 weeks and I was very pleased to note they were devised by a UK firm. So I got my first, BMW 7 and I have had the odd problem, nothing serious, and doing thousands of miles a year – I continued changing every two years or so, until my seventh in 1994 and doing less mileage – my eighth in March 1999 is in my garage, immaculate, having only done 25,000 miles, but I have been run about mainly locally, in a smaller car, so if anyone wants to buy a Series 7, for a fair price, I will then get a smaller 3 series, ready for my old age!

Whenever my car goes in for service I make a point of telling the person responsible, that I don't mind if I can't start, (I lie, I do mind!) but I have to be able to stop – so check the brakes.

William FitzGerald Suttcliffe was a long time friend whom I mentioned when discussing Richard Sutcliffe Ltd at Horbury, earlier, in our conversation. He was also the last chairman of the company, until his untimely death in 1979. Gerald was also a life long bachelor, and also a life long friend of myself and my family, Maria (RIP), and Timothy Baines Walton, my dear son (RIP).

We met at the new house which I had designed in 1953 for one of the company directors, Mr Harold Streets, in Horbury. Gerald bought The Grange, Badsworth near Ackworth, about 6 miles from Tree Garden at Sandal Magna, and en route to Horbury a couple of miles away, so he would drop in on his way home, for a chat, stay for dinner, or stay the night, as may be arranged. Or we would do the same things, and follow him up to Badsworth Grange, and stay the weekend, or have dinner there prepared by Mrs Pickering and return home. I designed alterations for our bedroom at the Grange, and for both Gerald's bathroom and en suite bathroom, using an adjacent room, for Maria and myself. Gerald had the same en suite accommodation at Tree Garden, and these arrangements were to continue until Gerald died, in a London Hospital, with Maria and I staying with friends nearby.

During these 26 years of our relationship, we both entertained our mutual friends, Gerald had his obligations to travel, on company business

148

to South Africa, America, Canada etc., but otherwise wherever and whenever Maria and I were going on short breaks, in the UK, or wherever, Gerald was invited. We went in my Jaguar, I did the driving! Which he much preferred, as I did – reason, Gerald, particularly when driving, was very impatient, (drove in bare feet, had foot troubles, by the way) and on one earlier occasion, alone, had run out of road, driving his Bentley on a bend, and not done his car, or himself, a lot of good. Main thing was, he walked away, the Bentley was only metal, that served its purpose in protecting him.

I completely redesigned, and re-equipped, the large kitchen laundry, and storage areas, adjacent to the Pickerings and their children's house, also part of the main building of the Grange, complete with a range of AGA cookers, Aga central heating boilers etc., kitchen storage cabinets and laundry room cabinets, ironing boards, drying room – and all, as always for my friends, free and with my compliments.

Gerald, was one of five brothers, Richard Desmond Suttcliffe, 1914–1950, Richard Suttcliffe, Dermod Suttcliffe, and Edward Suttcliffe – (High Court Judge, Old Bailey.) All very pleasant company, including their wives. I rang Lois, (Richard Desmond's wife) an hour ago to check how she was, the spirit, was very willing, she is an artist, but like both of us, the flesh was weakening. We are both about the same age she has her family, and grandchildren around her.

Over the years, as Timothy was growing up, whenever possible we visited various parts of the country, and soon after I was demobilised from the RAF we rented a house in Primrose Valley, Filey, for the summer months, as Timothy was very seriously affected by hay fever which lasted all summer, and made his life a misery. The main culprit was apparently Timothy Grass. Timothy's grandparents, Frank and Alice Baines, and Maria and I, decided to buy a similar property that we could use throughout the year at our convenience. I still own it, but when Timothy, thank goodness, was about 18, he gradually grew out of his hay fever and later married my dear daughter-in-law, Sandra Elizabeth Walton, and took up residence at 'Tree Cottage', Crofton, Wakefield on the 22nd of October, 1966, when Timothy was 24 years of age. Thereafter, things began to change.

For over 20 years, particularly, in summer time, school holidays, when Maria and Timothy were living there, full time, I was driving daily, from Leeds, Wakefield, Huddersfield or Tree Garden and returning the next morning, at 6 to 7 am. Staying until Monday at weekends, I was busy redecorating, repairing, making alterations etc., rarely ever visited the beach, but everyone was enjoying it, even me. Timothy had his tricycle, three similar age friends, two girls. Timothy was never without girl-friends. Rohais (Rolly), Wendy and David, who lived in the next house, but was a complete little horror, to put it mildly. David and his mother lived there more or less permanently. In later years, he owned a leather goods factory in Filey. Unfortunately, he was to have a heart attack and die at Heathrow airport, some years later, going to Europe on business.

The next house, further down the road, belonged to Mr and Mrs Faust, who had two children Peter, and Patricia ('Pat'). Mr Faust was a small man (about 5 ft tall) who drove a very large Austin car, cabriolet type – H.M. the Queen Mother used to favour. Always immaculate, he was also a very good business man – he invented and was the founder of, InterFlora, the world famous company delivering flowers internationally. Mrs Faust was a relative of Sir Yehudi Menuhin, also world famous, the greatest violinist of the twentieth century. Mrs Faust was a very fine pianist, with a concert grand, Steinway & Sons piano, in her sitting room. Mr Faust also, at least twice a week sometimes more, drove himself there and back to Manchester where his florist products company was situated, alone. They were a fine Jewish family, but unfortunately had a very unhappy past. One of their children was born with serious problems and died in infancy, and their eldest child Peter (who was about 25 when we first bought the house next to them) was autistic, and required continuous care, which was provided by Mr and Mrs Faust, and younger sister, Pat Faust, then still a student at art college, now still our next door neighbour in Primrose Valley.

Pat Faust 'The Filey Artist' is indeed, a very fine artist, and her maybe unusual name is from German forebears, of architectural talents and she does in fact paint very fine exterior and interior paintings of stately homes and buildings. One is of Scarborough Art Gallery Museum during a snowstorm, and it now hangs in the gallery as part of the permanent collection. By 1960, when she was then 26, she had already had five acceptances by the Royal Academy London. Her amazingly detailed painting of the Chinese Room in Burton Agnes Hall, East Yorkshire, has been exhibited in numerous galleries, along with other works over many years – she also in one stage of her career designed scenery for Emile Littler. Miss Faust was educated at Culcheth Hall, Cheshire and was an art student in Manchester.

Pat works alone, in her studio upstairs in her home at Primrose Valley and is a very private person. She also travels at home and abroad alone, but I believe I am the only person she invites into her studio. She has many talents ever since she was a girl, she has invited me virtually all the time I have been there and Timothy was a five year old and she also got on well with Maria, and my in laws. Subsequently her mother passed away and later her father died, and Pat was obliged, for obvious reasons, to place brother Peter in a very good, special home, where he had friends, and where she visited regularly. She also sent me various pieces of artwork she had done there with him until, after some years, Peter died and she continued living alone, but as they say, getting about.

Autism is a terrible affliction for all those involved, but sometimes, just sometimes talent emerges. You may, perhaps, have heard of one autistic person, Stephen Wilshire, whose work appears in a calendar published by *The Architects Journal* 1994, which I bought, and still have. Along practically the length seven inches deep, above the five inch deep length of calendar, is the entire length of the Liverpool waterfront view, from the docks on the left side, to Gilbert Scotts magnificent cathedral at the right side, including Frederick Gibberd's Catholic cathedral, and other famous buildings in between. Stephen, then 16 years old came by ferry across the Mersey, and on the way heard the still very popular song, Ferry Cross the Mersey, for the first time. When he got on shore, he played the song on the piano, for which he had never had a lesson! This freehand drawing, which took three hours to complete, is astonishingly complex, and Stephen's pen strokes are two dimensional, and also in perspective, three dimensional – fantastic!

I wrote the lines immediately above on 1st of December 2007 – it is now the Sunday, 2nd December, and my angel was obviously reading over my shoulder, at the same time. I have just received my *Sunday Times*, had my breakfast, and opened the magazine haphazardly, at page 35. There is 'Stephen Wilshire, who is now 33', it says, under a picture of the 'young Stephen as a boy in the 1970s' with an open book on architecture on his lap. 'His autism diagnosed at three, and an exceptional talent for drawing from memory was discovered soon afterwards'. 'Top: Wilshire in his studio in 2005, working on a 10-metre-long drawing of Tokyo that he completed within days after a short helicopter flight over the city.' He is photographed from behind, seated on a draughtsman's stool, at a 40-inch deep curved white sheet of paper, fully supported on framing, with the central 20 inches, all along the 30 metres, covered with his black pen strokes of the buildings of Tokyo – again, fantastic!

I know I have gone on far too long about Stephen, when I should have gone on about Peter Faust. Now I will do the same about Peter, whom I first met a few days after we occupied the house next door to him. We arrived, parked the car in front of the garage, had a look around, just the three of us, then we notice a head and shoulders, leaning over his gate and then his sister, Pat, the artist, came and introduced us to the quite well built Peter. At first I was rather worried about my 4 year old son, Timothy and his other play friends, but not for long. Peter may be autistic, but he loved children and we were soon to find he had other remarkable qualities. For example he had a fantastic memory – for many years, until his father died, whenever we went to stay at Sunny Cliff Primrose Valley (later to be renamed by me Sea Garden) although Sandra has not yet changed the name, and occasionally at Christmas, and we went many times, for short, and longer visits, Peter always came out to welcome us with delight – he was probably lonely on his own, particularly after his mother died – and every time he would remind us that the last time we were there was Saturday, September 6th, at 3 minutes past four o'clock, and it was raining at the time – and he was always correct!

Mr Faust, as founder president of InterFlora, always took Peter along when he went to overseas countries like Australia, New Zealand, Europe and America, to present the new country 'president' with his gold chain of office. Reason – Peter would remember every person introduced to his father, name, where he came from, and whatever else was necessary, and would remember all of them for the next time they met – and for the rest of his life!

Peter was also taken to various classical music concerts, Brahms, Beethoven, Mozart, and Peter would have a copy of the full score, for piano concerto, sonatas, etc., so that he could check for 'mistakes' and make sure he remembered it correctly himself. There were also, unfortunately, other reasons for Peter to accompany his father as he was unable, for example, to shave himself, and needed adult male assistance for some more personal matters – hence the reason for Pat to have to place Peter in a special care home on the death of her father, after her mother died. What a life – but I believe they were all very happy together.

To continue with Timothy and his Filey friends who, as children do, began the process of growing up, and things like toys, as with food, were rationed, and, as I may have already mentioned earlier, I had built a rocking horse/push horse with wheels, and also, a year or so later, out of the thin wooden sides of an orange box – a rarity then – a motor boat with search light, pilot at the wheel and towing a small rowing boat, towed at the stern. At the Filey children's pool, he and his friends and other children would rush to get it in the pool, and I still have the photos. Wish I still had Timothy. One year, out of season, Timothy now about five or six, and down on a deserted beach, we could see him from our living room window, came rushing into the house. Daddy, daddy – come quick – he had dragged up the beach, path and road a large lobster pot, with half a dozen lobsters live inside, washed from the buoy onto the beach, after the previous stormy night. Flotsam and jetsam – a few of our neighbours had a lobster for dinner that evening.

As I have been known to tell my new house clients, when they have six children, (but, say, finance for four bedrooms) – 'children grow-up, they don't grow-down'. Funny thing, but they do, and then some fly the coup, as the Americans say – and to my surprise Timothy eventually, did just that. Under duress, Maria agreed to let him go to primary school, or whatever they were called at that time, less than a mile down the road from Spinkwell. Where we were living at the time, 1946, in Horbury, 'The Sisters of Mercy Convent' (C of E), with mixed classes, and dedicated nuns, doing the teaching. Next, he was a prep school pupil at headmaster Mr Shaw's, private school, in the fine orangery, (Grade 2 listed building), near Wakefield library and opera house, and HM Wakefield high security prison – so at least, he had the choice between the devil and the deep blue sea, at the start of his education!

Mr Shaw's school later moved to a large house, with grounds in Horbury, and Timothy later went on eventually to Wakefield Technical College, Huddersfield Polytechnic, and qualified as an architectural technician, and then came into my office in Wakefield and later Huddersfield.

Mention of HM Prison, Wakefield, reminds me that after WWII I was invited by the prison education officer, to meet him at the prison to discuss his idea of asking me to lecture to prisoners. His office was a cell on the ground floor, with a connecting door to an adjacent cell, in the row of cells, which was for his assistant who, at that time, was Dr Klaus Fuchs, atomic scientist, and traitor, who was there serving sentence for betraying the secrets of the American atomic bomb to the Russians. When I met him, he was not over communicative, understandably, but was obviously very useful to the education officer. He was released a few years later.

We continued, whenever possible, to take Timothy to Filey at weekends, or to other coastal places, in the battle with hay fever, and, thank goodness, things for him gradually improved as he got older. In the process he became a model railway enthusiast, assisted by Paul White – you may recall him as one of my very first enrolments at HSA earlier – also a model railway expert. Paul, when qualified, worked in my office, and built his own house, with his own hands, and the help of his wife to be, in Almondberry, near Huddersfield. I made the timber base support tables – they did the clever bit, track layout and landscaping. All this was on the first floor playroom, taking up half the space of the floor, and later to be converted to two rooms, when Timothy flew the coup. I also made him a full size lamin board, ¾″ thick, table tennis board on 3′ × 1″ folding timber leg sets, and also included a competition dart board – so neither he, or his friends could say they were badly done to. However, the racket, din or general mayhem was quite another ball game!

Around this time the Mecca Locano ballroom in Wakefield was being demolished, to make way for The Ridings, multi storey car parks, shops and tower block housing, etc. So, I bought some of the beech wood planks of the ballroom floor and had the joinery firm that had done the joinery at Tree Garden make a rather posh garden shed for Timothy to breed various birds, exotic or otherwise, which he became very good at, to such an extent that he had a favourite parrot, in a cage sometimes, in the playroom. One day, there was an absence of parrot – no means of escape except through one of two chimney flues, accessed via a 9″ × 9″ cast iron removable plate – a little heavy for a parrot. Someone had left a window open – we had a few parrots in the garden for weeks! Timothy was gradually growing out of the curse of hay fever, thank goodness, and he had his only brush with the law at 13, when we had a visit from a police officer, to inform me that he had, along with his pals, been caught on the railway embankment train spotting and it was dangerous etc. No action was to be taken – this was a police sergeant at that time, and also the coroners officer, he was an ex WWII officer tank commander, decorated – Douglas Williams, and his wife Jennie, and young family, a son and daughter, were to become our life long friends. Their son Edward Williams is still my solicitor, unfortunately his father died over twenty years ago and his mother Jennie 4 years ago. RIP.

In the summer of 1958 I had a letter from Ingolfur B. Guthmundsson, in Reykjavik, Iceland, inviting us to visit them for a couple of weeks in order to go fishing for salmon, and meet other mutual friends there, etc., cordial. Unfortunately I was very involved at the time suggested with projects in my office, and arranged to make the visit a few weeks later – big mistake, as I was to learn. Timothy was all in favour, the sooner the better, he was 16 and of course had heard my anecdotes on my service there. Maria, was not. 'I have been as far north in Scotland as I wish to go,' and that was that! Timothy and I duly flew from Glasgow airport, after a 6 hour delay and no means of communicating – only to be met on landing at my airport, Reykjavik, 6 hours late, by a posse of 10 people still waiting to welcome us – Icelanders are that kind of people! After celebratory drinks all round, we left for Ingolfur's house in Reykjavik in the late hours, and on arrival at his home we were first introduced to a large chest type freezer or, more particularly, to the large prime salmon in it. It was half full at least. I was informed that if I had arrived on the original date, I would have been able to catch the same amount, and there was even more to regret later.

Iceland is unpredictable. Nowhere is the sun brighter, cleaner, or more crystalline when it shines, nowhere does nature show herself more calm, more submissive, inviting when she chooses. But such whimsies are rare. Nowhere can the elements whip themselves into such a frenzy of agonised savagery, nor of heaving wind and whirling water and biting ice. Nor of spewing geysers and boiling springs and underground infernos of fire and water and molten metal. And overhead shafts of midnight light. Nowhere else can the elements so nearly approach a cataclysm – and don't even mention global warming here, they have been there, done that for over one thousand years!

Iceland also has statistics. It is the fourth largest island in the North Atlantic. It is 40,000 square miles of volcanic earth, and it had, during my times there, about 120,000 indomitable, independent people (remember the North Atlantic Cod War with the Royal Navy of the UK? – we lost, but we are still their best friends!). It is the oldest democracy still extant on Earth. It has been one since the year 930. And it was settled long before then, by Vikings, by Celts, by Monks and noblemen and pirates and also by determined men seeking surcease from oppression.

Conditions of life in Iceland are not good compared with those in more southern climes, as the country is bare and desolate. The greater part of it is barren plain, glacier and mountain, desert and lava field. It is a land of contrast: the land of the greatest glaciers in Europe, and at the same time the land with the largest volcanic areas. In this world of the greatest contrasts known to geology, boiling springs sprout from beneath rolling glaciers, and volcanic eruptions occur in the centre of the glacial belts which comprise one tenth of Iceland's area. Quite some amazing country! But Iceland is a beautiful country. Here are fertile valleys down which rivers flow, broken by torrents and cataracts, while in the distance the mountains are blue and the glaciers shine white. And in the various landscapes are a wonderful variety of colours and shades unequalled in other countries. To add to this beauty are the nights: in winter illuminated by the amazing Northern Lights; in summer bright and magical; and of such beauty, once experienced are never forgotten.

And now, from all this, in 1959, has come a modern civilisation and society, modern cities, with expensive hotels, office buildings. Swing bands and nightclubs, motor cars and telephones. Décolleté gowns (long before the rash of designer experts of today). Our hosts, the Gudmandsson family had arranged for a most impressive programme of visits, meetings with other old friends etc., which I of course fully remember, but not in the case of Icelandic place names, which all Icelanders know by heart – and there are masses of them.

I find I have noted on the map's margin – MULAKOT – Olafur Tubals – his home was near MyrdalsJokull glacier, and he had a plantation of fine trees – very scarce in Iceland. He was also a very fine painter, artist. He was some 70 miles away from Reykjavik – wish I had been able to afford to buy one of his paintings. KELDUR, 30 miles north of Mulakot, the site of a very old farm. HVOLSVOLLUR where (apparently) Timothy had a dance – with some of the local pretty blonde girls.

GEYSIR – GULLFOSS – 'ate LARUS' canned Mutton' (Larus Oskarsson) you may gather there was no one – just sitting about! The next two days or so we recuperated, visiting old friends and families with the usual warm welcome typical of Icelanders – getting back to our genuine eiderdown, the worlds lightest of light feathers – in the early hours!

One day we awoke to find a large ex US army truck with a seagoing power boat complete with fishing radar scanners, etc., on the attached boat launching trailer, part of the original ex US army package. The sole purpose of this turned out to be to transport Timothy and me, driven by Ingolfur and his wife Helgar, to their fishing lodge, on the lakeside of Thingrallavatn, a 9 mile long by 4½ mile wide lake at Thingvellir – the site of the original, 1000+ year old Althing, Iceland's democratic parliament and a very special place to them. It is 30 to 40 miles from Reykjavik – the site, by the way is also phenomenal, being virtually surrounded by vertical stone cliffs, very high, with only one access down a very steep narrow roadway alongside, a first class defensive position, particularly in Viking times.

We arrived about ten o'clock in the evening at the lodge, with a high wind blowing and very high waves crashing onto the huge rocks all along the edge of the lake on our side. Visibility was poor mainly due to water spray – but Ingolfur immediately said we should start fishing for supper! So, clad in oil skin kit and sou'westers, we three braved the storm, while Helga prepared the table in anticipation of a fish supper. I thought we had the proverbial cat in hell's chance of catching fish in this storm on the rocks – I was wrong. Timothy was back in his childhood form, landing fish for a banquet, seemingly every few minutes. Ingolfur and I didn't do too badly either. There is nothing more satisfying than catching and cooking, and eating, fish on the riverside, as Timothy and I had done when he was much younger, with his uncle, the Rev. Tom Watson (Vicar of Monyash and other parish churches in Derbyshire) on the river Dove where Sir Isaac Walton fished, so he should be good!

Next morning the lake was a vast mirror, dead smooth and still, completely opposite in every way to the day before. We launched the boat to go to the small island in the centre – Ingolfur pointed out, in the distance, a flock of huge white geese on the still water, and signified he would steer towards them to cause them to rise. What a magnificient sight it was, touching the still water only with their wing tips at every stroke, nothing else, flying in V formation, very slowly rising in their stately silent manner – slow, beautiful motion, and not a sound, unforgettable.

Our next pre-arranged visit was to the home of the sheriff of the 'county' or area – and here I must warn you, of the errors I will probably make – we visited in the late 1960 and it is now 2008, I am using a Map of Iceland, with practically everything on it, but you need a microscope to read it.

The area we were to visit was most probably the Bogarnes area on the west coast and the sheriff's home was probably Vogalekur, on the coast. Nothing much else except sea, and a number of very small, grass-green, islands, each with one or at the most two grazing cattle – all in its own way very beautiful. We had driven well over 70 miles, not including our diversion for lunch to a hotel on the side of a deep ravine, with river running through below, and Ingolfur informed us that this hotel, and its salmon fishing rights on the river below, was the finest in the world. Membership was very selective, almost sacrosanct, Kings of Norway, Sweden, UK, and probably Winston Churchill, and saintly Citizens of Iceland *only* (and he happened to be a member) and this happened to be the place where he had caught the salmon in his refrigerator that he had shown us when we arrived, and this also happened to be the place where even high paying members were very restricted in the times they were limited to, and which they had to book months in advance, and probably arrange with even Higher Powers, to ensure the weather was in a good mood. Oh yes, one other thing, this also, by good chance, happened to be the place he had booked, a month ago, for Timothy, me, Helga, and himself, when he first invited us to Iceland and I had asked for the month's delay! As I have said once before, how daft can I get? I felt like diving into the ravine, there and then!

Somewhat mortified, but excellently wined and dined, we eventually arrived in the evening at the sheriff's home, and were introduced to his wife and two blonde Icelandic daughters, who were preparing potatoes boiled in their jacket, with the jackets while still scalding hot expertly detached, and a joint of their own farm lamb etc. We had pleasant conversation until bed under the usual eiderdown duvet. Next morning was a beautiful sunshiney day, with the mass of small islands extending, uninhabited except by the odd cow, as far as the eye could see – but also, at the sheriff's private small timber jetty, a full size sea-going fishing trawler, complete with captain and crew for Timothy and me, (and of course Ingolfur and Helga), to go fishing for halibut, the expensive, and most delicious of fish. In these waters these flat fish, bottom feeders, can be very large indeed, but I need not have worried as it turned out.

After breakfast we put to sea, going south – south by what, we were not in a position to ask. After 10 to 12 miles we arrived probably at Akranes a small town on the coast with whale landing ramp and jetty, and also a fish processing factory. Here men were busy, flensing a recently landed whale, not a pretty sight, but life, if you are a northern island fishing nation with 97 per cent of national income dependent on international exports of fish production. We then went to the modern fish processing factory nearby, and the only employer of the small towns inhabitants. Here we were shown round the immaculate factory, with the female staff also in white uniform with face masks and hair completely covered working with the latest automatic processing machines to fillet, skin, at high speed, and then pass flat on a vertical, strongly backlit, moving belt. It was being carefully scrutinised by three or four blonde girls armed with special tweezers, all darting forward removing from the white plaice fillets very small white worms, parasites, fairly obvious, when you know what to look for. I commented to the manager that I had not ever seen those before! He replied, 'Oh yes – they are harmless if eaten, just more protein, but these are going to England and they are very particular there, so we have to be very careful!' I refrained from telling him that 90 per cent of people in England would probably not even know what fish it was regardless of where it came from.

Returning to the trawler, the two crewmen were busy loading on board large cases of herring – for Timothy and me to go fishing! It was incredible – of course if the fishing was successful the trawler crew would benefit most, but we would be six line fishing and technically what we four caught was ours. We were also presented with an Icelandic special treat, which was pieces of whale blubber that had been buried, as they say in the sand. Helga said it was 'good, try some.' We did, not my best taste experience, but you must try it, to test it. Timothy chickened out – he preferred fish not 30 ton mammals, the largest beast ever on earth!

The trawler headed out to sea with the two crewmen busy cutting up the herring, to bait the hand reeled lines we were to lay on the seabed. The bait was attached to hooks on the very long lines, some apparently up to one mile, hence the very strong large reels, four in our case, slotted into the ship's side and requiring no mean effort to wind in. As it turned out, we spent the whole day at sea, backwards and forwards for many miles – my miles not nautical miles – and after reeling and reeling, apart from masses of crabs, and various other not very good denizens of the deep, not one single halibut. Even Timothy's previously mentioned junior fishing skills had gone on strike, and in this case, doubting my veracity as you may still be, I have in my mass of photos a single photograph of me, apparently holding up by the head a huge halibut, 6 feet long × 3 feet wide (approx) taken on our return to the jetty of the sheriff's house, purely for 'publicity purposes'. Of course, there is behind it a very stout post to which it is hooked, it's bigger than me, and hopefully more palatable, and I had not landed it! But again a most memorable trip for both of us.

During our two week visit we were guests also of Larus Oskarsson and family, and son, called of course in Icelandic manner, Oskar Larusson. So it has been, for probably the 1000 years since the first Larus or Oskar, arrived on the first or second Viking ship. We stayed one week with Ingolfur, and one with Larus, and we were entertained by mutual friends of theirs, and mine. Reykjavik is a small capital, where everybody knows everybody, and this probably extends to Icelanders country wide. The total population nationwide, was a little more than 120,000 when the British army invaded in 1940 – and were ignored by the population for some time. The population in Reykjavik is not Iceland, it is vastly different, and in WWII it had to be occupied. Thank god we then had government that was desperately trying to do the right thing, unlike the present situations in Iraq and Afghanistan – it had to be occupied, and if Germany, who had for some years been wooing the Icelanders by various means, had taken it first, the subsequent Battle of the Atlantic would have been won by Germany.

We were taken to some of the best hotels at that time in Iceland, such as the Borg Hotel, Island Hotel, and others, also particularly one of the first Icelandic equivalents of a night club, good restaurant, dance floor, etc., but to the best of my memory, no gambling, and, in our case, very good company, a dozen of us at least and all at one table.

I am very pleased to report, as part of the Good Life of my life, that I was able in the following summer to invite Ingolfur and Larus, and their respective wives, to the then reasonably united, United Kingdom, and able to take them round to admire our country then, with pride, while staying at Tree Garden, and/or Gerald's Badsworth Grange, at dates of their choosing, as it was with myself and Timothy.

I collected Ingolfur and Helga at a hotel near Birmingham and drove them back to Wakefield by the most picturesque route possible, with plenty of trees, landscape views, including the Strines, south of Sheffield, an up hill and down dale and stream, masses of conifers, and many other types of trees Icelanders revere trees! Larus and his wife arrived at Tree Garden under their own steam, to the best of my recall, a month or so later including visiting our Filey house, a very good time was had by all, including Gerald, Maria, and Tim and me.

Girlfriends were on the agenda for Timothy, now age 19, and Maria and I were occasionally going for 'maintenance purposes' to Filey, alone – returning to Tree Garden to find the well camouflaged evidence of a clean up, after the 'party', but the damage was sustainable. I had, as yet, met no girlfriends, Maria may have, during my absence during the week, I don't know, I was not there. However, the day came when I was there, and Timothy arrived with his girlfriend, Sandra Elizabeth Nicholson, a very perky, very pretty, trainee hairdresser and stylist, at Wakefield's best salon. As the crow flies, she lived only about 200 yards from Tree Garden. I had no idea how long this had been going on, and of course I dare not ask, leaving it all to Maria, knowing her infallible judgement would prevail, after all, she had married me! Sandra was the first one, so from my point of view there was plenty of time, there may be others, who knows?

Sandra was the youngest, only daughter, with two elder brothers. Father worked for Slater & Crabtree, Precision Engineers, Wakefield, all upstanding citizens, and me a poor Yorkshire boy with only one vote. I kept quiet, I know my place, there could be three ganging up on me, possibly, in dire straits, even five more people, and Sandra alone had a no nonsense, firm Yorkshire accent. Poor Tim!

However, again, I need not have worried, all was sweetness and light. Maria thought she was fine, irrespective of any quibbles, and how right she was, Sandra was to become a paragon of virtue, in spite of everything, and thank the Lord, still is. Lucky Tim!

Timothy was by now working in my Huddersfield office as an architectural technician, and Sandra was continuing her training in the health and beauty field. They had their parties at Tree Garden, when Maria

160

and I were at Filey, or Maria, Gerald, and myself were otherwise engaged at Badsworth Grange at weekends, or on short breaks in Scotland, or Northumberland – sometimes very short. In due course Sandra was to open her own salon in Westgate, Wakefield next door to the Theatre Royal, architect, Frank Matcham, designer of Buxton Opera House and London Paladium etc.

HASS (Huddersfield Architects Students Society) was formed and originated in the early fifties by a small group of HSA students – who then presented me with the No 1 membership card enthroned in a clear plastic case. I still have it in my collection of various memorabilia presented to me by students at varying times over many years, culminating in an amazing and very vindicating occasion. I had escaped from my sick bed to attend a dinner and presentation on my retirement on December 31st 1971, details of which in a later chapter will (without any more Vs, hopefully) include probably the first 'student sit in' in modern UK history! Education Minister, MP Margaret Thatcher, later Prime Minister Thatcher, Director Durrands (ex Vickers Armstrong engineers Leeds) – ex Labour Party MP Minister of State of the DES Gerald Fowler (complete with his desk mounted, red dispatch box) Assistant Director Mr J.P.W. Mallalieu MP (Huddersfield East) the uncle of Tony Mallalieu one of my students, Chief Huddersfield Education officer Mr H. Grey, Dr 'Dirty Digger' Armstrong, (Australian visitor and Assistant Director) Alderman Sissons, Chairman of Governors, and, with greatest respect and sincere apologies, HM The Queen!

HASS initiated the Annual Architects Dinner, probably the first annual student dinner ever arranged, post WWII. Members of staff, wives, girl and boy friends, guests were invited to various hotels, restaurants and dining halls – dependent on the state of student finances at the time, but I am sure there was never a missed year. After a good dinner, with wine, coffee, the entertainment mainly consisted of a good going over of the staff, including various pantomime performances by the students at the staff's expense, my speech of welcome to wives, and guests – including staff wives, and my wife, and me, who were also, remember, guests. One year the dinner was held in a restaurant in the very centre of Huddersfield, owned by Mr Haigh, a building contractor, whose son was a student at the school. The restaurant was spacious with one quarter of its total length forming an entrance bar area, with sliding, folding, timber doors across the full width of the rooms. For this year, having been invited a fortnight before the event, I decided to do something different. I would write a poetic dissertation. Now I love good poetry, I have a very good collection – from Omar Khayyam to

161

Samuel Taylor Coleridge to Shakespeare, etc., etc., all favourites – but I am about as good a poet as I am a writer. If you have read up to this point, you will appreciate my problem. However, I decided to write a few four-liners as per The Rime of the Ancient Mariner, of which there are nineteen and one six liner. So I would keep it simple stupid – KISS – and write it on a pale blue toilet roll, one stanza per segment. Now there are a lot of segments in toilet rolls, as you will be aware.

Before I started at the college I was driving a Riley 9 'Kestrel' 1930 Model, vintage car, nineteen coats of paint on an aluminium body before leaving the factory, coach built, with ash upper frame, covered with top quality inner and outer fabrics, sliding roof, leather racing seats, headlamps as big as some of today's car wheels, and all today's mod cons etc., all from my dear friend, the late Ted Neal, master engineer, previously mentioned, for the princely sum of twenty pounds!

As I drove the Riley to and fro, on my mainly country route, I would think of a line, or even two, stop the car at the side of the road and jot down the line, or two, on my note pad then continue, until the next so called brain wave. Came the students dinner and my time to perform, I produced the pale blue, and allowed it to roll across the table somewhat, in a casual manner, put on my best poet's voice – and enunnunciated, in my hope of getting my own back, at least. So far so good, but as I was coming to the best bits, near the end, with an almighty crunching and crashing, the sliding wall partition came into the room, opening from the bottom of the doors, followed by the heads and shoulders of Trevor Drinkwater and A.N. other, third year students, now suitably wedged to the floor. Apparently the end door was locked and they wanted to get at me before I finished – they were duly extricated, and I don't think they ever booked that room again – good job Brian's father was a builder!

HSA students also organised a series of public dances, (proceeds to charity) as cuttings, ex *Yorkshire Post*, or *Huddersfield Examiner* show, with a photo of the Yellow Submarine and the following write up:

Students made a yellow submarine

HUDDERSFIELD architectural students had a yellow submarine of their own to sing about last night.

And if it wasn't quite big enough for them all to live in, it was certainly the "hit" of the evening at their Pop Pirate dance.

The 16ft-long submarine, suspended from the ceiling by steel hawsers and surrounded by floating model mermaids and fish, hung above the 350 dancers in the "Students" Union hall, Princess Street.

Students from the School of Architecture took a week to make the submarine and other decorations as "part of their studies."

The fancy dress dance, a sell out several days ago, was the first to be held by the Huddersfield Architectural Students' Society for a few years.

Victor Box and the Blue Train and Dino and the Travellers played for dancing.

In later years there were others, and again proceeds to charity, particularly the Nighty on the Nile, held at the Salvation Army timber meeting hall, which also had a fifty yard long enclosed, timber access ramp from the street to the hall, which students covered with a good layer of sand up to the hall level, with our few female students suitably attired in Egyptian artifacts decorating the hall and ramp.

There was also the Untouchaball following the very popular gangster TV programme with actor Elliot Ness, as the Untouchable G Man of the 1920s. For the promotion of this dance, a second year student Gillian Tewkesbury, Gnessy, cut out in fawn material, and machined, dozens of fabric mens ties on which Russell Lumb, an ex Leeds Grammar School young man, screen printed a design in black of a gangster with submachine gun and gangster car. Russell, by the way, is the head of my practice in Shepley near Huddersfield and has worked in this practice every vacation since becoming a student, and has continued so to do as a really first class person and architect ever since, one of the best cartoonists I know. They also made a near full size model of a 20s gangster car, suspended from the ceiling (as was the Beatles' yellow submarine). The greeters, on this occasion, wore dark double breasted suits, trilby hats, and were armed with submachine guns, also in timber, but painted realistically.

Then there was the Buccaneers Binge. For this HASS rented the St Patricks Catholic Church hall, a fine stone building with oak hammer beam roof construction, and which converted, internally, into the interior of a cannon armed, pirate's galleon, using the end rolls of the *Examiner* newsprint paper, suitably decorated, to transform the hall, into a galleon. However, the Huddersfield Chief Fire Officer decided to pay a visit the day before the date – perhaps also to get some tickets I am not quite sure – and decided that the fire hazard of so much paper was too much. As last resort, we decided to spray the lot with a fire retardant spray, the show must go on, and time was of the essence, but they managed to proof at a few points which were carefully marked and which he approved when he called back later. We made doubly sure by installing extra fire extinguishers, complete with willing, stout, first year volunteers. So that turned out OK then.

HUDDERSFIELD DAILY EXAMINER
1959

Huddersfield Student To Visit Rome

MR. JOHN KEITH MALLINSON TINKER, Oak Dene, Wood-house, Shelley, a student in the Architectural Department of Huddersfield College of Technology School of Art, is to visit the British School of Architecture in Rome next Easter.

Mr. Tinker, who has just completed the five-year course in the Architectural Department and will shortly be taking his final examinations, was nominated to go to Rome by the West Yorkshire Society of Architects.

This Society subscribes an annual sum to the Royal Institute of British Architects to enable a student-member to join students from all parts of the country who have been similarly nominated for the visit.

The purpose of the award is to encourage the study of the architecture of a different clime and to profit from an exchange of views between students within the study group.

In Rome a Fortnight

Mr. Tinker, who is twenty-six, was chosen from a large number of students who were eligible for the award in this area. He will be in Rome for a fortnight.

To gain the award he had to submit drawings that he had made while a member of the Department. Some years ago Mr. Tinker won the West Yorkshire Society working drawing medal at the intermediate stage. He is the second Huddersfield student to have won the Rome award.

The West Yorkshire Society's second choice for the Rome visit is also a Huddersfield student, Mr. J.B. Hickling, of Dewsbury, who is in his fourth year in the Architectural Department.

Answers to the petrol shortage – support the Huddersfield Technical College

HUDDERSFIELD DAILY EXAMINER
28 November 1956

Yo–Ho–Ho And An Empty Tank!

Architectural Students' Union "Buccaneers' Binge" and they'll most likely send along this motley crew o'cut-throats, long boat, cannon, Jolly Roger and all to tow your car there. That is if you and your car can stand the pace. "Buccaneers' Binge," for the uninitiated, is a fancy dress dance to be held at St Patrick's Hall on Friday night. Part of the proceeds will go to the Hungarian Relief Fund.

Enough of this student frivolity, but please sir, we did have a remarkable degree of academic success. To name just a few, and some record breakers:

Leeds architecture awards

Students of the Huddersfield School of Architecture have again taken most of the honours offered annually to students by the West Yorkshire Society of Architects.

The Society's president, Mr. Kenneth Warman, Deputy City Architect of Bradford, last night presented the prizes at the Leeds School of Architecture.

School scores top again

For the second year in succession members of the Huddersfield School of Architecture have won all but one of the student prizes offered annually by the West Yorkshire Society of Architects.

The prizes were presented last night at the Leeds School of Architecture by Mr. Kenneth Warman, deputy City architect of Bradford, the president of the Society.

Architectural award means study in Rome

For the third time in recent years one of the highest architectural awards in the country has gone to a student of the Huddersfield School of Architecture.

In the past two years the School has won all but one of the annual awards of the West Yorkshire Society of Architects.

The student is Mr. Keith Heywood, aged twenty-three, 171, Hill

Rises, Netheroyd Hill Road, Cowcliffe, who has been awarded the Rome prize of the Royal Institute of British Architecture and the West Yorkshire Society of Architects.

The prize entitles him to two weeks' expenses-paid study in Rome.

Mr. Heywood recently won the West Yorkshire Society's Bedford Scholarship. He takes the first part of his final examinations this year.

HUDDERSFIELD DAILY EXAMINER

22 November 1963

Architectural students achieve record

Seven prizes out of eight

Seven prizes out of a possible eight. That is the record of the Huddersfield School of Architecture in the eighty-eighth session of the West Yorkshire Society of Architects. And that is a record achievement.

The first prize of £100 in the Bedford Scholarship competition was won by twenty-three-year-old Robert Ian Cockroft, of Flat House, Linthwaite, and the second prize of £25 went to Richard John Bramham, also twenty-three, of the White House, Barnsley Road, Clayton West.

In this competition, three students had to submit designs for an ecclesiastical college library. Earlier in the session Mr. Cockroft won the Society's Rome Scholarship, which provides facilities for two weeks' study in Rome.

His winning of the Bedford award gives another opportunity for foreign travel to carry out architectural research. One condition, however, is that he must submit a report on his return.

Girling prize

His design for an M1 motel won for David Manton Ellis, aged twenty-three, of Mount Road, Marsden, the Girling prize of £60.

Other awards made to students at the Huddersfield School were: *Working Drawings Medal* to Dennis Boothroyd, aged twenty-three, New North Road, Huddersfield.

Senior Sketching Medal to Glynne Lincoln Shackleton, aged twenty-four, Highbury House, Lower Edge Road, Rastrick.

Essay Medal to Arnold John Pacey, aged twenty-five, Rainhill Road Barnoldswick.

Junior sketching medal to Michael Richard Hallas, aged twenty, Woodside Road, Beaumont Park.

The only prize which Huddersfield students failed to win was the measured drawings medal which went to a student at the Leeds School of Architecture.

Entries from architectural colleges throughout the West Riding were judged at a meeting of the Society under the president of the Society, Mr Richard Thompson, of Leeds. Entries were made under fictitious names, the names of the actual authors being in sealed envelopes.

A record

Mr Jeffrey Walton, head of the Huddersfield School, whose building is above the Passenger Transport Depot at Longroyd Bridge, said that the achievements of the Huddersfield students were a record.

The nearest they came to such an achievement in a previous session was the winner of four prizes out of a possible six. But only five students entered.

Mr Walton emphasized that the entries were entirely voluntary.

He was extremely pleased with what had been achieved. 'We like to see the students enjoying their work and I think this is self-evident. We like to see a good relationship between the staff and students and there is no doubt that this has been achieved'.

THE YORKSHIRE POST

21 November 1963

School left just one prize behind

The Huddersfield School of architecture has missed by one a clean sweep of awards in the 88th session of the West Yorkshire Society of Architects. It is thought to be a record for one school to gain so many prizes.

Entries for the competition were assessed at a meeting of the Society under Mr. Richard Thompson, of Leeds, the president. To ensure secrecy, entries were made under a nom de plume, the names of the actual authors being in sealed envelopes.

The first prize of £100 in the Bedford Scholarship Competition was won by Robert Ian Cockcroft, 23, of Flat House, Linthwaite, Huddersfield. The second (£25) went to Richard John Bramham, 23, of The White House, Barnsley Rd, Clayton West, Huddersfield.

In this competition the students had to submit designs for an ecclesiastical college library. Earlier in the session Mr Cockcroft won the Society's Rome Scholarship, which provides facilities for two weeks' study in Rome.

Another chance

His latest award provides a further opportunity for foreign travel, to do architectural research. One of the conditions is that he must submit a report on his return.

The Girling Prize (£60) was awarded to David Manton Ellis, 23, of Mount Rd, Marsden, Huddersfield. The subject in this competition was a design for an M1 motel.

Other awards made to students at the Huddersfield school were: The Working Drawings Medal—Dennis Boothroyd, 23, of New North Rd., Huddersfield; Senior Sketching Medal—Glynn Lincoln Shackleton, 24, of Highbury House, Lower Edge Rd., Rastrick, Brighouse; Essay Medal—Arnold John Pacey, 25, of Rainhill Rd., Barnoldswick; Junior Sketching Medal—Michael Richard Hallas, 20, of Woodside Rd., Beaumont Park, Huddersfield.

The Prize which escaped Huddersfield was the Measured

Drawings' Medal. This was awarded to Mr. V. M. Nelson, a student at the Leeds School of Architecture.

Juries Judge

Entries for the Bedford Scholarship and the Girling Prize were assessed by Mr. Arthur Arschavir, head of the Hull School of Architecture. The medal winners were selected by juries of architects.

Commenting on the awards, Mr. Jeffrey Walton, head of the Huddersfield School, said yesterday; 'This is a happy school and I think people who are happy do good work. Naturally, I am delighted that we have been so successful.'

Planning expert praises student architects

Yorkshire Post Huddersfield Staff

Mr. G. Grenville Baines last night adjudicated on entries submitted by students of the Huddersfield School of Architecture in a competition organized by the West Yorkshire Society of Architects. Mr. Baines is Planning Consultant appointed by Huddersfield Corporation in connection with the proposed redevelopment of the town centre.

A meeting of the Society, presided over by Mr. E. A. Johnson, was attended by members of Huddersfield Town Council together with Mr. C. Shaw, chairman of the recently formed Huddersfield Civic Society.

Competing teams, which each comprised four students at the school, were asked what they would suggest could be done to make St George's Square and surrounding fabric a pleasing and useful part of the Hudddersfield of the future. The square contains the Lion Buildings, the George Hotel, the Huddersfield Building society and is dominated by the railway station frontage.

Ten schemes were submitted. Dealing with them in detail, Mr. Baines said he was pleased that no one had attempted to tear down the railway station frontage. He added that in the Square was some pretty good building fabric which would be looked on with reverence even a 100 years hence.

"There is many a first-class architect who I doubt could have shown so much town planning awareness as these students," he said.

The prizewinning team was Ian Hirst 22, Tony Flesher, 20, Russell D Earnshaw, 19, and Russell Lumb, 19. Winners of the second prize were Peter Binns, 29, Miss Gillian Sharp, 20 Michael Ellerker, 19, and Frank Estcourt , 22.

In proposing a vote of thanks to Mr. Baines, Mr. J. Blackburn, Huddersfield's Architect and Planning Officer, said that the competition had shown that there was a new spirit abroad in Huddersfield so far as town planning and architecture were concerned.

Students' Work Exhibited in Art Gallery

Models of a county primary school and a church for a fishing community are two of the outstanding exhibits at the fourth annual exhibition of the School of Art, Huddersfield Technical College, in the Art Gallery, Ramsden Street.

In the interests of display and the need for a consistent level of quality the exhibition which began on Saturday and will continue until June 27, has been limited.

Therefore, all full-time and part-time courses cannot be represented, but there are examples of work from the courses leading to the final examinations for the National Diploma in design of the Ministry of Education, the Associateship of the Institute of British Architects and the Associateship of the Institute of British Decorators.

Display Works

In one gallery there are examples from the painting and decorating, printed and woven textiles, graphic design, typography, pottery and modelling, embroidery and lettering and illumination courses. Display works from the full-time and part-time courses leading to the final examination for the Associateship of the Royal Institute of British Architects occupy another gallery.

There are three-dimensional models of students' schemes, sketch designs (prepared in one or two days), historical, measured and working drawings, and complete design projects.

Examples of the pictorial arts of drawing, painting, lithography and etching are arranged in a further gallery.

Art students' display

Taste and vitality mark the exhibition opened on Saturday in the Art Gallery by students of Huddersfield Technical College. It is the work of 50 students, ranging from the first year to senior members and those in charge of the Arts Department can feel satisfied with the standard of the year's work.

There is an eye-catching display of textile design with an attractive range of colours; pottery exhibits have simplicity of line and good taste and there are some accomplished examples of typography and lettering. <u>The gallery devoted to architecture is outstanding</u>. Designs by Clifford Kaye and M.J. Honigsfeld attracted a good deal of attention on Saturday, and there is some arresting work by James Andrew Buck. The pictorial section is disappointing.

As I may have said before, 'Time is of the essence'. I know, it is probably a dozen times, so I will change it for you, just this once: 'Time like an ever flowing stream bears all its sons away, they lie, forgotten,' you will know the rest – but I am afraid it's true, and this piece of downright brazen, criminal, 'academic skullduggery,' must be exposed, if it is the last … it's wise not to tempt Providence!

The government at this time was considering upgrading suitable technical colleges, in due course, to polytechnics. This possibly happened at Huddersfield with the retirement of the Principal Dr W.E. Scott and/or, the renaming of the Technical College to the Ramsden College. I, as Head of the HSA was never ever involved in any aspect of the promotion to polytechnic status and it was only some time later when I had a meeting with Mr H. Grey, chief Education Officer and Secretary to the Board of Governors, that he informed me that 'Without your school of Architecture students there would be no Polytechnic!' Not previously having even had a visit by the college principal, Dr W.E. Scott, in all my years at Longroyd Bridge (I went to see him at his office, or wrote to him many times) at least someone with full information and involvement appreciated our efforts. And then we had a change of government. There has never been a Labour government, that has not left this sovereign UK since its inception last century in a complete and utter mess – and I am not a member of any party. We have only now, just finished a fortnight of an unelected Prime Minister, since the exit, after ten years, of President/Dictator Blair – and we had still better take very great care, it can still happen. There is also the

EU (European Union) striving to nullify every thing we in the UK hold dear, with fake constitutions promoted by the German president.

DAILY MAIL

25 July 2007

Price of Liberty

They defeated Nazi Germany, Imperial Japan and Fascist Italy. But now they've met their match – in the health and safety inspectors of Lancashire.

British Legion war veterans in Horwich have been told they can't hold their annual Remembrance Day Parade unless they stump up £18,000 for security. So they've had to cancel it.

Can you blame them if they look back on everything they risked for our liberty – and wonder why they bothered?

DAILY MAIL

25 July 2007

Further to the caning book of 1902, I was at a boarding school in the UK and then in Melbourne, Australia, from 1935 until I went into the Navy in 1942.

Caning up to six on the backside was common. House prefects and masters carried out the punishment.

At night time, caning was more painful, as one wore only pyjamas.

We understood the system and were quite happy if caught disobeying rules to receive the punishment, and, of course, compare wounds afterwards.

If we were caught being naughty in the dorm at night, the culprit was asked to come forward.

Sometimes the whole dormitory stepped forward rather than snitch, knowing we would be lined up outside the master's study and all given three of the best.

I am now 82 and it did me no harm, but taught me respect for others and for rules.

That is, of course, before we had the present dictatorship introduced by New Labour and the EU.

Now, nobody takes any notice of such things.

PETER FALSHAW,
Shuttington, Nr. Tamworth.

Some very funny things happen on the way to the Colosseum. Suddenly the Polytechnic had a Director, previously it was Head or Principal or even Professor, no Director. One was Mr K.J. Durrands (no affixes), just Director – apparently, he had previously been in the employ of the Leeds Engineering Firm of Vickers Armstrong Ltd, Battle Tank manufacturers to H.M. Government – which had only recently been kicked out of office, and he was soon followed by, surprise, surprise, an ex. Labour M.P. and ex. Minister of State at the D.E.S. (Department of Education and Science) Gerald Fowler, who, for all I know may have arrived by tank. I do not recall seeing any 'Educational,' 'Situations Vacant,' 'Appointments,' in any other National or Local Newspapers, – and then we had yet another one, believe it – Assistant Director. He came from Australia, where the government had driven out of the country architect Bjorn Utzon, designer of the world famous Sydney Opera House, of course aided and abetted by some more engineers.

During Session 1958/59, I had been appointed to the Schools Committee of the Board of Architectural Education and the Scholarship Committee of the Royal Institute of British Architects at Portland Place, London, a fine Building and Headquarters of the R.I.B.A.

Coincidentally, in the same session (1958/59), 'The Principal's Report of the College of Technology,' by Dr W.E. Scott, (page 9) reads:

Architecture Students visited Imperial Chemical Industries Limited, Billingham Works, the Manchester Building Exhibition, the Le Corbusier Exhibition in Liverpool and examined buildings at Fountains Abbey, Ripon and York. Smaller groups of students got further afield in the summer vacation e.g., Watson and George visited Greece and the Aegean. It is good to note the active participation of our students in the Huddesfield Branch of the West Yorkshire Society of Architects – not only in competition work but in the reading of papers to the Society. Other student activities included lunchtime debates, the showing and criticism of some fifty films of technical and artistic content, and a Dinner and Dance. The 'live project' mentioned in last year's report has now been successfully completed.

It is a matter of regret that this active and enthusiastic section of the College's work is housed so far away from the main College. Architecture embraces so many facets of art and technology that its study should take place in proximity to that of other disciplines, with mutual benefit to all concerned.

I agree completely with the statement in the above excerpt, but cannot agree with the last two lines – what 'disciplines?' The College is a perpetual daily mad house, morning to late evening, except possibly Sunday. I have not, I don't think, ever been there then. Also excepting, the Music Department which, should be School of Music, and perhaps the School of Art, which is in my experience often too quiet for its own good – on holiday perhaps? The passing mention of the 'Live Project' is of a unique project which I was able to have students undertake – a local businessman asked me if I would, as a wedding present, design a house for his daughter, on a site on his own small estate in Huddersfield. You will recall I insisted on being able to practise when appointed, and I had completed some projects, but this was the first time I had one, very local, client and I managed to persuade him to let me use third and fourth year students in a competition to design, specify and supervise the building under construction. The winner was Michael Butterworth, who was then to practise, and I hope still does, in York as I also hope the happy couple, still live in the house. Also on the same page is a reference to students going to see 'Othello' at Stratford on Avon with Paul Robeson, the famous singer, basso profundo, and stage and film actor – one of my favourites – whom I met that same year at the Queens Hotel in Huddersfield when he invited me to join him at lunch. He had just recently been allowed to leave the USA and travel abroad, after being restricted for many years, suspected of Communist sympathies – he was one of the nicest people I have ever met.

One of the assistant directors, the one with the red box screwed to the table, invited me to his office, for a 'chat'. I arrived, there was another assistant director present, and also a tape recorder running somewhere – in the red box possibly – it was early days, but I decided to come suitably equipped on my next visit, just in case.

The Polytechnic was designated in 1970, but due to increasing staff and student members I was obliged to agree to HSA being returned to the poly campus. Some two to three years earlier, in 1967/68 session, with Dr Scott as Principal, as there was 'classroom capacity' available in new buildings. We are now in 1970/71 session with the three directors, and Mrs Thatcher MP was Minister DES. She did in fact present the main academic, music, artistic awards, and other awards, at which event I was introduced to her, as were some of HSA students who received RIBA awards.

Since the arrival of the 'Board of Directors', meetings of the 'Board of Studies', of which heads of departments were members, were held. These I regret to say were by no means happy meetings – certain heads having been interviewed by the 'directorate' and left in no doubt about their position in the future, prior to the next meeting, and so they became yes men for the pre-arranged agenda. They even agreed with the four no men when invited to deny this 'dictatorial' assault on integrity, so meetings became superfluous, 'This is it, take it, or leave it, now vote', no need to discuss it, got to move on – those in favour. A typical Maxwell (*Daily Mirror* owner) style of meeting. After the meetings, with the die cast and we were dismissed, we few no men were 'apologised' to by a few of the very larger number, saying they agreed with our stand, but were afraid of the consequences, but unfortunately, as they say 'that's how the cookie crumbles', so that's it then, as they also say. Later in the weeks when I was barred from even attending at the Polytechnic, and before I was ill, I had heads of departments coming to my practice office at New North Road, to brief me on the disastrous situation that was developing – even yes men, but also the Head of Music – a dedicated and competent artist – and the other two no men who kept me informed on the worsening situation. I also had members of my staff, particularly independent part time members – Dr Arnold Pacey (Manchester University), Harold B Morris (Liverpool School of Architecture (University), Geoffrey Bray (Arch., Structural Engineer) local, and also local artist David Blackburn, Artist in Residence before he later went to Sydney University, also as Artist in Residence, and Ian Henderson, Artist/Designer, who was with the school at this time (and knew the Director, Australian, ('Dirty Digger' Armstrong) – Ian also left after the sit-in to go to Australia and was appointed to two of the University Schools of Architecture there, and taught in the same subjects as he had with me. He was very architecture orientated, and wished he had been able to study architecture at HSA. He continued to write to me and in one particular letter said that, 'if my ears were burning, not to worry, it was only that he and his wife were having dinner at that time with Charles Moss and his wife Susan. They had met the Mosses, never before knowing them, and they would be talking about me.

The 'sit-in' began in October 1971, instigated by HASS and as you will

175

see, already supported to the full by NUS (National Union of Students) and many other bodies. HASS were responsible for there being a Students Union in the College of Technology long before the present time as the first editions, Nos 1, 2, 3, of *FACT* – presented to me in winter 1964, *FACT* 1, in which the Editor is Keith L. Harrison, union editors are Brian A. Tetley, and Peter D. Jackson, Editorial Staff, Roger S. Sawyer, David Sunderland. *FACT* 2 – President, Brian A. Tetley, Vice President, Peter D. Jackson, Press Relations Officer, Keith L. Harrison. *FACT* 3 – President, Brian A. Tetley, Vice President, Peter D. Jackson, Treasurer, Ian M. Fletcher, Press Relations Officer, Keith L. Harrison, NUS Secretary, Mike Ellerker, House Secretary, Roger Sawyer. All HSA students!

You will also see from the following press cuttings at that time, that Director Durrands states that 'I had been informed by letter'. I never ever received ANY Form of communication from Durrands by ANY means – not even being barred from the Poly and the HSA and barred from seeing the RIBA panel visiting all the listed schools, comprising Alex Gordon, Jack Napper, Elizabeth Layton, RIBA Secretary – NONE of whom had been to the HAS before, EVER, for 23 years – Elizabeth Layton, a person I had met on a number of occasions during my 'Heads of Schools of Architecture Committee' meetings at Portland Place. On my last meeting I invited her to lunch at the White House Hotel, 300 yards away from the RIBA HQ, which was then very good. I have no idea what it is like now, but she will recall that, Mrs Fanny Cradock, the most popular cook on TV at that time (but not accompanied by 'Johnnie'on that occasion,) was shown to the next table to us.

Takeover threat by students

By MICHAEL PARKIN

Architectural students at Huddersfield Polytechnic threatened to take over the administration block at the polytechnic today unless the board of governors accepted their demand for the immediate enrolment of a first-year intake of students in the school of architecture for this year.

The governors rejected this demand. They stated that the enrolment of a first-year intake for the next academic year (1972–73) would depend on "a very considerable improvement" in 1972 on the results of the 1971 RIBA Part 1 examinations, in which only 33 per cent of the students passed wholly or in part.

176

The RIBA has given Huddersfield, and four other schools of architecture, until 1974 to achieve recognised status. Staff and students of the school complained that the directorate of the polytechnic recommended first-year applicants to look for places elsewhere even before the RIBA decided to give Huddersfield three years to prove itself.

Justifying this decision, the polytechnic explained that the absence of a first year intake this year would improve the staff–student ratio, one of the issues raised by the RIBA.

Mr. J. M. Walton, head of the school, said he had told the governors that the polytechnic had a moral obligation to take all 40 of its applicants this year. But the damage had by then already been done by the sending of letters recommending these first year students to apply to other schools. None of the four other threatened schools had rejected a first year intake.

Mr. Walton, officially principal lecturer in charge, calls himself "head of the school of architecture" because he has guided it for 23 years. He complained bitterly that neither he nor his staff nor his students were told of the decision not to admit a first year intake.

This was another slight to add to the one he received when the directorate, without telling him, advertised for a head of a new broadly based department, including architecture. The governors decided yesterday not to go ahead with this appointment.

The students marched to a demonstration at the administration block yesterday and left a coffin, draped with scarves and flowers, on a landing.

Mr. Mick Allison, an architectural student until recently, said: "Staff and students believe in this school and are going to fight for it. Its threatened downfall is the responsibility of the directorate which is pandering to the RIBA. The polytechnic claims to be making an effort, but there seems to be no sense in what it has done."

The director of the polytechnic, Mr. K. G. Durrans, or one of his assistant directors is to speak to staff and students of the school of architecture in an attempt to bridge the breakdown in communications.

Students lock out staff

By MICHAEL PARKIN

Students were in full control of the administration block at Huddersfield Polytecchnic yesterday, and they look like staying there until noon on Monday at the earliest.

The director, the registrar, and the administrative staff found all doors locked against them, and were forced to move into other offices on the campus.

A little man in a brown coat, a polytechnic maintenance worker, made a determined attempt to force entry by trying to unscrew locks, by trying to cut through a chain with a hacksaw blade, and, finally, by coming up through a manhole cover in a women's lavatory.

Startled women students saw the cover lifting and called for help. Other students stood on the cover, and subsequently covered it with a heavy box of paint tins. They believe that the last has not yet been heard of the man in the brown coat.

The dispute is over a decision by the governors not to take a first-year in architecture this year. The governors have emphasised that this does not amount to a decision to close the school of architecture.

The students, who seem to be existing on a diet of raw carrots, jam, baked beans, and an order at a shop for "fish and chips 67 times, please love," have given the governors until noon on Monday to accept a resolution calling on them to make immediate arrangements for a first-year in architecture.

They have also insisted that there should be no recrimination against any staff or student involved in the dispute, and they have demanded greater consultation with the staff and students before major decisions are taken.

Alderman Sisson could not understand why Mr. J. L. Midgley, a senior lecturer in architecture, should have said that he first learned of the decision on first-year students through the press. A letter on the decision had been sent immediately to the principal lecturer in charge of the school of architecture, asking him to tell his staff.

At a meeting with four of the protesting students Alderman Sisson warned them that they would be alienating public good will by interfering with a tea party for 400 distinguished guests, to be given by the mayor in the polytechnic Great Hall today, to mark the opening by the Queen of Scammonden Dam. Students are using the Great Hall as a dormitory.

He said they would be antagonising ratepayers and taxpayers, who were prepared to back the polytechnic in a 10-year programme to increase the number of full-time students to about 6,000. They were also destroying the good will of people with accommodation who were not likely to let flats and bed-sitters to students who were prepared to disrupt the work of their polytechnic.

After a short meeting the students said they would make available all the facilities needed for the mayor's tea party and for a concert on Friday and a playgroup on Saturday. But by that time the corporation had decided that it would be wiser to go somewhere else for the mayor's tea party.

TIMES HIGHER EDUCATION SUPPLEMENT
15 October 1971

ATTI backs listed schools in architecture row

The recent decision by the Royal Institute of British Architects to publish its view of the "listed schools" of architecture has met with sharp criticism from members of the Association of Teachers in Technical Institutions in the colleges concerned.

Last week there was a meeting between ATTI representatives in colleges with "listed" schools, and members of the ATTI executive. The representatives were very disturbed at the publication of the RIBA report on the five schools concerned. They emphasized that reports on colleges or departments were always normally made to the authorities in confidence. Not only had the RIBA not done this, they said, but they had issued the report before the colleges involved had had the chance to comment on it to the RIBA.

They also attacked the content of the report, especially the failure figures quoted by RIBA. RIBA say that only 23 per cent in the listed schools pass their examinations, and the ATTI members stress that "pass" in this context means "all eight papers at once". They claim that the majority of those in the remaining 77 per cent do become qualified architects (and members of the RIBA).

Their statement concluded; "The RIBA have by the publication of the report in this manner and at this time prejudiced the possibility of the schools gaining recognition. They have prejudiced the recruitment of the students, of staff, and of resources. They have cast unwarranted slurs on the professional abilities and qualifications of staff. Furthermore, they have given no indication, other than misleading statistics, of the standards they expect before recognition is granted."

A spokesman for the RIBA said that the Institute had been misrepresented enough already, and he had no further comment to make. The executive committee of the ATTI are meeting tomorrow to consider further action.

HUDDERSFIELD'S SCHOOL OF ARCHITECTURE

A proud record in spite of big difficulties

After the recent disagreement between the students and the authorities, the very mention of any sort of a sandwich at the Huddersfield College of Technology is probably still a thorny subject.

But, for want of a less controversial word, "sandwiched" could aptly be used to describe the life of one of the departments of the College – the School of Architecture.

Before the war, when it was run by Mr. Norman Culley and when there were not so many budding architects about, it was one of the smallest departments occupying one of the smallest rooms at the College.

The immediate post-war years brought a boom in the number of architectural students, particularly men returning after serving in the Forces, and so an old dye-house was converted to cope with the influx.

At the same time, Mr. Jeffrey Walton became the first architect to be appointed on the staff in a full-time capacity.

Accommodation "pretty grim"

"The accommodation in those days was pretty grim," recalls Mr. Walton, who has been head of the School since Mr. Culley retired. "The equipment was very poor and the roof leaked in sixty-six

180

places – I marked them all one lunchtime! For people who were studying how to design buildings that would stand – and were watertight – it was something of an architect's nightmare."

At that time there were about ten full-time students and fifteen part-timers, but as the number increased the need for more accommodation became imperative.

The result is that now the school – officially part of the School of Art – is far removed from the main College, and certainly in less ostentatious surroundings.

A solution to its "growing pains" was found by tucking it away in part of a building at the Longroyd Bridge bus depot.

"Ironically, the building was designed by an ex-student of the School," Mr Walton said. "The part we have now was intended originally as a social club for the bus men, but it turned out to be something of a white elephant, as they did not use it much.

Still cramped

"It is an improvement on the old place, but we are still terribly cramped for space, considering that the number of students has gone up steadily to eighty-five, of whom over sixty are full-time.

"We could have many more because the school has gained the reputation of being one of the best of its kind in the country, but the accommodation problem is so acute that applications for places have to be vetted very carefully."

Some of the more advanced students are able to work in the small studios, but the lack of accommodation is such that most of them, whether in their first, second or third year, are crowded in one room.

"In spite of the handicaps, I think we can be proud of the record of the school,' said Mr. Walton.

"We have former students throughout the length and breadth of the land working in practically every field of the profession – with banks, local authorities, breweries, the Atomic Energy Authority, nationalized industries and private firms. To name only two, Mr. Ralph Hudson was the architect in charge of designing the new civic centre in Huddersfield, and Mr. John Womersley became Chief architect of Sheffield.'

High standard

The School is one of only three listed in the country for twice-yearly visits by two examiners from the Royal Institute of British Architects.

The high standard set by the students is indicated by the fact that the lowest mark given by these examiners for design studio drawing is 93.7 per cent – and they have reached a peak of 99.3 per cent. And the pass level in RIBA examinations is more than double the national average of about 33 per cent.

As well as that, some of the top prizes in examinations and competitions have been won by students.

These achievements have been gained with what Mr. Walton considers is the smallest full-time staff for a school of its size in the country.

Apart from himself, there are two full-time lecturers – Mr. J. M. Midgley, a former Deputy Borough Architect of Dewsbury, and Mr. G. G. Furness, a Huddersfield man who studied at the School.

In addition, there are five part-timers – Messrs. G. B. Bray, H.V. Morris, J. S. J. Horsfall (all ex-students), Dr. A. Pacey and Mr. J. Carruthers.

Big reputation

They are in charge of a pretty cosmopolitan bunch of students – from afar afield as Poland, Greece, Iraq, Lebanon, Kenya, Ghana, Sierra Leone and Egypt, as well as from many parts of England, Scotland and Wales.

"With people from so many places working together, I think the interchange of ideas helps their studies," Mr. Walton says.

"I don't think the importance of the School is fully appreciated locally.

"But its reputation is known throughout the country. Only recently, I had a letter from a man of fifty who is prepared to give up his job as a senior civil servant in order to take a course in architecture here.

"We may be handicapped for space, but that sort of thing makes us appreciate the high standing the School enjoys."

3 JOBS HELP WIN PRIZE

STUDENT BEATS 800 COMPETITORS

Yorkshire Post Huddersfield Staff

Because he wanted to do something creative, Mr. Dennis Boothroyd, 23, of New North-Rd., Huddersfield, decided to return to full-time study. This meant exchanging one job for three to help pay his way.

Mr. Boothroyd, ex-GPO engineer, became a library assistant, a petrol station attendant, a newsboy and, of course, a student. Last night, Mr. Boothroyd, who studies at the Huddersfield School of Architecture, learned that he had won the Sir Bannister Fletcher prize for 1963.

The prize is awarded to the student with the highest marks in the intermediated examinations – there are two each year – of the Royal Institute of British Architects. It is the first time it has been won by a student at the school.

Mr. Jeffrey Walton, head of the school, said last night: "I am delighted with this latest prize, for it demands a great deal of enthusiasm for someone to give up a good job to return to full-time study.

HARDEST PRIZE

"I think this is the hardest prize to win. This year 845 students took the intermediate examination, so it is a real achievement."

Mr. Boothroyd has spent five days and two evenings each week at the school. When he enrolled he was awarded a bursarship worth £50 a year to work in the library of Huddersfield Collge of Technology for 10 hours a week.

"That occupied each lunchtime and two evenings a week," he explained. "For Saturdays I got a job as a petrol station attendant, and on Sundays a newspaper round. I still have these last two jobs."

In a few weeks' time Mr. Boothroyd leaves the school. He will join an architect's office in Exeter. Then he will have a new spare-time activity – house hunting.

Architects argue

THE ARCHITECTURAL ASSOCIATION has just appointed a new principal for its School, the oldest biggest and probably the best school for architects in the world. He is Doctor Otto Koenisgsberger, head of the School's tropical department.

This news marks the latest development in a row which has split the School for the last three years. The argument is, should the School become part of London University thereby losing some of its independence but gaining financially?

The new appointment is temporary, because the School's future is still not officially certain. But bar the shouting, it appears to be all settled, says Tim Heald.

"There seems every reason for confidence that the School will be absorbed into Imperial College," says Mr. Edward Carter, the School's Director. 'We are just waiting for the final word from the Government.'

There are still, of course, some architects who are not sold on the idea. One of its most convinced opponents is Mr. Cedric Price who recently left the school after teaching there for seven years. "Personally, I would rather be tossed into a vat of crazed elephants than join the University structure.

"Instead of the amalgamation, I would like to see much closer links between the existing schools of architecture in the country."

Mr. Price has evolved his own solution, his "National Schools Plan", which will be published shortly in an architectural journal.

"Whatever happens", he says, "I want to keep architectural training *out of the hands of University wine and food Socialists from Hampstead.*"

Throughout my years at the HSA at Longroyd Bridge, I had been responsible, of my own volition, for all the various arrangements necessary for yearly visits by RIBA Examiners and sometimes twice yearly, by them, and other distinguished members – including meeting them at railway stations and transporting them to the school, and eventually back to the station on return, taking ALL of them, and at least one member of my staff, for a very good lunch, with wine at my own expense every time. I never ever was offered, asked for, or received one penny in expenses from Mr Grey's Education Dept. which I have no doubt he would have given had he known anything about it, which to the best of my knowledge he did not. By this time, what with directors and presidents – Alderman Sisson is/was a local solicitor, now President of the Polytechnic he was also a senior member of Huddersfield Conservative Party as was also Gordon Furness a member of my HSA staff for 13 years. According to the HAAS members, 1971 Christmas Issue on the cover of which I am cartooned as Father Christmas with a Medal for 23 years service, and Gordon Furness is shown as having two faces, one on his body, the other a 'mask' held in his hand – two faced! And so it was to turn out – just as it had 13 years earlier with the same personalities Sisson and Furness. The Technical College under Dr Scott, following my request for another member of staff, had advertised the position for the 1959/60, session, and I was of course a member of the interviewing panel, along with Dr Scott, and some of the governors, including, I was later told, Alderman Sisson, whom at that time I did not know.

Most unusually, there were only two applicants for the position, neither of whom I had ever met, or knew anything about, before this meeting – I had not even seen any application forms or CVs, perhaps not surprising, when there were only two! I regret to say, I have no record of the name of the first applicant interviewed – I cannot forget the fact that this person's attitude, qualifications, bearing and personality were all first class, and schools of architecture far more fortunate than mine would, I am sure, welcome him on their staff. I wish I knew who he was now, particularly at this time. The second applicant was a very different personality, and – please remember I had no knowledge of either – was Mr Gordon Furness. His interview was much shorter – and I do not know now whether it was at this time I learned that he was a one day, 'part time' lecturer at Huddersfield Technical College, Building Department, or some time later, when I was also to learn that he was also a member of the aforesaid Huddersfield Conservative Club and Friend of Alderman Sisson. Interviews ended, I left the governors, and Dr Scott, in no doubt whatsoever that I considered the first applicant most suitable for the position, and, as is not usual, I was asked to leave while the governors discussed the matter.

To say I was staggered by their decision to appoint Mr Furness is mild, compared with my true feelings – *I simply could not believe it!* I had been waiting with both applicants for the decision, so the immediate shock must have shown on my face, I regret to say. With a nod to Mr Furness – and 'I will see you at Enrolment' – I at once began to commiserate with

185

the other applicant and offered to drive him to the station, which he accepted, so I was further able to express my feelings and assure him of his certain success in his future career. I meant it, but it was a very sad blow for me at that time, and little did I know it was destined to continue for some 13 years – although I did get very good full and part time staff there after. At first, unfortunately, the students knew more about Gordon Furness than I did, due to the Student Union connection, ours and theirs – but I soon started learning. At the beginning of enrolment I asked him to take our Acoustics of Buildings, Auditoria. Sorry, he had never done that. History of Architecture? – no not that either, and so it went on, until in desperation I suggested Building Construction and Materials – which I later discovered he had 'lectured in', one day per week.

Again, unfortunately, from the HAS and the students' and staff's point of view, and professional reputation he was a disaster. Lampooned regularly and in no way respected – which of course, particularly in university level education, is vital. All I could do was use him in areas where he could do least damage. I was not able to fire him – and there were times when I had 'all on' to prevent him being used as the guy, on the annual charity bonfire we held each year, on Castle Hill, by Victoria Tower, south of the town! The following is an excerpt signed by *SPLAT!* from 'the HASS Christmas Issue – printed on red card. On the reverse is 'How to make your Director Work for you': a cardboard cut-out, 'pin jointed' with pull string control, to work the arms and legs of 'Director' Durrands. So much for respect!

You will recall, I had been barred from meeting the RIBA examiners, and also the HAS which was, you will also recall, no longer at Longroyd Bridge, but at the 'New' Polytechnic – now even more of a madhouse than the Technical College had been. I was coming from my original office at 14A, Bond Street, Wakefield to my office at New North Road, Huddersfield, on a daily basis. I was kept well informed on the state of the sit-in by both heads of departments, and some members of my staff and of course students.

You will I hope be interested to learn, that within (approx) the next six months, I was to read in the press that there had been another sit-in warning by the HAS and polytechnic students. Reason – the Minister for the Department for Education and Science, the Polytechnic Governors, Huddersfield Corporation, The Defence Minister (Tanks), even the Royal Institute of British Architects, unfortunately I know not who, had decided perhaps enough was enough, and proposed to terminate Director Durrand's employment in education, with apparently a generous financial

186

payment, to facilitate this most unusual action. But the Students had had much more than enough, this was an insult to them, and many others receiving an education, at the taxpayer's expense, and already grossly under funded, long overdue action. They would not accept he be 'paid off' with such a large sum of money. It *must* be reduced, considerably, and more than halved – and it was. What happened to the rest of the directors and their hangers on, I do not know, it has had 'university' status for some years, and there was no possibility whatsoever of my ever agreeing to going back to the polytechnic with the then Board of Governors and the Directorate in charge, and I have never been back there since.

Of course, all this skulduggery, previously mentioned, was just part of the 'Directors' and ex Ministers and even 'hangers on' objectives, not for a polytechnic, but, knowing the late governments forward planning legacy, for a university.

I did, however, have one very interesting experience when University status had been given – I received a phone call from the new Professor of Architecture Mr B. Edwards, who informed me that he had recently bought the house in Almondbury, near the university, that I was architect for, from Mr Ron Sample a quantity surveyor friend of mine, who did our quantity surveying, before we got our own quantity survey staff at our Huddersfield office. He was ringing me to tell me how delighted he was, and Ron Sample had even left him my framed, full colour, perspective drawing, of the house – long before computer-generated colour perspectives of today. He would be very pleased if I would join them for dinner as soon as convenient, he would ring me again later to arrange, etc. – or as usual, words to that effect – as I have had many times over the years from clients, all of whom I am pleased to say are at this time my friends, that is of course, those who are still with us. There was only one difference in this case – he never contacted me again – I wonder why. But now we may have something else in common, other than a house and a school of architecture.

Since the 1940s I have pointed out, sort of, in passing, that students in the USA have all been to college – when they mean possibly, at best, equivalent to our *then* grammar schools, and even these days, also, in my opinion, you can't 'build' universities – remember, 'It is not what you call a thing, it is what it really is that matters'. Children go to kindergarten, primary schools, secondary schools, grammar schools, in this case, hopefully, but not perhaps for long, to 'learn how to learn', as pupils. They then, some of them, are accepted at our traditional universities, as students and adults, simplified, they then have the free choice to either get on, or get out, be successful, or be sent down or fail. Universities also have traditions – as do similar institutions world wide, Oxford, Cambridge, Edinburgh – M.I.T., Harvard, Yale, Sorbonne, at the close of the fifteenth century, the University of Paris could boast fifty colleges and 20,000 students.

I recently, June 2007, received the well presented and colourful booklet 'Architecture Week' 2007 – June 15th to 24th. Yorkshire's Urban Picnic – 'Eat in the street' (the pages are sprinkled with small ants everywhere) 'featuring the ever-popular RIBA Architect in the House' – (Founding Patron) Janet Street-Porter, no less, and five others – 'Views expressed are not necessarily those of Arts Council England.'

On the back and cover are listed 80 Diary of Events – Yorkshire, including all universities, the entry for Huddersfield reads – Architecture in the Gallery Huddersfield Art Gallery 15, 16, 18–23 June. The Education of an Architect University of Huddersfield 18–21 June. HSA exhibited every year, for nearly 20 years for weeks, with models and first class projects in this same gallery, many of them transported by pony and flat cart, by Trevor Drinkwater from his family farm, then on to the gallery. As for education, HAS had done that, been there, for 23 years and got the accolades – and it is the *only* mention of architectural 'education' in the booklet!

And with that, I will bid a bitter sweet, fond farewell to what has been over one quarter part, continuous, of my life, to this day – Sunday August 19th 2007. On which, by sheer chance, I have been very happy to have the company for lunch of Russell Lumb ARIBA and his wife Susan.

Turning over a new leaf – you will I am sure have noticed that things can happen together, in parallel, in and out, up and down, rich and poor, then and now, good and bad, and even if and but, amongst very many more so far in these pages. I have been guilty of inserting sections and items because I have just remembered them at that time and it is convenient to me and saves having to remember later on. I am also guilty of digressing in my face to face conversation – something apposite comes to mind. Very few people phone you (except by arrangement) at your convenience – it is usually at theirs, like my insertions, my apologies, as I am sure will happen again!

So to inventors and makers of underground mining machinery of all types – Mr Richard Sutcliffe 1849–1930, arrived in England for the first time in August 1885, and worked in the coal mining industry in Ireland from leaving school and eventually as manager. In 1905 he returned to

England and patented a number of inventions and also eventually selected a factory at Horbury, 2½ miles from Wakefield. Actually, the Universal Works as he called it, was mainly in Horbury and partly in Wakefield (he invented, amongst other things, the world's first underground mining conveyor) and it was at the rear of this factory where the old mill dam was situated, that I worked one Summer, on hols from Crossleys and at Danum Mount, just 300 yards from the factory, which at the rear overlook the rolling fields of the Stanard Well area, Horbury.

The mill dam was about 30 yards long and 15 yards wide, lined with york stone paving slabs 2 inches thick, with sloping sides and was fed by a continuous supply, summer and winter, from a spring (Stanard Well), which also maintained a fixed temperature the year round – not that we checked it much in the winter! And I know this because I helped, during my long summer hols from Crossleys at age 14, to clear away the accumulation, due to long years of disuse, of mud and detritus which was a good topping for the very fortunately, adjacent, large allotment of Mr Raby, father of my good friend Billy, who also helped, and lived near me on Benton Hill. The good supply of strawberries etc. was very much appreciated as an incentive, and also convenient, as was the private swimming pool, the 'well' washed york stone slabs provided.

Nearby, at the end of the single storey, north light bays of the factory, Mr R. Sutcliffe had bought over 30 years earlier, was the gas engine he also bought to power his machinery, in a corrugated iron protective enclosure, and this on occasion I was able to use as a changing hut, along with my lifelong friend and later client, Miss Molly Hartley, Head Girl at Wakefield Girls High School, and a few years older than me. Like the adjacent strawberries, very pleasant indeed –the only snag was the loud TERR-PUTT, TERR-PUTT, TERR-PUTT of Mr Sutcliffe's gas engine!

I had started practising in the early 1950s, as a one man band, and one of my early commissions was a house for Mr and Mrs Harold Streets. Mr Streets was Director of Engineering at the Horbury factory of Richard Sutcliffe & Company Ltd. I produced, as I always endeavour to so do, the preliminary, ⅛″ = 1 foot drawings, in colour, of plans, elevations, sections, landscape gardens layout. All were to presentation standards, and after some time spent in describing them, for example, pointing out to Harold that on the terrace, 'there he was, on a deck chair with a parasol and a glass of gin and tonic on the table,' (at ⅛″ to 1 foot) he said, 'They are just what we want, first class, I am delighted,' or again, words to that effect, only more so. 'There is, I am afraid, one thing wrong – I am a Chapel lay preacher, and I do not drink!'

In due course, the house was well built by a local contractor, ready for Queen Elizabeth's coronation in 1953. I had designed various mirrored pieces of built-in hardwood furniture, dressing tables, wardrobe mirrors etc., engraved with the date and royal emblems, which Mr and Mrs Streets were very pleased with, along with en suite bathrooms, fitted kitchen, with Aga Cooker, Aga central heating and hot water boiler long before fitted kitchens were even thought of. Eventually my wife Maria and I were invited to the house warming party – all very pleasant.

There was, however, a not pleasant, even if slightly amusing incident, some months later Mrs Streets, having prepared breakfast (Harold having walked the 200 yards to his office at RSL) locked the house and went out shopping – but fortunately decided to return home, unlocked the door and found the house on fire. She had left the lower draft door on the Aga fully open. I don't know whether she closed it then, I do know she rang me (long before mobile phones) to inform me the house was on fire, and would I come quickly. I asked if she had rung the fire brigade. No! By now I hope you will know I always try to do my best, but I am not superhuman. I told her I would do it, and to get out of the house at once. I duly arrived, as soon as possible, to find she had followed my instructions to the letter as the saying goes. The firemen were approaching the front door with axes at the ready. I asked her if she had the keys? 'Oh yes, but I have locked it!' Just in time, but these things are all grist to the mill, as they say.

Here comes the 'connection' I mentioned earlier. Amongst the guests, naturally in this case, was the great grandson of Richard Sutcliffe – Mr William Fitz-Gerald Sutcliffe, youngest son of Mr R. J. Sutcliffe, Barrister-at-Law, and almost exactly my own age. Gerald had recently joined his brothers Thomas Desmond, Richard, and Dermod as a director of the company and eventually, he became chairman of the company, following the death of their eldest brother, Desmond. It is due to this simple chance meeting at this party that Gerald and his brothers' families were to become life long friends to my family and in particular, Gerald Sutcliffe. All Gerald's brothers had married and had families, unfortunately he never married, but he had the pleasure of mainly a good family relationship with his brothers and all their children, although, as with many families, there were ups and downs. Gerald eventually bought The Grange, Badsworth, West Yorkshire, then the home of the Badsworth Hunt, a small village between Wakefield and Doncaster, as a company property with grounds, and of sufficient size to entertain and lodge, if necessary, directors, customers, in the mining industry both in the UK and abroad, Canada, South Africa, Australia – and friends and family of course.

After the initial employment of a dishonest couple as housekeeper and gardener, who only lasted in his employ for a few weeks, he was fortunate, as it turned out, in obtaining the services of Mr and Mrs Laurie Pickering and small family. He was a former Yorkshire coal miner (due to pneumoconiosis) and his wife, Mrs Pickering was the very epitome of the genuine Yorkshire housewife – the best in the world. Laurie was the quiet odd job man, and gardener. Both excellent people who looked after – and were also looked after by – Gerald, until unfortunately Laurie, after many years, passed away. Mrs P. eventually retired to live with her daughter and husband in the area. We all however, were very fortunate in having many happy years Christmas, birthdays etc., countless breakfasts, lunch and dinners, cooked by Mrs P. My wife and Mrs P. exchanged recipes and gossip on a weekly basis at least! I educated Laurie on the finer points of asparagus, strawberry, and tomato culture, and tree and rose pruning, and he tried to catch me out, and get one up, as is said in Yorkshire – Boycott country, just down the road from Badsworth, near Nostel Priory – with all the Chippendale cabinet furniture and fine art and – history!

Believe it or not, I am sitting in the dining room of my house, Tree Garden, Sandal Magna, near Wakefield, writing this, with the sun shining and trees all around the house over 36 different varieties, some of which I have planted or propagated myself over the last 55 years including apples, pears, fig, walnut, horse chestnut, magnolia soulangiana, sumac, 'staghorn', elm, rowan, sycamore, hawthorn, laburnum, plum, greengage, to name but a few. While still blowing my own trumpet, I have exhibited at Covent Garden and also been a Fellow of the Royal Horticultural Society and if it had been winter with many of the trees leafless, I would be able to see Sandal Castle (300 yards away), Battle of Wakefield, 1460, where the Duke of York was killed. This is where Gerald's great grandfather Richard Sutcliffe, who also lived in the Sandal area, used to take his sons to the top of the Castle Hill, and point out to them the beauty of the Calder river and the rolling countryside, and the railway viaduct, as adding man's skills to the beauty of the scene, not the contrary. I myself, as a boy, often went to the castle to play – I am afraid, after writing these words I find it hard to believe how now, amazingly. I have checked on events in my life, and the Sutcliffe family, and factory, and Gerald and I, despite virtually living in each other's family pockets for so many years, have never ever discussed any of the various things I have just mentioned.

I wish he was here to agree that he had in fact no knowledge about any of them, in any case! Thinking about it, it is understandable. I was born in Sandal, but soon moved to Horbury, at about the same time Gerald was born in Hampstead, London and more or less stayed there, until he came to Horbury to work with his brothers at the family business, Richard Sutcliffe Ltd., in his late 20s having unfortunately failed to graduate at university, and not having in any way participated in WWII, I don't know why. Come to think of it, as I write, this again was never ever discussed, at that time or any time later, and was probably due to my personal presumption of ill health, in both cases, graduating and service in WWII, and not my business anyway, as I am sorry to say later events were to perhaps give credence.

So, from the age of 7 I had been living near the factory, knew some of the senior staff of the works, George Senior, managing director, and more particularly his daughter 'Girlie' Senior – Girlie, friend of one of my friends on Benton Hill, 'Fatty' Oddie who by the way was also to manage to evade service in WWII, in his case by subterfuge. He was older than me and in his late teens was responsible for some serious motor car accidents involving pedestrians etc. A few years later, he was to marry Girlie and they both eventually acquired, with substantial subsidies, Heath Hall, a fine stately home which had for many years been unoccupied, as their residence and had it restored. I could go on, but will refrain, he was part of my life – unfortunately.

In the late 1920s, the RS Ltd. works started slowly to expand from the single storey mill and the warehouse building which had been alongside the swimming pool, and both were eventually demolished. Gradually the works expanded, and in fact produced machined items for WWII, for Spitfires and Rolls Royce etc., and it was only after 1946 that Gerald, still in London, may have occasionally visited although his eldest brother William Desmond, was actively in charge of the 'works' from 1937, as a director, under his father as chairman, who as well as being a distinguished company law barrister, (company law book author), and his son, Edward D. Sutcliffe MA, Oxon., who was to become a High Court Judge at the Old Bailey, in later years, were both living in London. Also my mentor and friend, from my engineering years at Charles Roberts and Company, Henry Stead, became works manager at RS Ltd., and the majority of the directors and senior staff were comparatively local. Many had been friends of my dear wife's family (three generations), the Bains' of Horbury, special wool yarn manufacturers, Addingford Mills, Horbury and my dear mother and brother Ronald for years. So Gerald had a lot of catching up to do!

192

I was of course, in the early years, developing the HSA and also my private practice, both of which were, by this time, improving, the main effort being made at HSA and gradually my efforts in both fields began to improve, more than somewhat!

Russell Lumb is now the senior partner in the practice I started in the early fifties (John Horsfall having retired) and ever since I met him, as a first year student, he has been outstanding, both in his student years, and in all the years since at the office. He is without question our best artist architect, including me, and John Horsfall. I hope he will not object to my mentioning that, a few years ago, he underwent a triple heart valve operation, and I am delighted to say he is now his older self, with two fine graduate sons, who have since flown the coop. Russell expressed to me his despair in the state of once Great Britain, and also the attitudes of the ever growing bureaucracy of national and local authorities, in all fields including architecture, town planning, construction, public services, to name a few! So am I, and he emphasised, to my surprise I must admit, that he was really looking forward to his retirement in ten and a half months' time, things really must be getting bad! Russell was also particularly involved with me in the late sixties, in preparing, to our standards of presentation, my various sketches, for my ever more various ideas. And it was Russell who by chance pointed me in the right direction, for one of my better efforts, Speeduct. But I will start with Imperial Chemical Industries, ICI, our bluest of blue chip companies. One of their companies was interested in my recently patented group of products, as I had used and in fact specified some of their best products, and their best products are very good indeed. The ones I had used were their plastics and Melinex, a film similar but far superior to polythene, and with a much longer life in the open air, years longer, and other special properties.

ICI at that time, and to simplify, consisted of a number of 'group' companies, amongst them, chemical products, paints, fertilisers, domestic products for homes and garden products etc., all of them separate – but owned by ICI, and their success was the responsibility of each individual company. The company I was contacted by was responsible for all domestic, garden, and professional horticulture products, and their headquarter offices were in Farnham Surrey. They came to my offices at Huddersfield and were very impressed by all my different prototypes for different applications including cold frames, cloches, gro-stiks, gro-cubes, clipstik, domestic and greenhouse double or treble glazing. For over 40 years, all these products have been, and still are, in use, and without replacement, in my house and garden, Tree Garden, where I am writing this, and they are all the original items – and how about that then?

There was an exchange of visits, them to us, and us to them, and one other visit to them, but on this visit I was surprised to be introduced to a room full of people, not the two or three as usual. Some were from the continent, one a French professor, some were salesmen, all were interested in our products, which they knew all about, except greenhouses on a big scale. I then remembered that they were referring back to a telephone arranged visit by a gentleman from ICI, sales manager who had brought a series of aerial photographs of the landscape in Holland, where they *really* grow things, and from them it would appear that Holland has a big greenhouse, all over it! Polythene sheet greenhouses need re-covering after a year or two due to misting – whereas ICI Melinex was guaranteed a life of up to 15 years – could I design something to facilitate this? And I probably said Yes, or I would do my best, I can't remember. I might still have in my car boot an early model for this project. I had, so I was able to show something, it helped, and eventually near Farnham, we erected a large greenhouse with the system. The only snag was that, as built and fitted Melinex was so clear, John Lee and his small team were walking into the Melinex forgetting it was there!

ICI decided to market my roller cloche, as it was called, and they invited us down to finalise, John and I, to their town centre HQ, Farnham. They had booked at a good restaurant in the town for lunch, two of us, ten of them, ICI. All went very well, until I asked who was going to manufacture them. The general manager replied, 'I thought you were, Mr Walton!' Quick decision time, quick glance to John, across the table, 'Well all right then,' on certain conditions. OK, they knew we were architects, I don't think they were aware we also had a small company, Hobbimate Ltd. and works at Scissett, West Yorkshire, a few miles from Wakefield where we made various Hobbimate products.

We had bought the Scissett property from Mr Wray, a long established and very competent joinery manufacturer, funeral directors, builders, etc., with very good workshop premises, top class machinery, and timber storage building and stock, and, a 'chapel of rest' on a good site in a very rural setting, with a stream on one boundary, and trees all around. Mr Wray was retiring, he had two remaining tradesmen, locals whom I employed, all pleasant and peaceful. But now we would need much larger premises, and particularly in 'handling' the rolls of ICI Melinex – and a fork lift truck – and more staff!

John Lee was manager at the Hobbimate works – a man of complete

194

John Lee   Me   Paul

Hobbymate factory staff and me

integrity, very skilful in many building trades, a hard and dedicated worker. What he didn't know he very quickly learned, and he was an excellent teacher and task master. I first met him pointing a very old stone wall at the entrance to my own property Tree Garden, which needed attention, as I was driving into my drive. I went back to compliment him on his skill. I now realise how exceedingly fortunate I have been in my life in the qualities and friendship of my school friends, pupils and masters – engineering years, colleagues, 6 years RAF friends, architectural (Leeds) school friends, and 23 years of my own LSA students, friends, all my partners and staff member friends in my practice, client friends, family friends, and my very personal friends, I just can't believe it. John Lee was in the very top rank! He once said, 'You are as good as a father to me,' and I am sure he was as good as a second son to me.

Paul Hobson was originally working at my new North Road office in Huddersfield as a junior trainee technician and general factotum. I promoted him, with his agreement, to be John Lee's assistant at Hobbimate – Paul was 18, and a devout Wesleyan. I was a guest at his wedding at Scapegoat Hill, Golcar, chapel on the outskirts of Huddersfield, some years later, surveyed and advised on his house. He now has his own print works in the town, and he still keeps in touch.

Getting on with it necessitated finding a suitable factory unit, preferably near to our Scissett Hobbimate site. Amazingly, the solution was on our proverbial doorstep, less than a mile away, in the small town of Skelmanthorpe where one of my clients the Fields family had their very successful and international business making high quality rugs from tumbletwist to superb mohair rugs, in a large mill that we had recently extended. Consequently they now had vacant an older, large, north light roofed bay unit, which I was able to rent, which only needed a good clean up and internal provision of office and toilet facilities, and my brother Ronald also happened to be Chairman of Skelmanthorpe & District Council at that time!

I had connections with the Fields family from the early 1950s you may remember. Earlier, I mentioned Gordon Berry ARIBA, who accompanied his pupil at enrolment at HSA. He had married one of the Fields family after WWII, and it was after his untimely death that my Huddersfield accountants, who were also Gordon's accountants, rang me to enquire if I was interested in buying his Huddersfield practice and offices. My offices were at that time in Wakefield, a Grade 2 listed Georgian, three storey terrace house in the centre of the town, and they continued as our Wakefield office until I retired, if that is what I have done.

The offices were situated at 2 Spring Bank, New North Road, Huddersfield, a Victorian House, three storeys, design studio and car parking at the rear. I eventually bought the practice from Mrs Berry, and we later designed for her a new home, her home was nearby, on the outskirts of the town.

John Lee located a fork lift truck, which we bought, and we soon had a sparkling factory. John and Paul, together also with our expert joiners from Hobbimate works down the road, soon erected the office and toilet facilities etc., we didn't need an architect. Mr Barry Kemp, an expert one man band in the plumbing, central heating, gas installation, air conditioning trades, who had done many jobs in these trades for John Lee and myself was, as usual, quick to get on with it and we were soon off-loading heavy rolls of ICI Melinex and returning finished products – on a weekly basis. Also arranging for the supplies of my patented, plastic extrusion components, from a factory at Wyke near Bradford, Yorkshire as well as my Patented, Injection Moulded Components from another Factory in Midsomer Norton, North Somerset – a case of near and far, when I was visiting them, to make sure things were going according to plan.

I was now committed to visiting my Wakefield office, the Scissett works, and the Skelmanthorpe works, all on my way to the office in

Huddersfield on many occasions, particularly in the early days. We now had the machines installed at Skelmanthorpe, and a staff of nine people, working there on the ICI contract for the roller cloche in the triangular section boxes – like Toblerone chocolate – for ease of stacking, rather than round section tubes. This was our main contract, and we supplied a very large number of the cloches to ICI and they were demonstrated on TV, at the famous Chelsea Flower Show by one of the then TV gardening greats, Peter Seagrove, each day of the Show. We had tried to get a stand or site at the Chelsea Show in order to sell, display, or promote the various Hobbimate products in horticultural fields, but in the Royal Horticultural Society (RHS) there is a waiting list of years – and even then someone has probably had to die! John Lee and I, on our last visit to the show, had to suffer seeing practically everybody walking round carrying 6¼" diameter by 24" long wooden dowel rods, and three plastic plant pots, in some cases, instead of Hobbimate grow stiks which can be any size in green or white plastic, virtually last forever, with integral grow pots they have been in use in my garden, all year round, for 40 years – at least– and they are just one of our gardening products!

We also exhibited products at Harrogate Yorkshire Flower Show, where we could get a stand, and we sold out all our stock on each day before lunch time. We even had one person who threatened to sue us, because he didn't win the one cold frame we had on display only by raffle – if you bought a ticket before 12 midday. He hadn't. We only did this as they were larger, and we had only space for one!

The mention of cold frames, also reminds me of the superb – previously mentioned – Nostel Priory, where these days, due to inheritance tax the Priory grounds were opened for trade fairs for all types of product. We were showing my 'Clip-Stik' double glazing system – 'So simple, a child can make it' – and one can and for only 50 pence a square foot! I have had them, age 10–12 years, assemble it, and install it in the windows. I have it installed on my own entrance hall door, two panels, 6' 0" × 6' 0" glazed area – it is a small hall – 12' × 12' – and on the north side, and it has been there for 50 years – and no one entering or leaving has *ever* noticed it!

To attract the attention of the public we had made a special cold frame, size 4' × 3' which had 10 opening 'doors', 8 on four sides, and 2 on the top, to show the versatility of the product. I also had 4 baby, white rabbits inside, and we soon had a considerable crowd fascinated by the antics of the bunnies. This was particularly accentuated by the fact that from 10 feet away, the Melinex was so clear that the whole frame seemed open. We were not there to sell the rabbits, but to sell double glazing. Those were the days of the start of the plastic window frames and Pilkington Glass double glazed units and three of the largest manufacturers were there with big stands and sales reps, but we had the unique experience of having sales reps, from all three firms, saying they would rather be selling our system than theirs !

We also had the cold frames exhibited at the famous Leipzig Trade Fair where of course the stands are very upmarket and well designed. The stand next to ours was Messrs Mellows, greenhouses and cold frames with glass and aluminium frames, a well known maker in the lower priced area, I don't think it is trading now. The Mellows rep came over to our stand to inspect our plastic and Melinex competition, made suitable condescending comments, went back to his own stand and started vigorously polishing one of his cold frames. Suddenly disaster, he had very badly cut himself, blood was spattered across the carpet, the cut had been caused by a sliver of aluminium, which had not been removed in the proper manner when the frame members were cut in production – not properly dressed is a trade name for it in a foundry. It is partly the job of the saddle maker's bottom knocker! This was not funny! But it cannot happen with plastic and Melinex. All Hobbimate products sold very easily in the gardening and horticultural fields. All were quite unique, and new.

BUILDING DESIGN
October 22 1971

WHY HUDDERSFIELD IS REVOLTING

What happens when RIBA wields its stick and a polytechnic loses heart: the background story of a rebellion in the north

A large poster across the façade of Huddersfield Polytechnic's school of architecture last week read "Durrands' expansion policy starts here.'

For the 100 students barricaded inside the administration block it was an expression of sarcasm, or hope, or perhaps both.

Nominally, the rebellion is a protest against the polytechnic's refusal to admit a new first year to the school of architecture. Actually, it is the inevitable autumn of a long summer of discontent at this troubled school.

For nine months the school has been involved in a series of intrigues, manoeuvrings and headlines. The obvious victims have been the receding number of students (now 80). To them, director John Durrands' refusal to their call for a 1971/72 entry was the straw that broke the camel's back.

That students should be so concerned about the absence of a first year is mildly surprising until the situation is seen in the general context of this amazing year for architectural education.

Ultimatum

Huddersfield school of architecture is one of the five listed schools to which the RIBA gave, on July 21, the choice of either closing immediately or trying to "improve" to an (undetermined) standard within three years.

The other four schools all have the total backing of their directorates to carry on, and seem convinced that despite the grave difficulties facing listed schools they will have no trouble in achieving RIBA recognition in 1974.

Huddersfield, however, has been bedeviled. Not only has it been attacked by the RIBA, it has also been uncertain of the support of its own directorate and governors. The insurgencies of last week are seen as the direct result of this uncertainty.

The occupation began after a pandemonic meeting on Tuesday between the students and the directorate. Originally, the architectural students had hoped to meet Mr Durrands ("Bigdee") on October 6.

This wasn't convenient, so on Monday, October 11, they held a "peaceful" demonstration outside a room where about 30 polytechnic governors were holding a meeting. (There would have been 31, but one governor changed his mind when he saw the milling students, saying that he wasn't really interested in going in, and anyway, his car was double-parked.)

The two leaders of the students were called in to talk to governors and their request to admit a 1971/72 first year was deferred until November 15, which, of course, meant forever.

Mr Durrands then agreed to meet the students on the following day. He had hoped for a smaller number from the school of architecture, but to his dismay over 400 from various faculties turned up.

The meeting broke up in disarray after Mr Durrands had tried to explain that the reason for not admitting new students was to improve the staff/student ratio, and that existing students should see this as a 'fallow year for consolidation.'

He refused to give an assurance that the school would continue.

The matter of Gerald Fowler, Minister of State at the DES in the last government and assistant director of the polytechnic, shouting down to a senior architectural lecturer that he was a liar also went down badly with the students and staff present.

After successfully ensconcing themselves in the admin block, the students issued a six-point statement outlining their grievances:

- We deplore the lack of a first year and still believe one can be obtained. Failing this, negotiations with other schools should take place to ensure a second year next year.
- The school of architecture should be granted proper staff and equipment facilities.
- Co-operation with the other four listed schools should take place to fight present RIBA policy and form a common education/examination policy.
- There should be significantly improved internal communication between governors, directorate and academic staff.
- The headship of the school of architecture should be immediately resolved.
- There should be no recriminations against any student or member of staff.

The first intimation of trouble at the school came at the time of the Alex Gordon/ Jack Napper/ Elizabeth Layton visit in mid-March.

For some extraordinary reason Jeffrey Walton, principal lecturer in charge at the school for 23 years, was instructed by the directorate not to discuss this crucial visit with the RIBA visiting board. It was handled, instead, by John Durrands.

The next disaster came in the spring. Following a January decision to reorganise the school of architecture as part of a "broadly-based CNAA degree course incorporating management, architecture, construction and interior design", the directorate advertised for a new principal.

This had effectively been Jeffrey Walton's job for 23 years (in 1949 the school had 12 full-time students); the directorate told him that he was free to apply for it, but that he would have to provide references.

Understandably, students sent a petition to Margaret Thatcher and local MPs in protest. Some felt that it was a case of the RIBA angling to get a fierce critic out of the way, and a member of the staff was told that the RIBA had two nominees for the new job.

There is talk of Jeffrey Walton issuing a writ against the directorate.

Fighting

By late summer the directorate and the school of architecture and some of the other departments in the polytechnic were barely speaking. There was even a case of a fight between a lecturer and a director.

Typical, too, was the fact that the head of the school of architecture learned that he wasn't to have a new first year this year by reading it in a newspaper.

Paradoxically, it looks as though the "broadly-based" department will not now get off the ground. Last week the directorate said that it would be "inappropriate" to proceed as the future of architectural education in Huddersfield was no longer certain.

To say that the future is uncertain is an anathema in itself to the students who talk and listen enviously to the confident noises generated by the other listed schools.

But what is even more worrying to them is the fact that they have the impression that the directorate and the governors don't want the school to have a future.

Damned lies

They point to a press statement issued this week by the directorate which shows the school's pass-rate in the worst possible light. Jeffrey Walton commented that "there are lies damn lies, and *these* statistics."

The directorate goes on to say that the future of the school will be reconsidered in the light of next year's mock-examination results. A second influence will be the contents of a course submission and detailed syllabus Jeffrey Walton has been asked to prepare by November 15.

The rebellion of last week was inevitable indeed, however discomforting it was to city aldermen who found they were landed with a student revolt and a visit from the Queen on the same day.

For the moment the RIBA is doing no more than watching worriedly from the sideline. After its starring role in the national press earlier this year the Board of Education is unenthusiastic about getting involved in bad news.

Tuesday's news that the National Union of Students has backed the occupants of the administration block – last week it was so keen to do so it sent an encouraging telegram even before the polytechnic's own student union had blessed them – could mean that the RIBA will find itself sharing the headlines again.

Architects and Interior Designers

M Kenard Longfield Practice

Glynne Lincoln Shackleton
Dip. Arch.   A. R. I. B. A.   Chartered Architect
10 High Street,   BETHESDA,   Caernarvonshire
Telephone: 0248 . 82 . 632

Alderman Sisson
President of the Polytechnic
Huddersfield

16 June 1971

Dear Alderman

A little while ago I saw an advert for the position of
Head of the School of Architecture and assumed that Mr.
Waltons health had broken and he was forced to retire.

On a visit to Huddersfield last week I looked him up
and to my suprise and DISGUST found he was being asked
to apply for his own job.   As the original Huddersfield
College of Technology has been "up graded"into a
Polytechnic is Mr. Walton no longer considered worthy
of leading a department within such a body? It is my
opinion that the high standards attained by his department
were the prime factor in the up grading of the college.
One has only to consult the records of the school of
Architecture to see what a powerful influence Mr. Walton
has had on Architectural Education andArchitecture in
general.
When I left Grammar School I was told that I had no
chance of achieving my ambitionas an architect as it was
just not in me.   By chance I met Mr. Walton whose
enthusiasm not only injected new hope but enabled me to
complete what is without doubt the most difficult of
studies embracing the widest field and the longest period
of time of any Degree Course.
I know I am not a world beater but I now have my own
practice within a group of Architects who are recognised
for their abilitiesand I know that I have a training
which enables me to act with confidence in any situation.
The full credit can only go to one person.

On my first enrolment at Huddersfield the department was
very badly equipped - in fact one had the impression
that the authorities did not take it seriously- despite
this Mr. Walton's tremendous enthusiasm and shear hard
work has built it up into a school which no one can
afford to ignore both from its academic achievements and
its system of Student / Staff relationship.

I therefore wish to make the strongest possible protest
at the way in which the Polytechnic Authorities are
treating a person who has given over twenty years of
dedicated enthusiasm and LOYALTY.   A man without whose
efforts the Polytechnic might never have been.

Sincerely

Shackleton (Pensaer)

M Kenard Longfield ARIBA
E A Miller Done LSIA
In association with:
Arthur Hewitt & Jones (Llandudno)
(LTA Foinette VRD B.Arch ARIBA)

Prestatyn Llandudno Bethesda

203

'What a Life' is fundamentally about time —my time, and even, at this moment in time, as people say these days, when they mean NOW. I have enough trouble trying to put words together, from the vast number there are, without adding to the list unnecessarily. While I am in the process of thinking how to say this to you, it is slip sliding away, tick, tok, tick, tok, tick – and so is your time, and I don't want you to waste any of it. There is no way you can save time, or buy time, if there was there would be a hell of a long queue, waiting to buy it, and then they would have sold it all, long before it was your turn. It would be an even bigger con than buying stock market shares in CO_2, global warming, to save the planet, (Earth) by 2020, or 2030, or 40. Keep the cash rolling in, like the infamous 'South Sea Bubble' of yesteryear.

There now follows the Doctor Camilo Servin MD – Donald Free Story, and if I have bored you enough already, do feel free to skip the next few pages. It is all going on in the USA, and I am not even there, and you probably won't believe it, anyway!

THE DONALD FREE (aka DONALD J. SYKES-FREE) AFFAIR

The following letter from Dr Camilo Servin arrived on my desk, precisely as depicted below, as will be the case with all the letters both to and from Dr Servin and myself. He also sent me an audio tape, which I had my secretary transcribe, and it is also included. I never met or spoke to Dr Servin, throughout the entire period of my time involvement, and not a dollar remuneration or gift of any kind, except his thanks expressed in his letters, did I ask for or receive from anyone, irrespective of what you read in his letters. So you may now read on, as you have already decided to do, in spite of my previous offer – be my guest.

Camilo Servin, M.D.

509 BROADWAY ARCADE BLDG.
542 SOUTH BROADWAY
LOS ANGELES 13, CALIF.

June 22, 1964.

College of Technology,
School of Architecture,
Huddersfield, England.

Gentlemen:

I would like to verify whether Mr. Donald Sykes-Free, born 8.20.25, attended your school in the late forties and early fifties. If he did not graduate, was it due to the fact that he dropped out or was it due to his inability to keep up on his studies or to misconduct?

I would be very glad to reimburse for any expense or time lost. I would appreciate very much, an answer in the near future as it is very important to my daughter and to me to have the true facts.

Thanking you very, very much,
I remain

Yours truly,
Camilo Servin M.D.

CAMILO SERVIN, M.D.

509 BROADWAY ARCADE BLDG.
542 SOUTH BROADWAY
LOS ANGELES 13, CALIF.

July 13, 1964.
Re Donald Sykes-Free
JW/GMD

Mr. Jeffrey M. Walton,
College of Technology,
School of Architecture,
Huddersfield, England.

Dear Mr. Walton:

Thank you very much for your letter of July 4th. You are right in wanting more information about me and the reasons for writing. Indeed we would appreciate more data.

My daughter, Maria Teresa, is suing Don for divorce, something she should have done long before. He has been very onery to her and insolent to me. My daughter would like to cut down the visitation rights to the child. We have good reasons to believe he intends to kidnap her and hide the child in England. My daughter would like to have basis for annulling the marriage.

I am a practicing physician in California since 1927, a member of the Los Angeles County Medical Association, for many years an instructor in Medicine at the College of Medical Evangelist. My credit is and always has been A1.

Donald Free has been a bad influence on the grandchild and has predisposed her against the mother and the grand-parents. We desire to prevent him from taking her out on week-ends, and to visit with her alone.

He was the "architect" on a speculative house for resale with disastrous results financially. At times there are reasons to suspect sex abnormalities.

For the annulment and further limitation of visitation rights we would like to have all possible information. Please don't worry about the letter being long.

If some of the information should be certified or notarized, please don't hesitate to do so and all expenses will be refunded. For expenses I am enclosing $10.00 on account. If there are other persons or places I should write to, please let me know.

My daughter, my wife and yours truly thank you very, very much.

Sincerely,
Camilo Servin

P.S Please address the letter "<u>personal</u>"
so my office assistant will not open it.   CS.

CAMILO SERVIN, M.D.

509 BROADWAY ARCADE BLDG.
542 SOUTH BROADWAY
LOS ANGELES 13, CALIF.

Oct. 6, 1964.
ref. JW/GMD

Mr. Jeffrey M. Walton,
Transport Bldgs., Longroyd Bridge,
Huddersfield, England.

Dear Mr. Walton:

Since my last letter many things have happened. On July 21st my daughter received an interlocutary divorce. One week before he decided not to contest it. I believe this was in part or mostly to the fear we would bring up embarrassing material we had, part of which you graciously gave us.

He had said to a friend and to the child he was going to take the child to England where mother couldn't find her.

He kept his new British passport which he had obtained in June 1964 even though he had become an American citizen. He had court orders to give his passport to the attorney for keeping and also court orders not to take the child out of Southern California. On Sept 26th he flew to New Jersey (Idlewild airport) and on Sept 27th he phoned from Puerto Rico he was returning to Los Angeles on the 28th. He must not have had all the necessary or correct papers to leave the country. He had shipped to Puerto Rico his work table, part of all his baggage and the child's tribicycle. We are sure he is going try again if he thinks he can get away with it.

My daughter is bringing contempt of court charges asking he not be allowed to take her out of the house and limiting his visitation rights and possibly eliminating them if he continues his mis-behaviour.

He has not kept up the payments on the house, refused to sell the house (sign the papers after my daughter had done so) and he has tried to mess things up. (He is living in the house). He has quit his job as he had predicted to a friend months before that he would do so.

We would appreciate very much more facts and materials even though not notarized and even though not useable in court, including any abnormal or unusual sex activities, etc. etc. a threat that this material would be made public court record may make him more accessible and willing to half way come to terms. This seems to be the only way this insolent, unscrupulous person can understand.

My daughter and I would very much desire to have this material before the court appearance which may be in two or three weeks. This favor would be deeply appreciated. If he were to take the child and hide her, he would win her. Please, Mr. Walton, help us.

Sincerely yours,
Camilo Servin

JEFFREY WALTON CHARTERED ARCHITECT · SURVEYOR
Dipl., Arch., (Dist.) A.R.I.B.A.   DESIGN CONSULTANT

14A · BOND STREET · WAKEFIELD · YORKSHIRE · Telephone 2121

Camilo Servin, M.D.,
542 South Broadway,
Room 509,
Los Angeles,
California.   10th October, 1964

Dear Dr. Servin,

First, I must apologise most sincerely for not replying to your previous letter, this is due partly to my being ill, partly to being exceedingly busy in my practice, and partly due, naturally, to some apprehension regarding becoming involved in what after all is only very remotely, of any real concern of mine. I was also even somewhat apprehensive of the fact that perhaps any information I might give may fall into the hands of Free and perhaps in some way be used against me at some future date ... I know Free of old! I even had the thought cross my mind that your letter may have been initiated by him to involve me in some manner to his advantage, he has I feel this kind of mind!

However, your letter of the 6th October, and your strong appeal has lead me to decide that I must do what I can to assist in what is obviously a very unhappy experience for your daughter. Further, in my opinion, his influence on your grand-daughter, were he to have sole control of her would, I regret to say, be far from the best! That is, unless he has changed radically in the last few years and from my experience in various matters of him and your own communications, this would not appear to be the case. He always seems to bring trouble to those around him.

You will appreciate that it is some ten years since I myself saw Free, although I have had communication with him and contact in different ways over the last ten years. Also, his elder brother is at present a student at my School and to use the old expression 'is as different as chalk from cheese'.

This brother, studied on his own for some three years under very difficult circumstances before he telephoned to me asking for assistance with his Intermediate work for the Royal Institute of British Architects and even on that telephone conversation endeavoured to avoid giving his name, he subsequently told me that he new of his brothers bad record at the School and elsewhere and in consequence was, shall we say, ashamed to attended at the School as a student because of this record.

I must hasten to add, that the elder brother has, I believe, little or no knowledge of these recent happenings to Donald Free in America and also the elder brother is in every way completely acceptable as a student and potential member of my profession.

I have of course had many students and trained many architects over the past fifteen years and of all these students I can honestly say that the only one who has caused me any trouble or has in any way brought discredit to this School, that person is Donald John Free.

Free was always exceedingly clever in his 'operations' in that it was always very difficult to prove that he had committed various misdemeanours. On reflection though, he only appears to be clever due to the fact that he was in contact with ordinary decent people who were not expecting his kind of person to operate amongst them. In my view he has committed a number of errors which a really competent 'con' man would not do. I do however consider him to be this type of person and I list below, chronologically, incidents which have occurred in my experience of this man in order that you may judge for yourself. From the official Record Card which he filled in when he first entered this College and which I regret to say is probably in part untrue. I list the following entries:

Date of entry: December 1947
Age at entry: 21 years 4 months
'Details of previous education':
Primary School: Paddock Council, Huddersfield. 1931–37
Secondary School: Royds Hall Grammar School. 1937–40
Other Training:
Huddersfield Technical College. 1940–43 (Part Time)
'Examination Successes':
College of Preceptors (Senior)
Intermediate R.I.B.A. 1951

Free apparently attended as a full time student at the School of Architecture from December 1947 to the Session 1952–53. Leaving from recollection during that Session.

Regarding the examination 'successes' listed, it was common knowledge that he had passed certain examinations in the College of Preceptors (Senior) by having a substitute candidate sit for him, this of course I was unable to prove. Further, he is not listed in the R.I.B.A. Calendar which lists all the fully qualified Architects and in addition those who have passed the Intermediate Examination of the R.I.B.A. which is taken after three years full time study, the Final Examination being taken after six years full time study. He is not now therefore entitled to use this Intermediate rating with the Royal Institute of British Architects.

To the best of my memory, Free first caused me concern by his influence over a much younger student (sixteen years old) by the name of Stewart, this student was a very promising student of good character, his father was at that time serving abroad as a Senior Officer in the Royal Air Force and sent to his son a generous allowance, a lot of which, as far as I could discover, went into the pocket of Free, as also did on one occasion a new watch which Stewart was sent.

Within the year Stewart ended up in the hands of the Huddersfield Police charged with breaking into a Coffee Bar and stealing money. He was given the option by the Court of doing National Service with the Forces or going into Borstal Prison. The opinion was held that Free's influence had brought about the downfall of this young man.

During Free's last year at the School we received a letter from the Secretary of the Royal Institute of British Architects informing us that he had received an anonymous letter claiming that Free had submitted work for the Final Examination of the Royal Institute of British architects that was not his own but was that of another student who he had forced to exchange Final Design Schemes with him, that is Free allowed this student to use his Design Problem in exchange for Free's use of the students Design Problem which had already been accepted by the R.I.B.A.

Free denied this charge and in fact swore out an affidavit with a Notary Public stating that he had not committed this misdemeanour, however our evidence of the matter led us to believe that the information placed before the R.I.B.A. was correct.

Free next obtained employment, again with forged references, with the West Riding County Planning Office at Huddersfield under the direction of Mr. Woolley, the Planning Officer for the area. While at this office, on Mr. Woolley's information, he disrupted the staff, used the office telephone for his own private long distance telephone calls without paying for them, removed plans that were the property of the Planning Office etc., etc.

In particular a very good set of plans of a very modern house called 'Farnley Hey' near Huddersfield were missing, at the same time Free also left this office! Mr. Woolley is of the opinion that Free took these plans. I also am of the opinion that he would take them with him to America to show as his own work in order to obtain employment there. The actual Architect for 'Farnley Hey' was a now well known Architect in England called Peter Womersley – he of course knows nothing of this.

I yesterday rang Mr. Woolley at his office and acquainted him generally with Free's activities in America with your daughter, and he was most co-operative in corroborating information and expressed a fervent hope that Free would continue to stay in America!

When Free left for America he took a car without the owner's permission had the car filled with petrol and oil at the owner's expense, drove to South Hampton, left the car on the dock unattended and embarked on board ship for America!

Since Free has been in America he has corresponded with me on perhaps two or three occasions, each time with an ulterior motive in mind! One example particularly comes to mind where he asked that I give him a recommendation to become a member of the California Institute of Architects. I refused to do this but suggested he asked the Secretary of the California Institute of Architects to write to me and I would give him all the information I could! This, in due course, the Secretary did and of course I gave him my honest view on the type of person he may be considering joining his Society!

Again, something over a year ago the Registrar of this College received a communication from the Chief Security Officer of the National Aeronautics and Space Administration of the United States of America. This requested that we verify the particulars given on a Form of Application for a post with NASA for which apparently Free was applying. The Chief Security Officer went on to state that Free would have access to Top Classified Information! Virtually all the information given by Free to NASA was in fact wrong, even to

212

the extent of claiming a Degree at this School! Further, the Form had an error of date, had it been correct, Free would have been a student at this College at the age of five! (This may have been a typographical error.) I of course replied through the Registrar most strongly recommending that they did not accept Free for any post with such an important organisation. I would suggest that you contact NASA they may have a file on Free!

These briefly (!) are some of my main memories of Free and I regret that I am not able to give them in greater detail or further check with his contemporaries on other details as I felt it more important not to delay my reply. There was an instance during his student days when Free was paying his attentions to the daughter of the Editor of the 'Huddersfield Examiner', a now elderly man by the name of Elliot Dodds. Mr. Dodds rang me at the College to ask my opinion of Free and his suitability to associate with his daughter. I warned Mr. Dodds concerning Free and gave my opinion that Free's tactics were to find a girl with an influential and wealthy family whose daughter he could compromise to force a marriage and perhaps in this way gain some control of the family money. I have of course no actual evidence of this except the strong feeling regarding Free and my knowledge of him. I know you will forgive me for suggesting it, but it wouldn't surprise me if this was the case with your daughter. Free could be very charming when necessary!

I hope this information will be of assistance to you and your daughter and I rely on you to use it intelligently and with discretion. Should there be any other way in which I should be able to assist you then please let me know, I would thoroughly enjoy a week or two's holiday in California particularly for such a good cause!!!

Please let me know the outcome, and I would also be interested to have your views on this letter and in fact, be kept fully informed of developments. May I close by wishing you and your daughter every success and I hope that this unhappy period in your family's lives will soon be rectified to your advantage.

Yours sincerely,
J. M. Walton.

CAMILO SERVIN, M. D.

610 SOUTH BROADWAY Rm 810
LOS ANGELES 11, CALIF.
TEL. MADISON 6–6439

5–23–66

Jeffrey M. Walton,
Huddersfield School of Art,
Transport Building,
Longroyd Bridge,
Huddersfield, Eng.

Dear Mr. Walton:

I received today your letter of May 20th. Today I called the office of Richard Neutra, He has been away from L.A. one week. Today or Tomorrow he leaves New York for a two monthly trip to Europe. He may be going to England, His executive secretary was not in and I was told to call tomorrow. It is my recollection that he was called in as a consultant as a specialist in acoustics for a chapel or auditorium in or near San Diego.

I shall write soon and give you details of his past here. He has not changed a bit.

On May 11th I showed the letter hiding your address to one of his witnesses. He must have concluded that it was from you. The case was continued to the 18th of May. He thinks the letter was recent and for this hearing. In the hearing it was not mentioned, raised and much less recorded. It is not a public record. On the evening of May 19 or 20th he phoned me telling me I had that letter and he wanted a copy. That he had already started a suit against you and was going to have you fired from your position. He is not sure from who the letter is from. I told him (to gain time) that I would let him know in 1 or 2 wks if I would give him a copy of the letter. When he does call me, I shall tell him to write to me and I shall answer by letter, that I do not want to talk to him because whatever I say he will twist and lie about it. When he does write I shall notify him that I have written to the author of the letter and shall not give him a copy till I have had your authorization to do so. He did threaten to bring suit to force me to give the letter.

214

He is not well off financially. He bought a used Lincoln Continental and is behind on his payments. He rents an office for about $118 a month and lives in it. He is in arrears on child support & alimony. He will have to pay several hundreds of dollars for his lawyer and also idem for my daughter's lawyer. Any lawyer would be foolish to work for him if he was not paid in advance. Otherwise he would not be paid.

I shall soon write to you in detail and tell you facts that you won't believe!

I wanted to get this off in hurry as Richard Neutra was sailing or flying from New York. Free worked for him as a consultant for about 6 months according to Free. I shall investigate. He has been fired or "asked to resign" from his last 4 jobs. I do not type so please excuse my long hand. The coming letter will be dictated to a typist directly (without water) as it shall be much more in detail.

You may count on me for a full co-operation, I can bet you he will do nothing.

Sincerely yours,
Camilo Servin

P.S. Please note new address. 810 Story Bldg-; 610 South Broadway L.A. Calif. 90014.
Richard J. Neutra address is 2379 Glendale Blvd., Glendale, Calif.

610 SOUTH BROADWAY
SUITE 810 STORY BUILDING
LOS ANGELES, CALIFORNIA 90014
MADISON 6–6439

June 2, 1966.

Donald J. Sykes-Free
5170 West Beverly Blvd.
Los Angeles, Calif. 90004

Sir;

I do have a letter from a man in England, stating a few facts about Donald J. Free. I am writing to the author of this letter to authorize my giving it to you.

When I get his authorization, I shall send you a copy of the letter in question.

Yours truly,
Dr. Camilo Servin
June 2nd. 1966

cc: author of the letter.

Dear Mr. Walton:

Today I got his letter asking for a copy of the letter otherwise he will take "legal means to obtain same".

I may sue him for slander if he continues saying lies about me.

If he takes my daughter to court, we would like to know about any abnormal sex activities: If you came to L.A., how much of the passage would you want us to pay? You are welcome to live in our home.

I shall keep you informed.

C. Servin

P.S.   I am not afraid if he takes legal means to obtain a copy of it. I would like to find a way of making it a <u>court record</u> if you have no objections. Or another letter which are easy to prove as expulsion from school for misconduct etc.

If he kidnaps the child, how difficult would it be to bring her back to the States. He may decide to take her to Australia or to Argentina.

With his reputation could he make a living in England?

I feel his making all these letters are to show to his friends that the details are slander and not facts.

Sincerely yours,
C Servin

P.S. June 13th 1966 at 11 pm. on going over and assorting papers in my coat, I found this which I wrote late June 2nd to mail next morning. Perhaps my memory is being affected by 65½ years more that what I suspect. The letter dated June 13th was mailed 7 30 pm on 6/13.

CAMILO SERVIN, M. D.

610 SOUTH BROADWAY
SUITE 810 STORY BUILDING
LOS ANGELES, CALIFORNIA 90014
MADISON 6–6439

June 6, 1966.

Mr. Jeffrey M. Walton,
Transport Building,
Longroyd Bridge,
Huddersfield, England.

Dear Mr. Walton,

I received your letter of May 28th after I had mailed my last letter. Enclosed is the letter you asked for.

He was refused the $5,000,00 because of poor credit or lack of property or financial resource or both. He could not take out the child for eight hours until he got the bond. He is going to be irked about this and my daughter will be forced to go to court again –

217

worry, time and money. He will not stop pestering until he gets custody of the child (something I am sure he will not succeed in) or <u>has</u> had an opportunity to take her to England, Australia or South America.

We would appreciate very much having a letter stating the facts about misconduct which are easily proven as expelled from school of architecture, his forged letters of recommendations etc., etc., also a copy of his application to enter school of Architecture, and persons and institutions we could write to get information that we could present in court and help fight him. There is also the possibility that he may want to sue me or that I sue him for slander.

You certainly were right when you stated that he brings trouble to everyone around him.

If he went to England, would he be able to stay there and earn a living considering his past?

Sincerely your,
Camilo Servin

CAMILO SERVIN, M. D.

610 SOUTH BROADWAY
SUITE 810 STORY BUILDING
LOS ANGELES, CALIFORNIA 90014
MADISON 6–6439

June 13, 1966.

Mr. Jeffrey Walton,
Huddersfield, England.

Dear Mr. Walton,

He still continues to irritate the family, This ————!! It appears that he passed the polygraph test. Pathological liars confidence men & men without a conscience, usually do. He is going to go to court again to try to take out the daughter not only for 8 hours but also overnight <u>without</u> a bond because he did not qualify for a bond and he passed a lie detector test.

I am leaving tomorrow and shall be away for a week. I do hope nothing happens.

I would very, very much appreciate having a letter from you stating his expulsion from school for misconduct, forged letters of recommendations and other points that are facts and no basis for a suit, etc. In the last resort could we introduce a copy of this letter? I would prefer an original letter. I am sure he made all these threats to you and to me so that I <u>would not introduce the letter</u> or get you to write to me not to introduce the letter which he evidently fears very much.

At present he cannot take out the child until he gives up his passport, produces 5,000.00 Bond. The above may be changed without a court hearing if he passed a polygraph test.

In the next letter I shall include something in appreciation of your cooperation.

Yours truly,
Camilo Servin

CAMILO SERVIN, M. D.

610 SOUTH BROADWAY
SUITE 810 STORY BUILDING
LOS ANGELES, CALIFORNIA 90014
MADISON 6–6439

June 25, 1966.
Re JMW/GMD

Mr. J.M.Walton,
Huddersfield, England.

Dear Mr. Walton:

Things have not been going so well. Don repeatedly lied on the witness stand. By passing the lie detector test, in about 6–8 days the Judge will reduce an order he take her outside the home and will probably increase the visitation privileges. To counteract his passing of the lie detector test, we desperately need evidence to counteract this like: 1) He was expelled from school for misconduct, etc, etc. 2) His taking of car without owners permission, etc., and all other points that there is proof of. His purpose in his threat to you was to keep me from using that letter in court.

Last week His Lincoln Continental, which he bought used, was repossessed and he blames my son for this! This is the third car that has been repossessed from him for failure to keep up payments or for bouncing checks. He is definitely not well off financially and this, I am sure, will become worse and not improve as his reputation and bad credit gets around.

He, certainly, has caused a tremendous amount of anguish and bother to all the family. We certainly would like to put a stop to this and your letter would be of tremendous help.

Sincerely Yours,
Camilo Servin

p.s. I do not type, so please excuse the long hand.

Transcription of tape recording sent by Dr. Camilo Servin to Mr Walton – 8. 6. 66.

From Dr Camilo Servin, Los Angeles, USA

Dear Sir,

You may count on me for full co-operation in all this matter. I can bet 10 – 1 that nothing will come out of it and that he is making this threat in order that you may not get any more information for the present or future. He has made many threats to my daughter and to me that he was going to take the child away from her, that he was going to take my license away from me and so on and so forth.

On May, 24th, I called up the office of Richard Neutra and the Executive Secretary remembered very vaguely about Free and that he had worked on the acoustics of a Chapel at Mirama Naval Station near San Diego. This was an acoustical flop. I also spoke with Mr. Anderson, at the recommendation of the Executive Secretary, because he was at that time a partner of Mr. Richard Neutra.

Mr. Anderson kindly volunteered the opinion that may be it was not Free's fault for the flop as the Navy said to erase the acoustics for about 2/3 of the seats occupied and when it was tested with a full audience was much smaller and my wife and my daughter were there and remember it was a big flop as the Neutra Associates definitely stated. Mr. Anderson said that Free was an agreeable chap and that is all he knows.

I also spoke with Dione Neutra the son of Richard Neutra who dealt more with Free. He stated that he was never an associate of Richard Neutra, nor an employee. This was also stated by Anderson. Dione Neutra was at the wedding and at the reception.

At the hearing on May, 18th, as I said before, the paper of the letter was not introduced nor mentioned nor discussed. On May 11th I did show it to a Mr. Duncanson a friend of Don's who disapproved to a certain extent some of Don's behaviour on the divorce proceedings. I showed the letter but not the top so that I am sure that he did not get to see who the letter was from, I believe that Don put 2 and 2 together and presumed that it was from you. I shall not give him the letter until I have authorization from you and if he still insists I will go to court before I give it to him. This letter must have hurt him more than what I thought it would. He is such a cynic that he could commit purgery again and again and still stay as cool as a cucumber.

Financially I am sure he is not well off. In September 1965 he was to have appeared in Court at proceedings against my daughter which he started. He failed to appear because his Attorney refused to go to bat for him for some reason or other and we believe, yes definitely, he did not have the money to pay the Attorney and that is why he failed to appear, that was September, 1965.

For about 2 or 3 years he has been going around with an Argentinean girl by the name of Adella Lopez about 32 – 36 years of age and since the fall of last year began to go around with her more steadily, also he opened an office, as his letter head shows, Planners, Developers & Engineers, it does not say Architects.

He was evidently going to work as an Architect, Planner and Designer, also buy old houses, repairing them for re-modeling them and then selling them at a profit.

We knew that somebody was lending him money, whether it was his friend from North American Aviation corporation or a rich widow or some other future victim.

This Adella Lopez worked for a family, or rather for a man who was a widow, with 3 or 4 children, she cooked for the family and cleaned house and helped with the house work and taking care of the household. The granddaughter once mentioned to him about the 'domestic' Adella Lopez, Free corrected her and said that she was not a domestic that she was a 'governess'.

In February he called in my office to get some information and a 19 year old assistant that I have had answered. He dated her and made friends of her and made love to her, asking her to get information about my office while she was still an employee. He wanted any dirt or any information that he could harm me and use it not only to do harm but possibly blackmail me. Also the employee began to do less work so I fired her. Then she went to work for Free and began to visit the house to visit Elizabeth the grand-daughter to see what information she could get.

On Elizabeth's birthday, February, 21st, they met and they acted as if they did not know each other. This girl let her home and went to live in an apartment near Don, who later entered and went to live in Don's apartment as she testified in Court the May, 11th.

Shortly after the middle of March Adella Lopez left her employment in a town about 25 – 30 miles from Los Angeles, came to L.A. and threw out this young 19 year old redhead and moved in with Don. Shortly afterwards announced that he was going to marry Adella Lopez. In the meantime this 19 year old girl expected to marry Don. Don had told her that if she became pregnant he would go to England and have the child there. She understood that they would leave Adella here. This same young girl testified in Court that she had never touched any man before, that Free was the first man, that they had planned to take the child to England and had discussed it several times. Free testified in Court that he had never touched the girl and had no sexual relations with her and that he never intended to take the child to England.

On September 26th, 1964, Free took out the child for his visitation on the Saturday, that same Saturday he flew under alias names, Phillis and Richard Giles, to New York. There he 'phoned' and sent the message that they were alright that they would be back in 3 weeks. That was from New York. On Sunday about 11 he called from Puerto Rico stating that he would be back on Monday and actually he did come back and was in L.A. in the early evening of Monday, that is 48 hours later. He stated that he did not intend to go to England but only for a vacation with Elizabeth alone. He could have done that in California and still have been within the law. He spent on aeroplane tickets alone 596 dollars at a time when he left debts in L.A. amounting to a little over 2,000 and some dollars. Some of these he paid back, others he did not. Also he shipped to Puerto Rico the girl's bicycle and all his clothes and his work tables. Also he left the house cleared where they were living and threw away all his personal paper and other important papers if he were to come back. Evidently the way he threw out many of his personal papers he intended not to come back.

Furthermore, he did tell a person before the trip that he intended to go to England where no-one could find the child. About 2 weeks before the child had told us that 'Daddy is going to take me to England where mummy cannot find me'.

After that the court prohibited him from taking the child out of the house.

The young girl, let's call her 'red', said that she thought Adella's money for this business was being facilitated by Adella Lopez whom he married on May 3rd, 1966.

I do believe he is financially in difficult circumstances in September he did not have any money so he is living with money that somebody is lending him or investing in this business. He is not a hard working man, nor does he have a good business point of view so I am sure that he will sooner or later go broke.

He has difficulty in paying some bills. He is behind on the payments of a used Lincoln Continental that he bought, besides his credit is poor, he had two other cars picked up for non-payment of the installments.

In this recent Court Hearing on May 11th, and May 18th, he would have to pay 400 – 600 dollars for his Attorney and the Court has ordered him to pay part of Philisita's Attorney's fee to the tune of 400 dollars. He would also have to have a Court Bond before he can take the child out for the day. This bond is for 500 dollars and it will cost him 10% of 500 dollars a year.

His wife of less than 3 weeks is 6 or 7 months pregnant and he will have to pay doctor bills and hospital bills for delivery.

He married my daughter on May 31st, 1958. Some time after that he and I entered into the business of speculative house building. I would buy the lot, furnish the money and first receive 10% of the money I invested in, after that the profits would be divided 50/50. He would also get the Architect's fee in addition to that.

The first house we built I lost 10,000 dollars on it. After the house was being, Further the house was being constructed and he took our 825 dollars to pay some Consulting Engineers. He told me afterwards that he did need it to pay a 225 dollar bill, he said that the difference between 225 dollars and 825 dollars I could deduct from his Architects fee.

About a year after the house, or a year and a half after the house was sold and the notice of completion made I began to get bills from Wilson and Wilson for the balance due. I told the Secretary that I had given, or paid, 225 dollars to Free to pay the 225 dollars that they would have to collect from him. They tried to collect from him and also my daughter was urging me to pay him in small installments. One day my daughter calls me and tells me that the bill was due to house expenses and that Don thought that I should pay it and she thought so too. Then for the first time I explained to my daughter that he had taken 825 dollars from the construction fund to pay this 225 dollar bill and he had pocketed the money and not paid the fee. She really was flabbergasted. I am sure this will not take you by surprise that it is still the same Free you knew.

About the same time he was associated with a James Gibson of World Wide Construction Company. He saw the Black clouds on the horizon and withdrew from the connection with Gibson when he realized Gibson was going to be indicted for fraud for which he went to the penitentiary for several years and is still there. Before the indictment and before he was hailed to Court Free borrowed 1000 dollars from Gibson to get a down payment on the house that he was going to buy. Later he refused to pay back this money and said that Gibson had stolen it anyway. I do not know what Gibson will do when he gets out of jail.

When Free took the child out from Puerto Rico Philisita used a private Attorney and not the District Attorney as the latter would make it a felony and for Elizabeth's sake she preferred to do otherwise.

Don liked to take tub baths with the child when she was 4 or 5 and on one occasion, according to the story of a mother neighbour, stated that her 8 year old daughter had also taken a tub bath with Free and 5 year old Elizabeth and that Free had asked the 8 year old girl to touch his parts. He also used to go naked in the swimming pool with Elizabeth and another 6 year old girl and this 6 or 8 year old girl and also thought this was funny.

On July 4 1965, he was discussing something about the family with Elizabeth in my back yard so I went to read while they were there, about 15 or 20 feet away to see what he was doing. He got irritated and said "I will give you 20 to get out of the patio" I looked at him with a sort of grin and then without counting he came at me and began to push me into the house, I purposely did not raise my arm nor defended myself to make it a one way affair. I went to the telephone called the police and had him evicted from the house. He threatened me and told me that I would pay dearly for this.

After he had gone I went to Elizabeth to apologise and explained to her that I was sorry I had to do that, she said "Oh I know I understand". She was not hurt or irritated at me at all.

Before Puerto Rico when he used to take out Elizabeth for the day she would become very antagonistic to me, the mother, grandmother and to the uncle. Then it would take Elizabeth one or two days to come round and be friendly again. Elizabeth is not as affectionate or close to him as she used to be. He thinks it is brain washing on our part. He does not realize that frequently he has misbehaved in her presence, he has insulted the mother, threatened the mother and behaved in such a way that the daughter herself can see through him. She still likes him because he will give her 100% undivided attention and fulfill every wish she wants, whether it is a toy, candy before a meal or anything she likes. On one occasion he wanted to leave because he had an engagement at the end of the hour of visitation. She slapped his face and his only comment was "This makes grandpa happy". I told Elizabeth "Have not I told you, you should be friendly and courteous to daddy." She answered "Yes grandpa". I can assure you that he hates me more than my son and you put together and anything clever or intelligent that my daughter does he thinks is due to my suggestion.

Before marriage he stated that he was Ph. D. from Cambridge and then got his Architect's Degree from Cambridge. Of course, you know the facts. I wrote to the State Board of Architects Examiners of California and they stated he had applied to take a license or to get an examination but he was not allowed to take the examination because he did not have the necessary requirements and that the case was still open. In 1960 from May to July he worked with Edward J. Samanearo and Architect, as an employee. He used to state that he was an associate which was not true. He was fired from there for causing trouble and dissension and taking the plans of a client of Samanearo with him when he left the group and finished the house himself. This client Dr. Forrest did not know he was not an Architect.

He left owing two of Samanearo's associates or employees money for work they did on our speculative house on Malibu. After Samanearo Free went to work for North American Aviation Corporation. He had made friends with a top officer of the Company through an Australian girl that was a mutual friend and whom this officer of North American later married. Through his influence he got this job earning 1100 and later 1200 dollars a month. He stated that soon he would be a Vice-President of the North American Company. It was not long when he was told to either resign or be fired when he was under the influence of alcohol. He had an altercation with a guard. There may have been other things, or that his reputation was catching up with him, that is also a possibility.

Shortly after that he went to work with Rocketdyne another Aviation Company, a subsidiary of North American Aviation and probably therefore through the influence of his personal friend.

After a few months he was laid off there because they were laying off employees. When the Vietnam War came and they were actively hiring he was not re-hired.

CAMILO SERVIN, M. D.

610 SOUTH BROADWAY
SUITE 810 STORY BUILDING
LOS ANGELES, CALIFORNIA 90014
MADISON 6–6439

Feb, 6, 1967.

Dean of School of Architecture,
Transport Bldg., Longroyd Bridge,
Huddersfield, England.

Dear Mr. Walton:

My daughter and I would appreciate very much if you would be so kind as to give us information about Donald J. Sykes-Free (formerly Donald J. Free) and the circumstances for being expelled from the School of Architecture, and the date.

There is to be a court hearing on Feb 24th in his petition, among other things, to lengthen the time of his custody of Elizabeth, age 8. Ultimately he wants to have <u>full</u> <u>custody</u> of her. In the last court hearing he lied right and left and even passed a lie detector test!! He won the right to take her out for one or two days after posting a bond of $2,500:00. He, also, wants to eliminate this bond.

We would appreciate information that we could use in court to

226

show his lack of scruples, ethics and morality. For many reasons we know his plans of more custody time are not for the best interest of the child.

We would be glad to pay for notary fees, etc and remunerate in full for time used in arranging this matter.

Please, please do not fail us.

Thanking you and appreciating very much this favor, we remain

Very truly yours,
Camilo Servin
Maria Teresa Sykes-Free (by CS)

CAMILO SERVIN, M. D.

610 SOUTH BROADWAY
SUITE 810 STORY BUILDING
LOS ANGELES, CALIFORNIA 90014
MADISON 6–6439

2 – 8 – 67

Mr. Jeffrey Walton,
Huddersfield, England.

Dear Mr. Walton:

Today I had the time to go to the bank and get this $25<u>00</u> draft. This is only a token of appreciation. Please do let me know the time consumed. If there are other hints or clues that you could give me in a separate letter, just for me alone, or persons or places that we could contact to get data, it would be immensely appreciated. This separate letter would be torn and I would just keep the names and addresses we would have to contact.

Sincerely yours,
C Servin

I do hope you have enjoyed that 'interlude' in my life. As compensation for the effort, here is the sequel.

Donald Free, without the hyphenated Sykes-Free used to con the respectful Americans, arrived back in the UK, and in particular at the polytechnic apparently in high dudgeon, to sue me for defamation of character, etc., yes, all three. But, and I admit, at that time, I did not think of or even consider it, and I wish I had it now, to Spare, Save, or even buy, you may think, due to my present fixation, with time. However, in spite of all the heartfelt requests from various quarters, that he stay in America, I have since never seen, or heard, from anyone on the subject of Free, not even Dr Servin (including the above mentioned, 10 dollar and 25 dollar drafts he mentions). He probably intended to get them, but forgot to put them in. I would not have accepted them anyway. Free, I just assume, went back to his old tricks in the USA, but maybe, perhaps, dear reader, you may know more.

But, they all take time, and I hate sitting about, doing nothing, or not doing much, as I am now, wasting time writing this, for the last 12 months. Actually, it has not been so bad, there still have been many things done, visitors to entertain etc., and some still to do. Over the last two months intermittently, I have had the pleasure of the help of Neil Fallows (who is originally an Englishman but is also an Australian, his Yorkshire born wife, Cheryl, persuaded him to come back to Yorkshire). Perhaps unbelievably, from the very start, to the apparent end of this episode in my life, I have never met, or even spoken to anyone on the telephone, not even Dr Servin himself, or his daughter – excepting Donald Free.

Comprehensive as I have been, how on earth do you write your life story? Have it 'ghosted', or make it all up, for political or commercial profit to name a few, or imagine it, as I do only when I design? Or do you do it yourself, at the last stages, hopefully, of your life, and all you hope for is time, to finish before your time has finished, as I am trying to do, not exactly fingers crossed but doing my best, where there is life, there is hope, as the saying goes.

Dr Wilson was assigned as Timothy's consultant in the early spring of 1991, and he eventually started to slowly improve to a stage where he was able to return home, but with a lot of conditions and unfortunately for him he was not allowed to work. He had to visit his local GPs surgery, weekly, and must not go into the waiting room and wait with other patients in case they had some infection, colds etc., and must enter the surgery by the back door and straight into the doctor's by appointment time. By the way the said doctor was the very first one Tim had seen at the outset and who had

228

then just started at the practice, and Timothy was a first heart patient after qualifying. One Dr Johns, and yes, in spite of the name, she was a lady doctor, and thank goodness had the sense to realise, he was in an even more urgent state than usual and arranged his immediate transfer to Pinderfield Hospital after her own cardiac check.

He was also required to have very regular blood tests at the hospital, and some few months later he was to have the latest device from America, a defibrillator, (£20,000, or dollars, one or the other) inserted into his chest at the LGI (Leeds General Infirmary), by Dr Cowan, cardiology surgeon. This ten cigarette size box was designed to electronically restart his heart, in case it stopped and, if it did, and was extra urgent, would eject him from his chair or wherever with force. On I think a monthly basis he attended at the LGI for the computer printout to be checked, which he told me, 'went completely across the computer room floor'. On one other occasion, while he and Sandra were in the waiting room a well dressed person with a briefcase came into the room, and, oh dear, a rep, he thought, having many experiences of reps at the office, I will have to wait even longer. In fact, they both went in together for the test. He was the technical rep of the USA manufacturers, to check that everything was OK! Timothy was then allowed to drive but still not work, which was a good sign I suppose, as it allowed them both some freedom, and his relationship with Dr Wilson was obviously very good indeed, and he was, to all intents and purposes, as they say, living a normal life with me constantly worrying that he may have an altercation, perhaps when driving, and some yob would thump him in the chest and kill him! He also had bets with the doctor, five, or even ten, pounds, that he would, or would not, survive, until a certain time. I am glad, Dr Wilson appears to have always won, as later, when I did see him in his office, I was to see some pound notes, framed, on the walls. I had decided at the beginning not to bother Dr Wilson with constant requests to be informed on Timothy's condition, he always seemed to me to have enough on his plate as they also say, anyway, than me having to waste his time.

Then there was a time when a real crisis point did arrive. Doctor Cowan, shortly after he had implanted Timothy's defibrillator, asked me to see him when I next visited Timothy, who was at the time a patient at the LGI having had problems. This to me meant next day, along with Sandra and Sheila, ASAP. We arrived after lunch time and the ward sister informed us that Dr Cowan would be with us as soon as possible. It was now 1.30 pm and by this time both Timothy and we knew what this was all about. Dr Cowan wanted us to persuade Timothy to agree to have a heart transplant operation at the renowned Freeman Hospital Newcastle, as he had refused to accept – as he said 'He may as well die,' or words to that effect. I was not there then, and on every half hour from the time we arrived, to the time we left the Sister came to tell us that the doctor had just rung again, to ask her to tell us that he was sorry, but he was running late and would come as soon as possible, and that turned out to be no earlier than 9.00 p.m.! On my visit next day Timothy informed me that Dr Cowan had already been to see him before 8 am, and, from my short experience of Dr Cowan, that's dedication, or I don't know what I am talking about. When he did arrive, he was accompanied by four younger doctors, I remember particularly a very pleasant, handsome, properly dressed, doctor, Indian, I would guess, and his senior assistant but I did not know, they were all very purposeful. Dr Cowan had with him a large scan of Timothy's heart which he held up, as a transparency, for all to see, which I suppose we all agreed with, when in fact, none of us had a clue, until he explained, and even then not much more. We gradually persuaded Tim to agree to the proposition, and he was then, alone with Sandra, some few days later taken by ambulance from Crofton to Newcastle, Freeman Hospital. They were to be there for five days, during which Sandra was provided with her own flat and was of course able to visit Tim daily, she also had a female nurse, chaperone, to answer any questions she may have. Timothy had a similar male person to answer his questions and assist with his virtually constant special tests, and we later learned that on day one Tim had asked all the questions that could be asked on the whole process. Sheila and I went to Hexham, 20 miles from Newcastle to check the area for a place near to the Freeman, to stay in the event that he was accepted but we were not allowed to see him, obviously. We did two recces to ensure we knew the town area. Timothy was accepted, and they both returned home to Crofton where, when not in hospital, he was visited by Dr Johns who had also arranged for a local patient, who had a transplant heart operation, (and I think also another organ transplant, at the same time,) that had been successful to give him assurance and generally cheer him up – which she did very well indeed.

The arrangements made were that Tim was supplied with a dedicated, to be worn at all times, radio telephone device, I suppose, I don't think I ever actually saw it, and to have ready packed a suitcase of detailed articles, and be ready in three quarters of an hour, to be transferred, by helicopter, to Freeman Hospital. Unfortunately, the vital call never came, no suitable heart was to be available. I understand Dr Wilson gave lectures to other medics on Tim's condition.

It got worse. We were urgently requested to go to the hospital as Tim was in a critical condition, at 4 am on September 14th, 2000. Sandra and her cousin Diane were already there, and we were able to talk to him and after a few hours we all left, only to be phoned to ask us to return, almost immediately after we were back home. Sandra rang me to say the hospital had rung, it was critical, would I take her to the hospital, along with Diane, they were of course in no state to drive. We arrived but regrettably too late. Timothy once said to me, with Sandra there I think. 'If you pop your clogs before I do, there would be trouble,' to which I responded with 'If you pop your clogs before I do, I'll kill you!' I hoped it was funny at the time, I meant it to be so, it's not funny now. His grave is directly opposite and facing his dear mother, Maria, in Horbury Cemetery. By chance? I hope not. Although I could write a whole lot more about my lover boy, and lovely lad, bear with me, I am, understandably I hope, pleased to leave it at that. RIP Dear Son.

Trying to continue, after the foregoing, is not easy for me. Something in a much lighter vein, but in the arts field, 'music', in this case, that will be appropriate. 'If Music be the food of Love, Play on, give, me excess of it'. I am reasonably in 'time' sequence. Timothy passed away in the year 2000, and he would have been very pleased for Sheila and me to be able to enjoy ourselves, by lucky chance, on a prestigious occasion. I subscribe to *BBC Music Magazine*, and in the August issue, 2003, there was a competition coupon, for the Grand Concerto Final of Leeds International Pianoforte Competition 2003. I had done my observation bit, Sheila, provided the clever bit, by getting the answer right. She happens to know a lot more about music, than I ever will, I just wander, from swing and boogie woogie to classical music, all on HMV, Plum Labels, to show my wide experience. We arrived at the Radisson, SAS, Hotel on the Headrow, and near to the Leeds Art Gallery, and Town Hall, we were welcomed by the charming, lady manageress, and then welcomed again, by the automated TV, over the automatic drinks bar. What a welcome, particularly after we had struggled with the card lift operator/room suite door operator, 'staff shortages'. The hotel was formerly a large bank building on the corner of the Headrow and Cookridge Street.

The two nights of the Grand Concerto Final in the Town Hall were superb, with the Hallé, under the baton of Mark Elder. The Hallé is the longest established symphony orchestra, founded in Manchester by Charles Hallé, pianist and conductor in 1858, first concert in the city's Free Trade Hall. The very latest Steinway model D had been purchased

Sandra and Timothy

for the players by the Chairman and Artistic Director, Dr Fanny Waterman, CBE, FRCM, and Steinway and Sons also provided free 22 new Steinway grand pianos for the use of competitors' practice in private homes – and that's generosity, amazing. All this clever information I have garnered from the souvenir programme of the competition, in a mad splurge of research! The second prize was won by Rubinova Eugenia, of Uzbekistan, age 25, playing Tchaikovsky: concerto No 1 in B flat minor, Opus 23, silver medal and £6,000.

The first prize was won by Süralla Antti, Finland, age 24, playing Beethoven: concerto No 4 in G, Opus 58, gold medal and £12,000. But the whole performance was wonderful, and after the last evening there was a very pleasant, but as usual crowded, reception, for the winners and the various dignitaries etc., and Sheila and me, at the Radisson Hotel SAS, all of which was very enjoyable. But standing, holding a glass of whatever, was not my idea of the best use of time, particularly with my knee problems etc., and we'd had a busy day and time was going beyond midnight, but most enjoyable.

In the early years of our acquiring the house at Primrose Valley, Filey during the Leeds School of Architecture summer vacations, I spent all of my time there in refurbishment, alterations, re-decoration etc., while Maria and Timothy were on the beach, out and about etc., with their friends. Our transport at that time was the very reliable, Riley Kestrel Sports 1932 model. We visited Scarborough, Whitby, Bridlington, Hornsea and points inland and on one occasion we had been to a show or something similar in Scarborough, and had arranged to have a later meal at a good small shop, with restaurant, in Primrose Valley, we knew the owners. We duly arrived in the evening and were served an excellent three course meal, including fillet steak, and mushrooms, fine. I later went to bed, woke up sometime later in the night with a peculiar pain in my feet, of all places, which then started moving slowly up my legs and body. My wife, woken, realised something was very wrong, dashed to the phone to ring for a doctor and then brought me a glass of brandy and handed it to me. I couldn't take it as both my hands had 'curled', closed up, and I could not open them. I was paralysed from my feet up! The next thing I know, there is someone by my side pushing a hypodermic syringe into some part of me, and I am beginning to take notice. Turned out to be a doctor, but he was in pyjamas!

Next morning, the same doctor came to see how I was getting on. This will come perhaps, as something of a surprise to you, doctors don't seem to do that much these days – although they are very well paid indeed, under the NHS, funded by the tax payers, like me, and probably you.

The doctor was a WWII, ex Royal Navy doctor, young, about the same age as myself. Maria had already told me that he had arrived as quickly from Filey as I did in the Riley, thank goodness, but then he only had his pyjamas on, I was always properly dressed! He told me I had fungus poisoning and time was vital. He also informed me that in France, in each large town there is an inspector of fungus. All those funny things, some even popping out of the ground overnight, and some dug out of the ground, with funny spelling names, like truffles, dogs dig 'em up – 'orrible, 'in it! He went on to tell me that in Calais the Inspector was taken ill and died of the same mushroom poisoning that was afflicting me, that's why he had got a move on, coming from Filey, out of uniform, not to mention that he asked to borrow my pen to write out my prescription. A very special Parker '51', so named for the 51st anniversary of the Parker Pen Co. USA, and liberated by me from some US of A, PX, or Post Exchange overseas, and some few years (4) ago. An article in the national press, (probably on their centenary) said they were now valued as collectors items, at £150 and I didn't ask for it back, didn't want to embarrass him. It's easily done, done it myself, he was most welcome to it, my gift! He had earned it more than somewhat!

I may as well take this opportunity to include the full list, to this day 30/01/08, of my various ailments that have bedeviled my life, since I came into this world. Whether I should divulge this private part of my life, whether it is the done thing, or not, I do not know, I only thank the Lord that I have survived thus far. Here is the list: in hopefully chronological order!

1. Abscess, under chin (3 or 4 years) – fully healed, still have the scar.
2. Meningitis – Dr Simson, (4 or 5) miracle I made it! Thanks Mum and the late Doctor Simson!
3. Tonsillitis operation – at Danum Mount Nursing Home, painful, home, very good. But very sore mouth.
4. Appendicitis (13–14) Clayton Hospital (anaesthetic problem).
5. War damaged hearing – (hearing aid) – No Pension.
6. Bursitis, both elbows, Batley Hospital, (since closed). Consultant said he had never had a patient who had it 'symmetrical' before, they were in agony, and coming to him with it in only one elbow, so called tennis elbow.
7. Mushroom poisoning (very near miss,) – Filey. Thanks, RN doctor.
8. Insect poisoning – Dr J. Brandon Stoker, MB., ChB, FRCS, Brandon, virtually my life long friend, had spent some years in

Africa, knew a lot about photography, insects, and a lot more things as well, but did not know what had bitten me. I had to spend over two weeks in bed recovering, and he visited me every day he was that kind of doctor, thank goodness.

9. Jaundice – Dr J. Brandon Stoker. HRH The Duke of Edinburgh and I had this very unpleasant illness at the same time. I was at home. I suppose The Duke was too, I never enquired.

10. Stomach operation, Dr Ingolby, MB, ChB, FRCS, (success), he was later sued by a cancer patient who survived! And, after some thousands of successful operations at Wakefield and Leeds Hospitals, he was then suspended, later cleared, and is now practising on Harley Street, London. I am very grateful for his skilful dedication.

11. Both knees replaced – Mr Ian A. Archer, MB, ChB, FRCS, Consultant, Leeds, both in the same week, very conscientious person, I am still running, thanks to his skill.

12. Carpal tunnel syndrome – Mr Ian Archer, Consultant, Leeds. Both hands, one at a time, to allow me to drive home, each time. I am now driving without any pain, thanks again, to his skill, a charming and highly competent person.

13. Very urgent stomach problems, Christmas and New Year period, (it would appear that most consultants were on two weeks holiday, West Yorkshire Wide). Dr Mike Bennett, MB ChB, Leeds, my GP, played a blinder on my behalf, and probably saved my life, in finding Dr M.S. Freeman, BSc, MD, MRCP, Consultant, Dewsbury Infirmary, and my partner, Sheila, in her VW, immediately driving me from Wakefield to Dewsbury! Dr Freeman and his associates, first class! Infirmary, and some of the nursing staff, require the attention of what used to be called the matron. But now it is the chief executive, or director, like in a factory.

14. Endoscopy treatment – Dr Mike Bennett diagnosed, and sent me to the Pontefract Infirmary, where I was treated by a very caring consultant and was there for the day, and informed that I would be required to return in about a couple of weeks. They also informed me I must go prepared to stay in for possibly a couple of nights, in the event, it was a different consultant, but the same pleasant and efficient staff as before, they were, I think, mainly Thais, but I am not sure. They all did a very good job on me, and I managed to scheme out of staying for two days, or even more, and it took only one day.

15. Arthritis and sciatica, both at the same time, still have both of them, and I do not recommend them!

16. Dentistry, Mr J.A. Brain (JAB, note!), dental surgeon, (Leeds), kind, gentle, considerate, understanding, completely competent, etc. (I am due for a check up in a few weeks time, can't be too careful.) He is at it all day, every day, and keeps you fully informed all the time, so you will gather he is very good indeed!

17. Oh, yes! One I forgot to mention in the sixties, a 'spur', in my heel, like a large rose thorn on the scan – don't have one, it took a hell of a number of times to get the hypodermic needle into the bottom of my foot, as you may guess, due to instant reflexes, and no anaesthetic, on two occasions! Consultant, Halifax Royal Infirmary. We later completely refurbished his large Victorian terrace house, on the opposite side of the road.

Not wanting to tempt providence after writing this list, I find I have a few small twinges of writer's cramp, and, of course, the usual migraine, coughs, colds, flu, and tripping over things, etc., and on the whole list E&OE! And I hope there are to be no more!

Today, is February 26th 2008, and for once, I am able to be even more, from your point of view, infuriatingly exact. Yesterday, all my troubles seemed so far away, and I hoped I was here to stay, for that day, but that was yesterday, and very soon the postman came with a letter or two, to say, but that too was yesterday, February 25th Monday, and it's now, as I have already said, today, so that's enough of that.

I do hope I have not put my foot in it – today, is the 5th of March 2008, and you may recall my reference to Sheila, drawing my attention to a very small ad, 1¼″ × 1¼″, in the *Daily Mail*. I had been trying at that time to find a suitable publisher, preferably local, in Yorkshire, but, I had not been impressed, I rarely had any interest shown, even by the telephone receptionists, all female, one in Wakefield, was an exception, they only published local history booklets. The lady was, she told me, 72 years of age, and was both very pleasant and interested, quite a change.

However, Jan 18th or 19th, I had phoned Book Guild Publishing (The Independent Publishers) Brighton, and received a very much better reception, and a there it is again, the 'comprehensive' word, a package of first class information etc., and a letter from Carol Biss, Managing Director. It is now dawning on me, my dear son, Timothy, and daughter-in-law Sandra, 20 years ago (approx), gave me a small white plaque, I don't remember when, birthday or xmas, but it still is displayed, high up, on the wall of my kitchen,

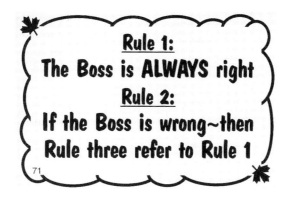

Rule 1:
The Boss is ALWAYS right
Rule 2:
If the Boss is wrong~then
Rule three refer to Rule 1

71

Now I know why, when I tentatively asked how I could address her, 'Miss, Mrs, or Madam,' (and hopefully not that ridiculous Ms!) she replied, 'Call me Carol.' Nice name, reminds you of Christmas (hope you don't mind Carol, please don't edit it out, or anything else for that matter, unless of course it is my bad grammar, spelling, bad language, continuity errors, wrong insert places etc., and typographical errors, quotes and apostrophes, I am only the poor boss here, you out-rank me.)

I met Andrew Peter when I was in the first (I think) Apple computer store in Leeds, called Raven, in Roseville Road, in 1984, when the first Apple Macintosh computer came on the market. I had recently bought one there and returned for more of whatever it was, I can't remember. The owner came from an adjacent office room to ask me if he could bring a gentleman, in his office, to meet me. That was Andrew Peter, and I was asked to demonstrate to him that amazing little product the Apple Macintosh, I still have one. We exchanged cards. He lived in Leeds, and that's the last I saw of him until 5 or 6 months later, when he phoned me to ask if we could meet at a layby off the M1 at East Ardsly, near Wakefield, which we did. He was then to tell me that the Raven manager had told him that I knew far more about the Macintosh than he did, so would he like to meet me? That was in 1984, but Andrew was soon to get far more competent than me on Apple computers and products.

Andrew was Jewish, always immaculately dressed, a small person, full of life, sharp as a tack, balding, overweight, ice cream connoisseur, appreciated good food but ate too fast, expert on Yorkshire beef dripping, fried fish and chips, played golf, liked to gamble at the club, hard worker, loved his family, married twice, all still friends, Richard, and daughter by first wife, son James by second wife. Andrew's father was a successful bookie, silver ring, and he also has a brother in London who was, when I last met him at Earls Court Apple Computer Show, now surveyor to all the

Catholic church properties in London. We had lunch together in the restaurant – very pleasant knowledgeable chap.

Andrew had racetrack sites at Aintree, Chester, York, Doncaster, Pontefract, Cheltenham, Redcar, Wetherby, Ripon, to name a few. Father retired, Andrew inherited the valuable sites and was already an expert bookmaker, silver ring, with his team of assistants, 'tic-tac man', book keeper, etc. Andrew gave the odds, and with a large solid leather Gladstone bag, took the money, called the bet, paid out after the race, all at lightning speed, virtually non-stop. He would on occasion invite me to join him at various meetings, after I retired. One such at York, I left my car at his home at Harwood and we then picked up his team, one of whom had his home in a new flat on the bank of the Ouse, York. Then on to the racecourse about 9.30–10.00 am, parking behind the main entrance to the main pavilion block, complete with spit roasted pigs, already revolving, quality ice cream vans, getting open for business along the roadways ready for the multitude to arrive. We entered the main foyer to be greeted by half a dozen bookies, comfortably ensconced in a small, well furnished open recess adjacent to the restaurant entrance, and with a small bevy of smart waitresses in attendance taking orders, and chit-chat, from their regular early customers, for drinks and light refreshments mainly in this case prawn sandwiches, and What's yours Jeffrey? Andrew and I got round to the ice cream stands later, before racing started.

Bookies' stands and sun umbrellas, erected by the team, and Andrew saw among the numerous bookies, an immaculately dressed, smart, trench coat, trilby hat, and polished, quality shoes, silk tie gentleman who he said was 95 years of age, and the doyen, of all bookmakers. Would I like to meet him? Yes of course I would, so we met, and after a most interesting, and for me enlightening, conversation, I was able to inform him, on pony race betting in Iceland. We parted, and walking away Andrew said to me, 'I can't believe it! I have known him for years, we all know him, and that is the first time ever that he never said one expletive, the whole time. Normally, they are non-stop! I can't believe it!' You can pause now, while I adjust my halo. Fine, you can read on now.

Also at this meeting was the well known horse racing presenter, in his usual, unusual, attire, John McCririck, moving around all over the place, but always in view, and in radio contact with, the TV camera team on the rooftop, of the then new pavilion stands. He came and stood in front of Andrew and me, and started broadcasting his commentary. Sheila spotted us, at Tree Garden, while watching the programme. Andrew's dry comment to me at the time was that John M. owed him a lot of money on lost bets, but he always collected when he won!

Another occasion, at Pontefract racecourse, a local famous racecourse, but then, not in York's class, timber two storey pavilion, with restaurant above and with rough terrain of ditches and gorse bushes etc. around, the restaurant had lino covered timber boarded floors, canteen, timber tables seating six or eight people, in short, ready for total refurbishment, but they served the most marvellous battered fish and chips, with all the trimmings. It was spotless and we had a pleasant meal, before the crowds came and racing started. It was an evening meeting and a nice day, and after paying out the winners, and knowing the score, he pointed out the busy, slow moving traffic, leaving the racetrack on the long adjacent main road, and decided caution before valour. His Gladstone bag, while not full, was by no means empty, and yobs could be waiting to stop the car, and grab the bag, so the four of us had a pretty fast and very bouncy, rough ride overland to another road he knew, and this not in a 'four by four Chelsea Tank' but in his BMW Seven Series.

Today is Friday March 7th 2008, and the *Daily Mail* has arrived, at 6.30 am. I may have already told you, I have read this newspaper since I was 7, at school, throughout my life, daily, when it was available depending on active service restrictions, and it has been, and still is, in my opinion, the best and only daily, to have consistently championed the British way of life, without being too left or too right, the not very common, common sense way, of the mass of those so called ordinary people who have, in the past benefited from teachers, who had the common sense to build on the bedrock of teachers, over the last few thousand years. Unfortunately only older people over the last century can tell you now how fortunate they were to have the essential basic animal discipline, and the dedicated teaching and learning, they had inherited from all those masters and mistresses through the ages. The system hadn't done too badly, look at the list in history, it didn't need fixing it wasn't broken, then along came governments, in our British case, over 670 something or other MPs.

But why go on? I am still just a poor Yorks boy, the *Daily Mail* has far better writers, satirical, political, humorous, distinguished and very serious, and more capable than I will ever be.

After that well intentioned homily, I continue with my further appreciation of my friend Andrew Peter, and our mutual friends, all Apple experts, some racing experts, hence, probably, the mutual connection. Four particular friends for years namely Gordon Sowden, at that time director of a Leeds engineering factory, we met together for lunch or a barbecue at Andrew's new house on the Harewood Estate, at Harewood, Tree Garden or other watering holes, over the years. Unfortunately, Gordon's company was to close down, as many others have since, and he started in a new business producing CDs, and DVDs in Leeds. Due to circumstances I have not heard from him for some time (must try to contact him). Some years ago I showed him my collection of the marvellous Studio Year Book and persuaded him it would make an amazing set of DVDs, or CDs. He agreed. My Studio books cover the years from 1914 to 1922 (approx), are international in scope, on quality paper, in full colour, and cover all the arts, and cost something like 5 shillings, that's 25p in our present coinage. I still have not had time to collect the book from him, or my DVD copy, in spite of my arranging to collect it on a few occasions, my fault, and he probably had more to do, getting his new business on course.

Another is Eric Sauce, who had an Apple business in Scunthorpe, East Yorkshire. My son Timothy and I used to visit, for help or products, and Tim took Sandra on one occasion, although she hadn't a clue about computers, and still hasn't (leaving it to her friend Christine to clatter away on a PC and Microsoft). She has managed to very expertly attend to keeping up appearances of Sheila's, Christine's, and my flowing locks, in my case, since she married her dear Timothy, RIP. That's over 40 years, what a treasure. Eric and his wife Lesley moved to Bempton, on Flamborough Head, a few years ago, and we last visited them, Sheila and I, about 18 months ago. Sheila had never met them before, and I rang their bell, and as I was introducing Sheila to Lesley, from the nether regions came the stentorian voice of Eric, 'That's Jeffrey Walton's voice!' and I didn't know he cared. We hope to visit them soon, early summer. Andrew and Eric were old mates, from a few years back. Eric providing the sauce for Andrew's pudding, probably, more so from his love of the race tracks than Andrew would need to buy Apple upgrades from Eric, I don't know, but the interdependency had certainly been fruitful. New garden he had created himself, with his own hands, and I sampled the huge raspberries, and other fruits and vegetables on what had been the builder's site to start with, when his house was built. The then latest Apple desk top, cable free, and with the latest, minute but wide ranging digital camera etc., built in, I asked to buy it, second hand, but no luck, must do better this next time.

And lastly, but by no means least, Paul Pierce. You have met him a few times already, he was a later comer, he is also close comer, having moved from just down the road in Milnthorpe Lane, to just across the road, a hundred yards from where I am sitting now, on Barnsley Road. Also a very busy chap, remember, he is a big help at times, like now!

Andrew had, by this time, retired from bookmaking and having sold off all his valuable race sites to other practitioners, started a new business, along with first son Richard, and other staff, in a nice set of offices at Armley, Leeds, designing Internet sites for professional and commercial business customers, fully equipped with Apple computers etc. Later he sold this business, and along with his second wife Brenda, took over an established multi product shop, including newspapers, refreshments etc., adjacent to a very large car wash centre, (which he would also have liked to buy), at Apperly Bridge on the outskirts of Leeds, and a few miles from his home in Harewood. Things were going fine, and they were considering extra staff, and I had also sketched out a café extension for tea, coffee, sandwiches, ice cream, etc., and they were very busy, both of them. James was at Fulneck School, and doing very well but not able to help, except on odd occasions. James, by the way, when they came to see Sheila and me at Tree Garden, apart from running round the garden, lawn, round the house, and jumping off the terrace at the high end, every circuit or lap, half a dozen times, was the only person, who could pass the ivory needle on the beautiful ivory ball with carved dragons, and at least six smaller, and, smaller, internal balls rotating. He could do it in just over a minute, and he also always enjoyed going through my numerous study drawers. We wish we knew what he is doing now, he's another redhead, and I have a soft spot for them as you know, he must be 18 by now.

Unfortunately, Andrew had suffered from indigestion for some years and when he came for a meal, or a visit, after a meal he would resort to a Gaviscon indigestion tablet. I regularly advised him to slow down, and see a doctor. Yes me, one who doesn't, and hasn't tended to take the same advice. At first he would not even consider the idea, but over a year or two I eventually managed to persuade him to see his doctor, and even discussed the problem of my friend, with Dr John Stoker, and he helped consultant wise. He was seen by a specialist consultant. He had cancer, serious cancer, and was more or less immediately operated on and the growth removed, 'the size of a grapefruit' he told me. He recovered and we visited him in Leeds General Infirmary where he was bright and cheerful and soon came out of LGI, to convalesce.

I am afraid the state of the LGI ward that Andrew was in was far from brilliant, in fact his ward was filthy, and the long ten foot wide main corridor, with the special fully powered brushing and cleaning machine, standing in a side bay, was there doing nothing, when we went in, and just

241

the same when we came out, a couple of hours later, filthy. Brenda had, during this terrible time for her, son James, Andrew's father, family and friends, and many more I don't know about, visiting Andrew every day, running the busy shop with help from family and friends, James, when he was able, due to Fulneck School, very good, and, along with driving to warehouses for stock, to and from home, and James to school, etc., she had a terrible time coping with all this.

Andrew gradually improved, and, typically set to and started thinking of Brenda and James, futures, organising the sale of his own fine house at Harewood, and the purchase of another for them etc., but all that was his business. All we were able to do, Sheila and I, was to go to Harewood, take him out for a nice quiet run to Harrogate, Otley, and Ilkley for him to do a little shopping. He always wanted the very latest technology in mobile phones, computers, and cars. He went to Orange, in Harrogate, for the latest mobile, and then lunch at Betty's restaurant, or at Ilkley, as the place may be, and he continued to improve.

However, the improvement was to be short-lived. He rang me asking if I could repair a film projector that had been his father's. He had films of his family when he was young, and he would like to be able to see them, after well over sixty years. Sheila and I went over at once. He was there in the garage, with his dressing gown on and his son Richard helping and was not looking well, but as usual, doing something. After checking, Richard and I reluctantly had to inform him that it was so much out of date and obsolete that there was nothing that I could do, and I regret that was the last time we would see him. He had to go back into LGI, and this time did not recover.

Monday, March 10th 2008, and, more or less, not unusual, I woke at six, usually do. We get up, about 7 am sometimes, wake up much earlier, visit the bathroom, and then go back to sleep for 3 to 4 hours, before waking, at the usual 7 am. My mind was as clear as crystal, and I was more than happy to lie awake, thinking. I will try to tell you what my thoughts were, like dreams, original thoughts, along with other bright ideas, in life, can be very elusive, come day, go, within half an hour, day. In my case, I had on Saturday March 8th, received a nice letter from Carol Biss. The letter's logo was apposite, and good omen, it was a Siamese cat, I think I may have told you Maria was a cat lover, and they loved her – we had two Siamese, the brain cat was Cottingley Crispin, to give him his full breed name. He would, on my return home to Tree Garden, jump on my shoulders, lying across the back of my neck, and tell me what had been done that day as we walked round. They are very clever cats, as you appreciate.

March 10th, 17.50 hours, Fiona, Sheila's grand daughter, has just rung me. She's on the bus from Morley to Leeds. Someone, has let the cat out of the proverbial bag – and she wants to congratulate me. Congratulate, me? I haven't won *Readers Digest* £300,000 plus prize, have I, at last? I have passed her on to Sheila, another silly mistake, on my part – within the hour all Sandal residents will be asking, who's he? and in large tracts of Armley, Leeds as well, never heard of him, so what?

Interruption over – sorry, – Sheila's just come crashing into my study, again – normally that's a courts martial charge. I have hung a 6″ × 6″ wall tile, with a green cat on it, and it clatters on the glass panelled door of the study sanctuary. Well one has to do something, you know, to warn me she is coming, you will understand. She wants me to come and look at a strip, along the mirror glass, in the dining room and, being also somewhat feline, takes me into the sitting room, lounge, drawing room, or whatever it is called these days, but then, will I go into the dining room? She's got it right this time. Fix a wall light that 'someone', (there are only the two of us) has 'knocked about bit'. I dare not say, 'Please Miss, it's not me, honest.'

However, apropos the foregoing, I realise that while the flesh may be willing, the spirit is still as strong as ever, and therefore considering, *just considering* mind renaming this opus, not, 'What a Life', but 'What, What, What a Life' (allegedly it may be useful if someone sues). That's how it stands at the moment – will keep you posted.

My brother, Ronald Douglas, whom I have mentioned at salient points earlier, had joined the RAF, I think in 1942, and ended up as an admin officer, in India, cushy job, at the end of the war, when I was in Germany, 84 Group BAFO, suffering the slings and arrows of HQ fortune, long past my demobilisation time. We were immediately back in the old routine, you already know most of mine, and some of the times when our paths have crossed – so this is mainly in honour of him – a hard working person, school headmaster, council chairman, family man, dedicated freemason, golfer, house builder, university gambler, chap who sometimes should have arrived at Crossley's, me waiting, on the cast iron teak slatted bench, it's still there. Funny thing, I never discussed with him later, or blamed him in any way, over all the years that have passed since we met occasionally, of course, but we both, after WWII, which thank goodness we had both survived, and during my six years in that, I had no idea where he was, or what he was doing, or where he was in the world, for that matter. A not I suppose very unusual predicament, or consequence after that unbelievable disaster. I mentioned golf as one of Ron's pastimes. He was a schoolboy champion, at Heath Common golf course, Wakefield, now long since gone. In his time, the horses, and horses with carriages, and the once or twice an hour, car, allowed you to wait a few minutes before driving from the tees, over the two or three main roads that crossed the heath. Now you would need a kalashnikov driver to aim between the cars, because they are all stopped by red traffic lights. The three storey, club house with balcony is still there, I hope. Since those days, a power station has been built, and there is also an official gypsy caravan, car, and rubbish site, so the club house may be the gypsy community centre.

After the war Ronald and I went our own various ways, but once we all returned to our homes, after a hard day at whatever, we were never more than 6½ miles away from each other, Ronald with his sons, and daughter, and then as grand parents, Ronald and Mary. Ronald's house was in the village of Emley (as you may recall, we were architects for various projects in Emley for the Skelmanthorpe District Council, our clients). The house, called One Acre. My dear mum, now a widow, Mrs Cass, had her house on the next site, towards the pleasant old village church, with the previously mentioned Remembrance Book, lectern in her honour. Ron commissioned it from the local woodworker. Ronald's son Christopher lives in Horbury and son Simon lives near Ronald in Emley, and Elizabeth is now Mrs C.D. Cutter, living near Salisbury, Wilts. She is the only person, in Ronald and Mary's time, who has telephoned me, and had conversations, person to person, at Mary's, later, Ronald's, funerals, at Kettlethorpe Crematorium. Hopefully, she is due to visit us at Tree Garden, when she is visiting Christopher in Horbury, this spring. Elizabeth is interested in things I may or may not know about, her father and mother before she was born etc. You know now if you have listened, I have been there, done that, even at school I had a few achievements in various fields, not a lot, but the odd few, sooner or later, then I engineered, and architected, and invented a few more things winning the odd Scholarship, only two given, studied a bit of architecture, volunteered, joined RAF, to help fight a 6 year war, been there, done that, got the odd medal or two, and parts of my uniform, No T Shirt, it was Serious. Had married and had a son.

Around 1997 Mary was having health problems, and needed a wheelchair and a stair lift. It was only then after asking them both, on a number of occasions, to come to visit us at Tree Garden for lunch or dinner, when Ronald excused my invitation, as Mary would have problems on my Barnsley Road inclined driveway. I had not seen Mary at that time, since I was 18, or thereabouts, at Danum Elmwood Grove,

Horbury, except on two occasions, chance meetings, in Wakefield on the pavement, if I hadn't seen my brother first, I would not have known her. The time came when they were on holiday in Hull and Mary had a bad fall, and broke her hip. She was brought later from the Hull Hospital to Pinderfields Hospital Wakefield, and then home, and from then on I called to see them quite often and two occasions met some of their grandsons, but fleetingly. My visits were always very pleasant as the three of us reminisced about our younger days, and friends then, Mary, often agreeing with me, when my brother, mid anecdote, claiming something was his experience, not mine. He had a habit of taking over and 'adopting' the incident, she always backed my account, not his, but it was also very amusing. Unfortunately Mary became ill, she had cancer, and she refused to have surgical treatment, due to her age, and handicaps, and later passed away. She was fine lady, and had a mind of her own and used it, as far as I know, to the end. The funeral was at Kettlethorpe Crematorium. Like everybody, I presume, I don't like funerals, but do like to remember the loved one, their family and friends, and this was particularly the case with Mary. After the cremation, I had all too short chats with relatives, some of whom I had never met before, and in all honesty had never even knew existed. Very strange indeed, and I haven't any idea why? I can't believe it has happened, either, but after a lot of mind searching, trying to reason with myself and my newly realised relatives, I offer the following possible explanation. I am probably wrong, and it is all my fault.

My brother was ten when I was five, and I had by then already had meningitis, so had no knowledge of him, or anything else, until he 'had to look after me', said Mum. He, probably, with his pal, had to take me along with them both, then I was to be whisked away to my Gran, when my father died. He was ten, still. I was then shuffled about a bit between three schools, on my own, after which I was installed as a newk at Crossleys, still on my own, until I was sixteen. My brother was 21, and at university, as you have read, and had his girlfriends and other occupations – just as I was beginning to be in full time employment, in engineering and architecture. Then, you may remember, in 1939 the Hitler war came along, and I volunteered to join the RAF when I was 19. Ronald was on his way to being married at 24 and I had probably not seen him for about the last 12 or 18 months, and I was by then involved in my extended war service, mainly overseas. No one told me my mother had remarried, or that Ronald and Mary were married, had a family, and grand children, and even great grand children, although by this time Ronald and I were, as you know, meeting on council business, etc. I was visiting my dear mum on a few occasions when I had, for miserable example, collected a badly smashed folding cake stand, from our days at Danum Mount, which I managed to repair and re-polish, back to its original state, and returned it. There were other visits, but should have been more, but I too had a family to look after, a child to bring up and the odd bits of work to do, here and there.

For over 20 years, Maria suffered ill health and we were on our own, my son Timothy having married Sandra, and they were on their own. When Maria passed away I was on my own, alone. My dear son Timothy and his dedicated wife Sandra were on their own, alone, when he was stricken with very serious heart problems, and awaiting a heart transplant and they were alone, as I was also alone, for the next nine years, as was Sandra, looking after Timothy when no suitable heart arrived, and he passed away. Sandra was alone again, and still is, in their house in Crofton, but with good friends and neighbours, I am glad to say.

Relationships are, as I am sure you will know or hope you do, a two way thing – you and me, father and son, them and us, mother and child, etc., but particularly in families; even when they emigrate, as some of mine did, to Canada, when I was a child. But how in heaven's name does a family of, initially, father and mother, with two sons, a daughter, one after the other, and they all married and, as far as I know, all may have had children, say, one each, I do not know, making a total of 14 (not including grand children, or even great grand) and me, to start with, I suppose, I do not know – the only, original, uncle, on my brother's side of the family! My dear mum never mentioned it but she, like me, would be doing her best, in her case continually babysitting, as probably the best babysitter in the country. She had remarried, and I did not know, even when her second husband, George Cass, and an old friend of mine died. She may have had her reasons, and I was overseas somewhere, I don't know. Ronald even phoned me, to make an appointment to see me at Huddersfield School of Architecture (probably during the sixties) and bring his son along, to see if he would like to study architecture. I was delighted to see them, and would have been very pleased to have him as a student, irrespective, but it was the 7 year length of study that put him off, or possibly the A levels required, I am not sure. I think the former one, but we had a happy hour, with only a cup of tea, and I was again on my own.

You will recall, I had invited Ronald and Mary many times to Tree Garden, even when I was on my own. Big head that I am, I can prepare and cook, a three or seven course dinner, and have done so for years, still do. Sheila does the more helpful job of gofer, and table layout, clearing up the aftermath, washing up with a dishwashing machine, to break the Royal Doulton, 'Queen's Lace', and at the same time fully able to chat up, or gossip, take your pick, with our guests, that's the floor show, continuous, but she *was* a Girl Guide and informs me she has the badges to prove it. Ronald was now also on his own, and with the district nurse looking after his health, and carers, hopefully, doing what carers are supposed to do, but 'no lifting'! Ronald, now nearly 90, had been in, and out of hospital, in Huddersfield Infirmary a number of times, since he had a very unfortunate accident in his kitchen. He was behind the kitchen door, bending down, doing something (I don't know what it was) when the chap who was now doing his gardening, part-time, probably one of his pupils from years ago, came in carrying a large box of something, backwards. And he sent poor Ronald crashing onto the hard floor and he was unable to get up, or even move, emergency ambulance and paramedics were called. He spoke very highly by the way, of his treatment, food and accommodation, nurses etc., during his stays in Huddersfield Infirmary.

I arranged to collect him from his home, but before I left home one of his sons, I don't know which, but assume it was Simon also in Emley, phoned to inform me that there had been some problem with his getting ready, or maybe shaving. However, when I did collect him I was completely shattered. His entire face was covered in razor cuts, each with a dried blood line. I immediately decided not to 'see' or mention them, to avoid any further embarrassment he had obviously suffered. He made NO mention of his horrible predicament, but immediately started to tell me how annoyed and hurt he was on I assume an incident that had happened earlier, this very day. He was fuming, I had never seen him that annoyed, ever. He said he had earlier given his son his Volvo car, of a size suitable for Mary's wheelchair and car seat turntable, he had given up driving, and was now his son's passenger, in the car and had made some 'warning' comment, to be told at once to 'Shut Up', 'he was no longer driving'. He was still obviously very upset, I am sure it had just happened, sometime that morning. I myself had never met my nephew, that was to come later in the day – but don't hold your breath, there was no ceremony or introduction.

We duly arrived at Tree Garden. Ronald, on his introduction to Sheila, was his pleasant, outgoing, and intelligent self – he was at this time, in his 90th year, by the way, and had never been to visit me and mine, ever before. I had visited him, and Mary, since she became disabled, had the odd cup of tea or a glass of wine, taken them plants, chocolates, bottles of port, and a 7 lbs case of properly traditionally smoked seahouses kippers from old friends Mr and Mrs Swallow.

Ronald, after introductions, kept pointing out things in the house, saying 'like that', and also 'that' and was in his element, as they say. We had roast duck, he said it was his favourite dish, nice wine, and he had I hoped forgotten his family and personal problems. I asked, when we had finished, if he would like to look round the garden. 'Oh yes', so we set out from the rear, kitchen, entrance, and then walking on the lawn, which due to the house being built on the old Victorian tennis court, necessitated slight changes in level. There is along one side a slope down to an apple tree, which diminishes in height as it extends across that area of lawn. I was leading the way, Sheila and Ronald walking behind me chatting, when suddenly, between the house and wall and me came Ronald, rolling, wheel-like, literally head over heels. My immediate thought was, NO, NO, NO, not now, not here, no way. But I need not have to blow my brains out, he stood straight up, immediately. 'Sorry, no, I am OK, don't worry.' Don't WORRY and I was already knocking on 'HELLS' DOOR! I still can't think about this brief moment without thinking, as I do now, for the first time, that the angel on my right shoulder, must have brought another one to keep watch on my left!

Eventually, it was time for me to take Ronald back to Emley. (I had recovered). On the way he jokingly said, 'Sheila is a very nice lady, does she have a sister?' No, she is an only child, Girl Guide and a musician under training! But problems were still to be dealt with, he was on his own, in his own home, and his son had his house key, and was not there as he should have been, so we had to drive into the far side of Emley to his son's home, to get the key. On the way Ronald asked me to turn right and into the housing development twice, until we found it, on the third right – why? I don't know, we arrived at the corner house he said was the one and we both went knocking on front and back doors, and looking in windows, all round, for at least 10–15 minutes, when, at last, an upstairs window opened and his son, five minutes later, came out to us sat in the car, and gave us the key. I drove Ronald back to his home, and saw he was safely inside, and phoned later to make sure he was OK.

Unfortunately, after more returns to hospital, during which time I phoned him and he assured me he was still being well looked after, but, in my further calls, and advice from the nurses attending him the prognosis was getting worse. Ronald, RIP, regrettably died in his 90th year. Soon after, one of his sons rang me informing me of his death, and the date and time, and also of his cremation, day and time, at Kettlethorpe, which I now appreciate. After the ceremony I again met Elizabeth and, I think, her university son, or he may have been one of her brother's sons. She also thanked me for being the only man there with the Royal Air Force tie on, as she had said, on our last meeting at her mother's funeral. She also informed me the next day, I think, that she had hoped to come to see me then, but there was some difficulty regarding her father's property, but she would make a point of seeing me, and asking me questions about the Family, that I may know something about, when she came back to Yorkshire, this spring, and that's due in fact, in two days. I too, have a few things, and questions to ask Elizabeth, that she may know something about in her family, and time is fast, running out, for all of us. It's no good forgetting to wind the clock, and, I hope we meet this time, in time, and I am able to keep you all posted.

However, it is now March 30th Saturday 2007, and I am doing one of my out of time context, with the last paragraph, but it is I hope apposite. I have, fortunately, just remembered that their daughter Elizabeth, my niece, and also a teacher, said on a phone call just before Christmas 2006 that she would call in to see me, when the weather improves in spring, when she was also due to visit her two brothers. One lives in Horbury, the other in Emley, a small village, and each just a few miles away from me, at Sandal Magna. Elizabeth lives near Salisbury and has no idea I am writing this, neither have her two brothers, or their children. If I tell her, I only hope it is a pleasant surprise.

There is another way to conduct our family relationships – even when we have a war on, and at present we have at least two, one with Iraq, and one in Afghanistan.

Regarding family relationships, the last eight months of my life, except when I am haggling with you, dear reader, has been dominated by the arrival of Sheila's great grand daughter, Emma. (I know it is 8 months, Emma's grand mama Sonia has 10 minutes ago rang to thank us for sending birthday cards to Simon, her son in Oz, he is going to get a sponsor, and become an Aussie so he's not so daft either.) I wish him well, and that is what I am getting at, keeping in touch, amongst many other things, and he is not even a member of my family. Hang on, unless I am mistaken he may well be soon, there's this business of leap year. Damn, I could become – perish the thought – his grandfather-in-law, and Sonia's father-in-law, and Emma's great grand father-in-law, and Victoria's grand father-in-law, and Penny's father-in-law, and Fiona's grand father-in-law, and Thomas's grand father-in-law – stop! STOP-THAT-TRAIN! Stop-That-TIME Train. I want to get ORF! PLEASE ?

Those Appendices I Promised

I have just now, come to the conclusion that I could end there, as Carol had asked me to complete the hard copy, to the end. But then, I realised that, hopefully, I would perhaps, live a little longer, after *What a Life*'s end. I would just like to hear what Elizabeth has to say to me, if she comes, and of course, if we all make it, and I have the best of hopes on that, and it is, today, Good Friday, March 21st 2008. Spring, the time when she said she would come. If I actually do get a 'Dear Reader' we may all have something to build on – who knows?

Assuming, you are still with me, I was talking about family relationships, and the business of leap year, February 29th 2008. Well, I couldn't get orf that 'Time Train'. At the beginning of April Sheila reminded me that we had to register 15 days before we could marry, on the 28th of April, and she had spoken to the registrar. We were both invited to visit her, Mrs Sally Clamp, at the Registry Office, Wakefield, to deal with all the necessary checks, birth certificates, previous marriage certificate, and even death certificates. However, we made it, and I realised what an idiot I had been in not 'doing it' much earlier. Sheila, had always been the most conscientious person in every way, she had stood by me, and literally done everything to help my recovery after my surgical problems during the 14 years we have been together – couldn't have managed without her.

The wedding was at 10.30 am on Monday 28th of April, and today it is May 5th Monday 2008, so this is our first 'weekaversary', another Walton first. Again, more by luck than good management, I have made it, and you will of course appreciate how up to date I am keeping my intelligent readers.

My first and only other wedding was during the war to my dear Maria, I would remind you, and then there were only five people at St Paul's Church, York. This time, there were eight including the two registrar's officials – Mrs Sally Clamp had particularly wanted to officiate, but unfortunately had pre-booked a flight to Italy the day before the 27th, but the two people there conducted the ceremony very well indeed. So we now had four guests for lunch, champagne, port etc., at Tree Garden. Sandra, my daughter-in-law, Sheila's grand-daughter, Fiona, and daughter Penny, and son-in-law, John Holliday, and our two selves, both looking forward to our first anniversary. And also to a short break in East Yorkshire in the near future.

'Dearly Beloved Womenfolk, the Scriptures Moveth us in Sundry Places to Acknowledge and Confess, our Manifold Sins and Wickedness.

Wedding, 28 April 2008

Wherefore, I do Beseech You, Humbly to,' etc. – from my days as, 'Vicar'. Please don't get alarmed, at this late stage, I am only joking, trying to be light hearted, when thinking of the ladies in my life – as I have already said, not many, but a well remembered few, from Nora, and my Mum, and to Sheila, some, regrettably, no longer with us. To Betty, my dear Maria's niece, no, not one, Betty was born in my dear Mum's nursing home in Horbury, and apparently I took her mum a cup of tea, (Helping my Mum), as a boy on summer holiday from Crossley's. Today is Tuesday May 6th, and two days ago Sunday 4th of May 2008, Betty phoned me to congratulate us, and the above is the result. We reminisced. Betty, who is also a retired teacher, first class hons., mathematics, plays piano, glides, in Yorkshire and Derbyshire, and long distance races over the UK, with husband Mike Fairman, TV sound technician. Kiri Te Kanawa the New Zealand opera diva, has had them both go to New Zealand, expenses paid, to surpervise her recording sessions. Son Matthew, violinist, coached by Menuhin, Bournemouth Symphonieta and others, last saw him at Buxton Opera House, with Julian Lloyd Webber. Emily an actress with Hull Truck Company, Coronation Street etc., Alice secretary – both ladies are very good violinists, both have young children,

Emily Ruby, Kitty, Archie, Alice, James and Alec. So Betty and Mike are now grandparents and are also possibly 'world class' babysitters. Unfortunately, she said there were some problems with three of them mostly 'baby' problems that are not pleasant, but hopefully, they will soon improve and grow out of them.

Being very attentive, you will have noticed already that I am up to date, except for about half as much again that I am suddenly remembering – but it is late enough already, and by now, you know enough about time. The publisher is waiting, and as I said at the very beginning page 1, but unlike me, 'very patiently'. I hope you have enjoyed our rather 'one sided' conversation. I have shown dates and time and place, because in a personal conversation 'jumping about a bit' is not unusual. People keep asking me questions, as you will have gathered, so I have tried to listen and answer them. I will have made mistakes – it has been a rush job – which I do sincerely hope you have enjoyed reading. It is definitely all non fiction – E & OE. Bye! – Sorry, and you will not believe it, but it is true. I have just spoken to Elizabeth, in Salisbury, Wilts – for over an hour! She is coming to Yorkshire in September and wants to know more about her Mother and Father – but it *is* a bit late Now!

Just in Time! It is 5 September 2008 and this letter from Elizabeth has arrived. She is bubbling with surprises, not least of which is twelve pages of research into our family tree, going back to Staffordshire, where we apparently came from in the seventeen hundreds, and our eventual arrival in Yorkshire in time for the 1841 Census. From then she gradually arrived at the 1891 Census, where John Ashton – my paternal grandpa to be – and his family went to live in the cottage near the Aire and Calder Canal and the Jolly Sailor Inn, at which cottage I was to be deposited on occasion a number of times, as you will have read in the earlier pages of my childhood.

Elizabeth, however, I soon realized kept her punch lines to the end. So, after a long pause, she said that in the 1891 census there were eight members of the family living in the cottage (pause) and - a lodger! The family comprised husband and wife, three sons and three daughters, aged one to thirteen(the one-year-old was my father!) and the lodger, aged 41! He worked for Grandpa Ashton as a boat sailor on the canal (own account). Please don't tell 'Elf and Safty' and Social Security, it is all gone now. The two semi-detached cottages each had one living room and one large cast iron cooking range and a staircase giving access to a bedroom of the same size above. There was a small wash kitchen with brick set pot and a front garden with paved path to the extensive 'green' area to

My Grandfather, John Walton

Doncaster Road. When I was a little nipper, it was my favourite place to be, in or out, and the food and home made ice cream the best in the world – then!

However, to my complete amazement, Elizabeth had a much more important document to present; she simply had no idea of its importance to me. Three weeks after her visit, she still has no idea of its significance and won't have until she reads *What a Life!* The document was the Certified Copy of an Entry of Death for my dear Father, RIP, on 14 March 1929 at 12 Cooperative Street, Horbury, UDC, aged 39. Cause of death: (a) Bronco-pneumonia, (b) Influenza. No PM. Certified by J.I. Simson M.B. Signature, Description and Residence of Informant, R.D. Walton, Son, in attendance, (same address), Witness My Hand this 27th day of March, 1930. Walter Gooder, Registrar of Births, Marriages and Deaths. (Mr Gooder was, by the way, Registrar for the Sub District of Horbury UDC in the County of Yorkshire, and he also had a good grocer's shop in Cluntergate, Horbury.)

But Elizabeth was not the only one with no idea; I was dumbfounded. My Father had not died before I contracted meningitis, as I had always believed, when I was aged between five and six. I went on to Crossleys in May 1929, aged 9, having been an orphan some six weeks! As you know, my Mother rarely sat about doing nothing and she worked wonders in my case. Until she had managed to get me accepted, I knew nothing much about her arrangements until a couple of weeks before the date of enrolment when she started to 'sell' me the idea. Duly sold, we were on the day driven to Crossleys and enrolled. At first it was not a success, I was homesick, but as usual she knew what she was doing and I was eventually very glad she had acted as she did.

Unfortunately, what now occupies my mind is where my Father was from 1924 to 1929. I was aware that even from our days living in Sandal, he was, I think, working at a local colliery, even though I couldn't 'see' him. (I do know that he went to work very early.) When we moved to Horbury, and I nearly got my eye knocked out by my father's WW1 bayonet, I believe he was also there, somewhere, but I still did not 'see' him. When we were at Cooperative Street, he was behind me when I 'pogged' the rabbits and when I had meningitis I did not 'see' anyone, including my mother or Dr Simson, until I recovered. I did not know that at that time he was working at the Horbury Quarry, probably in the office, because he was lung-damaged from WW1. As before, he did start early but by this time I had been sent to my Gran at Heath and been to the sweet shop. It must have been a false alarm and he recovered. He was, of course, an educated man and at least a sergeant in WW1, as his handwriting on his miniature Book of Common Prayer shows, but where was he from 1926 to his death in Horbury on 14 March 1929?

I do remember my Mother, on my first summer holiday from Crossleys, taking me to see my father's grave in Horbury Cemetery. I am sorry to say that since WW2 dozens of graves and gravestones have been vandalized, but I still think I know where it was. I am afraid that I still do not know where he was until he died as recorded and why I did not 'see' him. Maybe it is because my memory was damaged by meningitis. With the death of my brother, Ronald, there is now no one left in my family who would know why. He never mentioned it and I never knew otherwise until Elizabeth's visit.

I refuse to end this 'so far' part of My Life in this somewhat solemn manner. We will succeed in our unique and wonderful country in spite of the doom and gloom of the present financial catastrophe, which should have been avoided by a responsible government. All things end eventually but remember that 'the price of liberty is eternal vigilance'. The present dictatorship is already undemocratically installing control systems in the law of the land and has now legally removed the freedom of speech and movement, domestic traditions and personal activities in many fields.

Please don't let me down; remember that it is your time now and that it is still a free country, so God bless you all.